Your Role in
ORAL
INTERPRETATION

Virgil D. Sessions
Orange Coast College

Jack B. Holland
Orange Coast College

HOLBROOK PRESS, INC.
Boston, Massachusetts

Library of Congress Catalog Card Number 68–17284

PRINTED IN THE UNITED STATES OF AMERICA

Second printing ... May, 1970

Acknowledgments

The authors wish to thank the following for permission to use copyrighted material:

THE ATLANTIC MONTHLY COMPANY — for "Three Days to See," by Helen Keller. Copyright © The Atlantic Monthly Company, Boston, Mass. 02116. Reprinted with permission.

THE VIKING PRESS, INC. — for excerpts from *Sons and Lovers,* by D. H. Lawrence. Copyright 1913 by Thomas B. Seltzer, Inc. All Rights Reserved. Reprinted by permission of The Viking Press, Inc.

CHARLES SCRIBNER'S SONS — for an excerpt from *Look Homeward, Angel.* Reprinted with the permission of Charles Scribner's Sons from *Look Homeward, Angel,* pages 550-554, by Thomas Wolfe. Copyright 1929 Charles Scribner's Sons; renewal copyright © 1957 Edward C. Aswell, Administrator, C.T.A. and/or Fred Wolfe.

WALTER J. BLACK, INC. — for Edgar Allan Poe, "The Sphinx" and "The Tell-Tale Heart", *The Works of Poe.* (Walter J. Black, Inc., Rosyln, New York, 1927).

HARPER & ROW, PUBLISHERS, INC. — for an excerpt from *Life on the Mississippi* by Mark Twain, Harper & Row, Publishers, Inc. Printed by permission of the Trustees of the Estate of Samuel L. Clemens (Mark Twain), deceased.

DOUBLEDAY & COMPANY, INC. — for an excerpt from *I, Michelangelo, Sculptor,* by Irving Stone and Jean Stone. Copyright © 1962 by Doubleday & Company, Inc. Reprinted by permission of the publisher.

PAUL R. REYNOLDS, INC. — for an excerpt from *The Sea of Grass,* by Conrad Richter. Copyright 1936 by The Curtis Publishing Co., Inc. Reprinted by permission of Paul R. Reynolds, Inc., 599 Fifth Avenue, New York 17, N.Y.

EDITIONS GALLIMARD — for "La République du Silence," from *Situations, III,* by Jean-Paul Sartre, Editions Gallimard, 1949.

*To JEAN and JODI
who suffered the pangs of birth with us
as we have with them*

Preface

THIS TEXTBOOK, *Your Role in Oral Interpretation,* is one we hope you will find value in using. However, there are a few guides we feel you should have. The book is based primarily on a belief that a course in oral interpretation can do quite remarkable things for a student. We are aware of the student who takes the course mainly to get out of writing his own speeches or because a course in discussion does not interest him. But we have found, after some time in teaching the course, that students do respond, and quite well. Consequently, we have written our enthusiasm for oral interpretation into the pages of the text. Some reviewers have said that the text would be of real value to anyone who shares this enthusiasm. We hope you do.

We should say a word about the chronological order of the chapters. The text is arranged in two main parts — performance and literature. We have found it advantageous to assign at the start of the course the first five chapters in sequence along with a chapter on the type of literature we choose for the first reading — poetry, prose, or drama. Otherwise, chapters are not arranged according to any pattern of assignments.

We have discovered several ways to work for control of stage fright. One technique we have found useful through direct feedback from our students is to begin each session of the class from the first day through the first three or four weeks with a vocal exercise. The exercise is an old stand-by for improving voice projection. In short, the students, usually in groups of three or four, get up in front of the class, breathe in deeply, and make the "ah" sound, starting at low volume and gradually increasing volume to full range by count of ten, then decreasing slowly to total count of twenty. This exercise teaches projection, but it also reduces tension because students find it very amusing to watch others go through these vocal gymnastics — and even enjoy doing them themselves. We have found that over 75 percent of the class regard this exercise as the best ice-breaker there is. A second technique for alleviating nervousness is to adopt the theory of role-playing for the first two or three sessions. Since each student is ad-libbing a situation and a character, he does not feel heavily judged. At the same time he develops some idea of interpretation.

A third possibility is to read a piece of children's literature, such as "Three Billy Goats Gruff." We go around the class, encouraging students to exaggerate their characterizations of the trolls and the goats. The students do not identify the characters with themselves; therefore, they feel less tension, and they also learn to express emotion.

There are other aspects of this text which make it unique. Examples from literature are used to support a point in analysis. All excerpts are set up with effective oral interpretation in mind. In short, we use the preparation technique we advocate in the textbook itself, as far as this is possible within the mechanical limits of standard book typography.

We hope you find this an easy book to teach from. We have been told by reviewers that it is. We can only say we wanted to do a textbook that students could readily understand. Too many texts, at least in our opinion, seem to be too complex and abstract for immediate student comprehension. We definitely, however, were making no attempt to write down to the student.

We can only trust you will find this book helpful in your teaching of the course.

Virgil Sessions
Jack Holland

Contents

PART ONE

INTRODUCTION

🐦 CHAPTER 1

Is this the way to oral interpretation?

So you're taking a course in oral interpretation. What made you decide to do it? Academic requirements for future teaching? Extra credits to graduate? To fulfill a speech requirement at your college? Or did it merely sound easy?

Well, let's see what you have done to yourself. What kind of course have you slipped into? Here's what other students have said before you:

"I knew we'd have to read something." . . . "I took it because I didn't like to have to write my own speeches." . . . "I had no idea we'd have to put some feeling into the literature we read." . . . "I don't know why I took it—I needed three units and it was the only thing I could find open." . . . "I was afraid to get up in front of people."

Now let's look at some of the final opinions of students after completing the course—bearing in mind that these are actual comments made by young men and women like yourselves at the end of the course:

"I enjoyed this course more than any I've had in college." . . . "It made me aware of how beautiful and exciting literature is." . . . "I never used to like poetry, but now I can see its beauty." . . . "Drama was always something vague to me. I'd never read any plays, but now I regard this as an exciting new field." . . . "I feel as though I'll never be the same after taking this course because now I've been exposed to just enough new things in literature to have an appetite for more. I never knew what I'd been missing before." . . . "I'm no longer so afraid of reading before people. I have more confidence."

Let's see what this course can do for *you*. One thing is certain— you're not going to leave the course the same as you were when you came in.

For one thing, you will certainly increase your reading vocabu- lary. You will find a new interest in the varieties of literature from the search you make for material to be read—and from listening to selections read by your classmates. You will find that poetry is not dull and lifeless but is often full of suspense, adventure, excitement, and romance. You will find a new world in dramatic literature. And you will find that the more you read the more you will want to read—no matter how hard you may try to resist the temptation. You'll be exposed to many authors, both classic and modern— people like Carl Sandburg, Ernest Hemingway, F. Scott Fitzgerald, Jean-Paul Sartre, James Thurber, Robert Frost, William Shakespeare, Edgar Allan Poe, Eugene O'Neill and many others.

And last but not least—you will find that your own reading ability is vastly improved and this change will add materially to your accomplishments in other classes.

Four-Way Experience

Oral interpretation is, first of all, a bringing together of the author, the reader, and the audience. Even more than that, it is a four-way experience. There is, first, the author who writes the material and experiences the emotional impact of creativity; then there is the reader who searches for the proper selection to read and experi- ences various reactions, physiologically, to what he reads before making his final choice; the third is the experience of the reader as he performs before an audience, his reaction to his material and to his audience; and the fourth experience is the audience who, by its visible and audible response, lets the reader know how his reading is being received. This response, in turn, adds to the reader's total presentation since it serves as a guide to the effectiveness of the reading.

Now let's look at these four ways in more detail.

What do we mean by experience? Let us say an author feels strongly about a social problem. To express his emotions and principles, he puts them down in a language and style uniquely his own, so that others may share his views and either accept them or debate them. He is expressing his own experiences. For example, Jean-Paul Sartre in his "Republic of Silence" discusses the full meaning of freedom as seen by the French during the Nazi Occupation. In this selection he shows that every thought, every word, every idea of the French was treasured because freedom of speech, as an action, was denied them.

THE REPUBLIC OF SILENCE

JEAN-PAUL SARTRE

We were never more free than during the German occupation. We had lost all our rights, beginning with the right to talk. Every day we were insulted to our faces and had to take it in silence. Under one pretext or another, as workers, Jews, or political prisoners, we were deported EN MASSE. Everywhere, on billboards, in the newspapers, on the screen, we encountered the revolting and insipid picture of ourselves that our oppressors wanted us to accept. And, because of all this, we were free.

Because the Nazi venom seeped even into our thoughts, every accurate thought was a conquest. Because an all-powerful police tried to force us to hold our tongues, every word took on the value of a declaration of principles. Because we were hunted down, every one of our gestures had the weight of a solemn commitment. The circumstances, atrocious as they often were, finally made it possible for us to live, without pretense or false shame, the hectic and impossible existence that is known as the lot of man. Exile, captivity, and especially death (which we usually shrink from facing at all in happier times) became for us the habitual objects of our concern. We learned that they were neither inevitable accidents, nor even constant and exterior dangers, but that they must be considered as our lot itself, our destiny, the profound source of our reality as men. At every instant we lived up to the full sense of this commonplace little phrase: "Man is mortal!" And the choice that each of us made of his life and of his being was an authentic choice because it was made face to face with death, because it could always have been expressed in these terms: "Rather death than . . ." And here I am not speaking of the élite among us who were real Resistants, but of all Frenchmen who, at every hour of the night and day throughout four years, answered NO.

But the very cruelty of the enemy drove us to the extremities of this condition by forcing us to ask ourselves questions that one never considers in time of peace. All those among us—and what Frenchman was not at one time or another in this situation—who knew any details concerning the Resistance asked themselves anxiously, "If they torture me, shall I be able to keep silent?" Thus the basic question of liberty itself was posed, and we were brought to the verge of the deepest knowledge that man can have of himself. For the secret of a man is not his Oedipus complex or his inferiority complex: it is the limit of his own liberty, his capacity for resisting torture and death.

To those who were engaged in the underground activities, the conditions of their struggle afforded a new kind of experience. They did not fight openly like soldiers. In all circumstances they were alone. They were hunted down in solitude, arrested in solitude. It was completely forlorn and unbefriended that they held out against torture, alone and naked in the presence of torturers, clean-shaven, well-fed, and well-clothed, who laughed at their cringing flesh, and to whom an untroubled conscience and boundless sense of social strength gave every appearance of being in the right. Alone. Without a friendly hand or a word of encouragement.

Yet, in the depth of their solitude, it was the others that they were protecting, all the others, all their comrades in the Resistance. Total responsibility in total solitude—is this not the very definition of our liberty? This being stripped of all, this solitude, this tremendous danger, were the same for all. For the leaders and for their men, for those who conveyed messages without knowing what their content was, as for those who directed the entire Resistance, the punishment was the same—imprisonment, deportation, death. There is no army in the world where there is such equality of risk for the private and for the commander-in-chief. And this is why the Resistance was a true democracy: for the soldier as for the commander, the same danger, the same forsakenness, the same total responsibility, the same absolute liberty within discipline. Thus, in darkness and in blood, a Republic was established, the strongest of Republics. Each of its citizens knew that he owed himself to all and that he could count only on himself alone. Each of them, in complete isolation, fulfilled his responsibility and his role in history. Each of them, standing against the oppressors, undertook to be himself, freely and irrevocably. And by choosing for himself in liberty, he chose the liberty of all. This Republic without institutions, without any army, without police, was something that at each instant every Frenchman had to win and to affirm against Nazism. No one failed in this duty, and now we are on the threshold of another Republic. May this Republic about to be set up in broad daylight preserve the austere virtues of that other Republic of Silence and of Night.

Freedom became an experience and not just a word. Sartre's feelings are compellingly evident in this selection. One cannot help feeling, as he reads the essay, Sartre's surge of pride in his country, a sense of hope in a time of despair. He presents a theory that men are freer when freedom is denied them. It is an idea—but an idea fulfilled by the emotional experience of living that idea.

Now how about the author who writes a piece of fiction—or poetry? How does experience enter in here?

Richard Wright in *Native Son* may be dealing with a fictionalized plot, but the sentiments and the emotions underlying this story of a Negro caught in a web of prejudice and bias are those of Wright himself—the feelings, the experiences he has had as a Negro. The same is true of James Baldwin in his *Notes of a Native Son.*

In a like manner, Elizabeth Barrett Browning in her collection of poems, *Sonnets from the Portuguese,* expresses the love she felt for her husband, Robert Browning. Her writing is a part of her innermost experience. John Milton in "On His Blindness" also talks about his own personal experience.

But what about the books, the poems, the plays that are not directly related to a writer's experience? We cannot always presume to know the author's purpose in writing a selection—nor should we be tempted to attach a purpose, or a meaning, to every piece of literature. He is still experiencing an emotion that is familiar to him when he draws the word pictures of his characters and describes their emotions. He has undoubtedly felt love or hate or jealousy or revenge—or any of the basic moods—and he recreates them in his work.

The actual writing down of these feelings, these ideas, these principles is an experience on the part of the author.

Your experience as the reader begins with a visit to the library. You are looking for material to read. You pore over endless stories or articles. Suddenly one strikes you as exciting or moving or stimulating. It interests you—it means something to you. You have in this process taken the second step in communication. You have discarded some material as not suitable to you or not creating sufficient emotional response for you. You consequently select literature that appeals to you—that makes your spine tingle or a smile cross your face or causes a lump in your throat—or literature that recalls to you some similar emotion or event in your own life. Let us say you are a sensitive person. You express yourself openly, fully. You will undoubtedly be attracted to material that suggests the same feelings.

The third step is to convey, through the technical skills you will master in this course, the response you had to the material so that your audience will gain the same appreciation of the author and his work that you have—so that it will share in your emotional reactions.

Now you come to the fourth step.

It is conceivable that not everyone will share your response. Audiences consist of different types of people with different interests. Some may find elements other than those you selected to react

YOUR ROLE IN ORAL INTERPRETATION

to. Some may not smile or chuckle at a humorous moment. But it is your responsibility as a reader to create as uniform a response as possible. How can you tell whether you are succeeding in this purpose? By audible and visible signs—by a smile, a laugh, by complete silence during a sorrowful or suspenseful moment in the reading, by restless movement in seats—these and many other signs are there to indicate that you have communicated. When you have received such a response from your audience, you have achieved the fourth experience.

Such is the process of communication.

Oral Interpretation Is Not Acting

Oral interpretation has in many ways been rather like a wayward child. It has not been an unwanted child, for it has been adopted by both the speech and theatre departments of major universities and colleges. The theatre departments have laid claim to it because of its close relationship to the dramatic arts. The speech departments have zealously clung to it as an integral member of the speech arts.

So—what is all this to you? Basically, it poses the problem—do you "act" in oral interpretation or do you "interpret," and if you do the latter, what does that mean? What is the difference? Herein lies the conflict.

To avoid any confusion, let us make one thing clear: There is one significant difference between acting and interpretation—an interpreter reads a manuscript and does not "stage" his material while the actor's work is staged with scenery, lights, and an array of props. It is largely in the physical limitations that the difference exists.

To further understand the distinction, you have to know something of what the actor and the interpreter really do.

The actor is chosen, after an audition, by a director, to play a role that is part of the total reflection that is the play. He learns his part—memorizes it—after carefully studying the character's personality, his relationship with other characters in the play, the type of dialogue he engages in, where his personality changes, grows, and is motivated. All such refinements of the characterization are based on a thorough study of the total plan, on the director's constant observation of the performance during rehearsals. The actor moves about the stage, he wears costumes, he attempts to hide his identity and to create another person. At all times he is concerned primarily with his own role, although he, of course, must react to, and interact with, the other characters in the play. The audience, in turn, is asked to believe that the actor is the character he is portraying. Members of the audience participate in what is called a "willing suspension of disbelief"; they voluntarily accept the role-playing as reality.

In contrast to the actor, the interpreter chooses the material he wishes to read, studies it in its entirety, and without the benefit of a director, without the use of props, scenery, and lights, he must create a vivid and meaningful interpretation of the material. He is his own director, the sole judge, aside from his audience, of the interpretation. He works on a stage or platform with a reading stand. His rehearsals are conducted alone. He is not responsible for reading only the dialogue sections, as is the actor, but he must also bring to life the narrative and expository sections—those sections in literature which help to build the scene. He doesn't move about as the actor does, but he does use gestures and body movement to help add meaning to the reading. In all cases, the interpreter remains himself. But what does this mean?

Let's suppose you are the interpreter—a male interpreter. You have chosen to read the section in *Gone With the Wind* where Melanie is going through labor pains. Obviously, you cannot be taken for Melanie or for Scarlett who is in the scene. No audience expects you to. You are yourself. Yet you have to present the material in a meaningful and moving way. You must, therefore, involve yourself in that material—just as the actor must involve himself in the play.

But how much do you involve yourself? How far do you let your own emotions carry you? Do you submerge yourself into the mood, the feelings of the characters, into the dramatic content of the story?

Let's return to *Gone With the Wind*. You have to be concerned not only with Melanie's trial and agony and with her strength as a person, but you have to picture, through your own sensitive reading, the oppressive heat, the endless waiting, the "atmosphere" of the scene. You are dealing with all the elements in the scene, all the descriptions, all the character motivations and interactions. Each part is equally important. Melanie cannot become a full-bodied, understandable person if you treat her superficially or objectively. You can't make her suffering vivid without successfully handling the

YOUR ROLE IN ORAL INTERPRETATION

material describing the scene itself. Everything builds to the climax —the heat, Melanie's writhing on the bed, Scarlett's reaction to the scene.

If you read a play, however, you have to make your characters believable and lifelike. Suppose you are a girl and you choose the confrontation scene between the Grand Duchess and the girl posing as Anastasia in the play *Anastasia*. You must distinguish between the two women, make each of their personalities clear and vivid, and you must make certain you bring out the changes in the scene successfully. Yet no one expects you to be other than yourself while reading both parts. You are to show only the Grand Duchess' initial distrust, disbelief, and dislike and the girl's anxiety for the Duchess to believe in her. You must show how the little bits of information the girl gives about her past and her life in court begin to shake the Duchess' conviction that this girl is not Anastasia. Then you must finally bring the scene to a climax when the Duchess is convinced— and show her tearful joy at the discovery.

Since you must do all these things, ask yourself: Can I do all of this without involving myself, without feeling the characters as they feel?

What does "involve" mean? Or "feel"? Both mean that you physiologically react to the emotions in the story. When Melanie is suffering, you feel an ache in your own body. When the heat is described, it is as though you can feel beads of perspiration on your own neck and face. When the Grand Duchess begins to wonder if this girl could really be Anastasia, you feel a quickening of the pulse, an excitement, a conflict between believing and disbelieving. You "enter into" her emotions and become part of them. Such involvement is vitally necessary for the interpreter.

An audience can see a play—see people moving about, see the props and the setting. But they can only see such things in the imagination, in the mind, when the interpreter reads. They see with the eye of the mind and feel in the pulse of the heart—without any visual supports.

It is said that the interpreter should merely "suggest," that he should remain apart and not become involved. He must depict only what the author had in mind—to the extent that he knows what the author had in mind. Such a theory indicates an objective, unfeeling approach, a purely analytical one. As Bacon and Breen remark in *Literature as an Experience,* "Dry reasoning kills your imagination. The more you probe with your analytical mind, the more silent become your feelings, the weaker and poorer your chances for inspiration." In short, to communicate feeling both interpreter and actor must "feel."

It is true that the interpreter will find total involvement impossible, however, because of the many shifts of attention he must make. One minute he is one person, the next another, and then he becomes narrator or expositor. But with no involvement or with too little involvement, he cannot succeed in any of these roles.

Do not think for an instant that you can successfully move your audience by an indifferent, unfeeling reading.

Perhaps you are going to read James Baldwin's *Notes of a Native Son.* At some time in your life you may have been oppressed or hurt—or have known someone who has been. If so, you can share in Baldwin's despair, in his bitterness, his anger, his loneliness. You are able to give a more meaningful reading. Likewise, in interpreting *Death of a Salesman,* you need to feel the tragedy of Willy Loman's useless life, and understand Biff's frustration, and Lydia's loyalty. You or someone in your family may have experienced defeat or failure. Then you can know Willy. Or you may be unable to communicate with your parents—and thus know Biff's feeling. At any rate, you cannot read this play without involving yourself. It is a play of high emotions, of a relentless moving towards a climax. It calls upon the emotions of those who play it, read it, and see it. As the interpreter you must be all the people in the play—not just one. So your task is indeed formidable.

Such is a look at involvement and the responsibility of the interpreter. You are going to use emotions and feelings you didn't know you had. You will find that in the final analysis, you are in the business of making literature come alive to excite an audience, of giving them an experience. To do this you must transport yourself into the world of literature. This is your task, your responsibility. It can also be your pleasure.

ſ❧ CHAPTER 2

It's been around for centuries

CERTAINLY no one chapter can give a detailed picture of the history of oral interpretation. We do not presume to include here a thoroughly descriptive study, but it is important for beginning students of oral interpretation to have some knowledge of the background, growth, and development of the art.

Most records agree that Herodotus in 484 B.C. was the first professional storyteller. In the early Greek period, after Herodotus, poets were in the habit of reading their own poetry; most were known as rhapsodes. As such they were in the center of a controversy between the followers of Plato's ideology and those of others, such as Aristotle, who believed poetry and the delivery of it was in its own way art. To Plato, poets could not consider their work art because they were, in his mind, possessed; they were not governed by rules and discipline and hence could not be called artistic. He further condemned them because their goal was not truth.

On the other hand, Greek orators felt that poets were wise, that they were repositories of knowledge. To them, poets were teachers with the ability to impart knowledge. Aristotle, distinguishing poets from artists, placed the reading of poetry in a separate category from the art of oral discourse, or rhetoric, as practiced in the law courts. To him, poetry was the realm of the imagination; its primary characteristic was emotion. The aim of poetry was aesthetic pleasure, and the delivery of poetry more important than the substance itself.

To Aristotle, the essential difference between rhetoric and poetic seemed to be that art doesn't make the statement, rhetoric does. Art interprets, and reading poetry was classified as interpretation.

The art of reading achieved some of its greatest heights in Rome in the Golden Age of Literature—76 B.C. to 14 A.D. There was little activity in oral reading as such in the days of Cicero, but on his death in 43 B.C. the Augustan Age began, and a new emphasis was put on it. Before examining this era, however, we should consider the contributions of Cicero and Quintilian to what is now known as interpretation.

While Cicero and Quintilian were more interested in the matter of speaking, in fixing the arrangement of speeches and devising rules for the ideal orator, they did give some attention to such matters as reading. Like Aristotle, they stressed the need for training the voice. Cicero believed that rhetoric and interpretation by association belonged in a frame of a liberal arts education. He felt that the speaker or reader must possess talent and native ability and that he must be moved by "a passionate inclination, an ardor like that of love."[1]

Oral interpretation—though it was not called that—fits best into two of his five canons: elocution or style in written composition and *pronuntiado* or delivery. Cicero also felt that meaning influenced ideas and emotions and determined delivery. "Nature herself has assigned to every emotion a particular look and tone of voice and bearing of its own."[2] Quintilian in most respects is an echo of Cicero's theories. He proposed what is the Golden Rule for interpreters: "he (the reader) must first understand what he reads." His concept of delivery was based largely on naturalness; he felt that simplicity and naturalness were standards of excellence in performance. To him, the interpreter and the actor were much alike, and he advised the reader to observe *and imitate* the technique of a good actor. He added one bit of caution, however—to avoid a delivery that is too obviously theatrical. As he says, "that art is best which conceals its art." Or as Aristotle put it, "We should disguise the means we employ."

To return now to the Augustan Age—and to the beginning of a new emphasis on interpretative reading. Vergil, Homer, and other poets made a practice of reading their own poems and more courts engaged their own special readers; the Emperor Augustus even read works. Vergil detested any abuse in reading and was known to

[1] Cicero, *De Oratore,* I, p. xxx.
[2] Cicero, *De Oratore,* III, p. xvii.

YOUR ROLE IN ORAL INTERPRETATION

read only to select audiences. Horace followed Vergil in that he disliked artificial performances which stressed the performance more than the literary merits of the material.

Both the Augustan Age, which continued for about 165 years, and the Silver Age (14 to 180 A.D.) were glorious periods for the reading of literature. Around the year 359 A.D., the Golden Ages in Rome and Greece came to an end, and reading faded out as an integral part of cultural life.

While there was some reading of literature in the sixth century, there was no noticeable revival until around 1066 when a new minstrel type of reading appeared, accompanied by music, known as the Songs of Roland. Other forms of reading with song appeared with such groups as troubadours, jongleurs, the Dutch poetry guilds, and the Meistersingers in Germany. Through them, the art of reading took on significance in everyday life. These balladeers, who appeared primarily in Italy, Spain, and France, went from town to town commenting on the political and moral issues of the day through their stories and songs. The Meistersingers, for instance, traveled from one court to another and were highly paid. One of the favorite themes was the deification of women, and the plots usually centered around knights and languishing ladies.

The reading of literature attracted the attention of such poets as Chaucer, who often read his own works; he wrote mainly for court members. To him, oral reading was the elocution of literature.

It was, however, Stephen Hawes in the fifteenth century, the author of *Pastime of Pleasure,* who presented the first theory of oral reading in interpretation. He emphasized the importance of delivery. The Renaissance, then, brought with it a firm establishment of oral reading; it became popular to read aloud. One of the Renaissance's most notable figures was Boccaccio, who spent the last two years of his life reading and lecturing on Dante. Another figure, Castiglione, advised the reading aloud of poetry; he felt the practice added grace and distinction to a person's life.

For many years following the Renaissance, emphasis centered on the style of the written word rather than on delivery. In the eighteenth century in England, however, there arose a new interest in the spoken word and once again delivery became of paramount importance. Even before this period, though, there had been moves to read with the "performance" aspects, particularly in 1644 when John Bulwer wrote *Chirologia* and *Chironomia,* a detailed study of gesture and bodily action in which he stated that gestures were not perfect by nature and should be controlled. He taught by imitation and by adherence to systems used by the best "models." Since gestures are now considered an integral part of the communication process in reading, his contribution is worth noting.

In the eighteenth century, there emerged two schools of thought regarding oral interpretation. One group, loosely called the *Mechanical School,* was concerned mainly with rules for using gestures and managing the voice to acquire emotions. The other group, called, with equal looseness, the *Natural School,* felt that the meaning of the literature was the only important thing, that rules hampered any kind of natural expression and meaningful recreation of the author's purpose. However, both schools believed they were stressing the same thing—a meaningful interpretation of the literature.

The title given this new movement was the Elocutionary Movement, and it was born from a sudden interest in the English language and a revitalized awareness of the influences of discourse in persuasion, in swaying people to certain issues. Also of importance was the stage, which had presented a challenging, exciting new kind of language.

The voice and speech itself, the physiological aspects, began to be heavily emphasized and the tenets of science were applied to spoken discourse. Elocution was concerned with speech correction, the vocal physiology and the physics of sound production. Gesture was also emphasized, and elaborate principles and rules were devised for proper use of pauses, emphasis, pace, force, rhythm, and tone. John Mason in his *Essay on Elocution or Pronunciation* in 1748 stressed theories for pauses. He felt a reader should pause one beat at a comma, two beats at a semicolon, three at a colon; a period would require, of course, the longest pause of all. James Burgh's *Art of Speaking* formulated a guide on how to use certain emotions. It was his belief that if a reader followed his guide, he could find any necessary emotion in a reading by simply looking up the rule governing that particular mood.

The man who gave a definition to the entire movement, however, was Thomas Sheridan, a former actor, who turned to the study of elocution and pronunciation. He emphasized the need for qualified teachers and urged that elocution be placed in school curriculums. He felt the ideal delivery was characterized by grace, sincerity, naturalness, and he introduced a new code symbolizing emphases, duration of pauses, rapidity, and duration of long and short syllables.

There were other theorists, and each fell into one of the two camps. John Rice, for instance, felt you did not have to be affected by what you read. William Cockin, on the other hand, believed you had to feel what you read. All taught to a greater or lesser degree that the sense of what was read was the ultimate consideration.

The Elocutionary Movement also spread to America where Dr. James Rush and his *Philosophy of the Human Voice,* an involved and complicated study of the physiological aspects of the voice, became the center of attention. Others who made themselves known in this period were: Rev. Ebenezer Porter, who stressed sense and emphasis as necessary for sensible reading and felt the worst faults of elocution came from lack of feeling and errors in pronunciation; William Russell and James Murdock, both former actors, who stressed early training in elocution and decried mechanical, unfeeling reading; Samuel Curry, whose "think the thought" method proposed the theory that the mind had to be trained first for there to be any creativity in thought and imagination; Delsarte, a French actor and singer, who devised an elaborate system based on the Holy Trinity with Man being divided into life, mind, and soul and with the vocal sounds expressing life, words the mind, and movement the soul. His theory was used in many of the American schools with attention given primarily to the theories regarding the physical movement of the body.

Towards the latter part of the century oral interpretation became an impressive movement. Schools arose which taught basic exercises for the voice, diction, and frowned on stereotyped delivery. It was felt that man must speak through all his being, and that the voice was subservient to the idea being expressed. Among these were schools run by Samuel Curry, J. W. Shoemaker, May Blood and Ida Reilly, and Leland Powers, one of the most prominent figures. Powers was an actor and a recognized interpreter. He felt that speech should be the process by which avenues of expression could be freed and barriers to clear expression eliminated. To him, oral interpretation was the art of embodying the spirit and essence of literature, but both could be conveyed only when the reader understood the material and his voice and body responded to it.

The schools had almost identical aims: developing character, enriching personality, studying fine literature, freeing the voice from restricting habits and tensions, developing good articulation and variation in pitch and tone.

As time went on, elocution fell into disfavor because of the excesses taught by some of its leaders. Today the term "elocution" has a rather unfortunate connotation. It is often associated with the term "ham" as applied to theatre. Exponents of oral interpretation today prefer subtlety and suggestion, and emphasize the emotional aspects of the literature being read. Contemporary poets have read their own works. Dylan Thomas and Robert Frost are excellent examples and many of today's top actors and actresses have entered the interpretation field, mostly via records: Julie Harris with her album on Emily Dickinson; Judith Anderson with her album on Edna St. Vincent Millay; Sir John Gielgud with his Shakespearean reading in *Ages of Man;* Paul Scofield with his recording of poems by Dryden, and many more. In addition, a new kind of oral interpretation, called Readers' Theater, has emerged, which more closely resembles acting. In this field, several interpreters read poetic works, such as *Spoon River Anthology, John Brown's Body,* or a play such as *Don Juan in Hell.* One such group under the direction of Charles Laughton read *Don Juan in Hell* to audiences all over America, featuring Charles Laughton, Agnes Moorehead, Sir Cedric Hardwicke, and Charles Boyer. Mr. Laughton, incidentally, did more than any other single person to bring a new interest among the public in interpretative reading. His cross-country tours on which he read various types of literature revitalized interpretation as we know it today.

As you can see, even from this brief survey, the course you are about to take is founded on a resplendent history; the art of oral interpretation has developed over many centuries, guided by the ideas of many great minds.

PART TWO

THE PERFORMANCE

ᔚ CHAPTER 3

Let me out of here!

STAGE FRIGHT is a traumatic experience known to almost every individual. Even seasoned performers have experienced the disease —feverish brow, rapidly pulsating heart, cold, sweaty hands, dry mouth and throat, shaking hands and knees.

Some students are affected by it more than others. Some break into visible drops of perspiration; others have said they felt as though they were going to faint. Another remarked, "So this is what it's like to be a teacher." Still another commented, "My doctor suggested I drop the class to cure my nerves." On the other hand, there are individuals who seem to "breeze" through the situation without much more than a slight case of butterflies, a sensation that lasts only about a minute or two.

Many studies have been made on stage fright. Attention has been focused on the problem in psychological journals as well as in texts on acting and speech. And yet the problem remains—with no sure cure ever offered. Unfortunately, it is not possible to take a shot so the disease will not occur.

Stage fright, to reiterate an old saying, is good up to a point. The extra shot of adrenalin and the nervousness often provide a spurt of energy that gives a reading more interest. This is no new theory. But it is a theory few students will believe.

They are more concerned with such things as: How do I get over the dry mouth? How do I stop shaking? Can't it ever be cured? Consequently, they live with it and find their reading effectiveness cut in half by the results—a fast pace in reading, a colorless and unfeeling presentation, a lack of variety, and a noticeable drop in projection and vitality.

From a survey conducted by the authors among 150 students of beginning speech in a first semester oral interpretation course, it was learned that the biggest reason for stage fright in a classroom situation is fear of not doing a good job. No one wants to make a fool of himself in front of his peers. The second and third reasons, according to this survey, were the attitudes of the class and the instructor. The emphasis put on making a mistake ties in with the fear of class reaction. As for the attitude of the instructor, it was found that an instructor who is very formal, reserved, and highly critical creates a tense atmosphere that causes an increase of stage fright. It is for this reason that many professors purposely work for less formality as the key to better results from their students.

To enable the class to become a cohesive group is important. Consequently, it is wise for students to make it a point of getting to know each other as soon as possible in the semester. Association with fellow class members provides a feeling of "belonging" and significantly reduces tension.

Controlling Stage Fright

There are differences of opinion on how to handle stage fright. Some teachers refuse to discuss fright at all in their classes, believing that any discussion only magnifies the problem. Others feel frank and open acknowledgment of it helps by showing the students that everyone is in the "same boat," that the class is anxious to compliment rather than criticize, and that concentration on fear makes it impossible to concentrate on the task before them—giving the reading—so that increased fear is all that results. The first criterion, then, in overcoming stage fright is to concentrate on the material rather than on yourself. This is the surest way to control nervousness.

You have a choice; you can devote your time and energies and emotions to "Oh, I'm so frightened," and end up a petrified specimen, or you can put your mind and energies into the process of bringing a reading to life. This latter theory adds considerable support to the premise that a student can "talk himself" into believing he will do a good job.

In classes where free choice of material is the rule, students should choose only selections in which they are vitally interested: doing so has proved to be a most effective control of stage fright because it enables the reader to involve himself more in his material than in his nerves.

One student walked to the stand each time for a reading practically frozen with fear. It was a physically exhausting effort for him to finish. One day, in a drama-reading assignment, he chose Edward Albee's *The Zoo Story*. Suddenly, he became "unfrozen." He brought the incisive irony and bitterness of the play into focus for the class. His body relaxed. His response to his material was complete, meaningful. He was a different person. When he was asked why he was able to handle this assignment so well, he simply said, "Because I liked the selection, I guess."

Another student who spoke softly and without any feeling found a different situation in the reading of James Thurber's "University Days." He liked the selection, and when he got his first laugh from his audience, a smile came over his face. One could see the tension drop away, and he went on to give a most accomplished reading—just because he had liked the material and had received that greatest cure of all for stage fright, a favorable visible and audible response from the audience.

The next criterion in overcoming stage fright is solid preparation. No one can feel secure interpreting a selection he has hurriedly prepared. Only when you have prepared thoroughly can you feel confident in your reading. When students were asked, in the survey mentioned earlier, what helped them to overcome stage fright, they overwhelmingly said preparation was the big factor.

Oral interpretation offers problems to a student which are not always found in other courses of speech. In a speech fundamentals course, for instance, the focus is on making arguments clear and in presenting material in an organized manner. True, there is emotional content, as in speeches of persuasion, but not to the extent found in oral interpretation. Discussion courses deal with group efforts, so there is far less concentration on any one individual. Oral interpretation not only focuses direct attention on the reader, but it also calls for him to project emotion. He must deal with comedy, drama, tragedy, farce, all the significant moods and emotions of literature. Some students may not find it difficult to deliver a speech, but many exhibit great reluctance to show any feeling. Let's face it—many people are taught not to show emotion. Because these students cannot express feeling, fear is increased. However, it is generally true that the student who is at ease in oral interpretation is at ease in all speech courses.

Stage fright is magnified in the minds of some students who are

THE PERFORMANCE

certain everyone can see how frightened they are. One student asked, "Didn't you see my face turning red?" When he was told that his face was not red, he could hardly believe it. Another convinced the entire class throughout his reading that he was completely at ease, but all he could say at the end was, "But I was scared stiff! I thought everyone noticed." So it does not pay to assume that your audience knows you are nervous; the chances are others see you as in control. Generally, only you know how frightened you are. Don't prejudge yourself. In the same way, do not assume that everyone is thinking of your reading in a negative way. There is the distinct possibility that the audience will find your reading effective. In short, you cannot be critic and reader at the same time. If you split yourself in half in this way, the reading is bound to suffer. Be a critic during your rehearsals.

There are other criteria for controlling stage fright. One good way is to get in the habit of breathing properly. Try this experiment. Grab hold of a stand or the side of your chair. Make your body rigid. Then take a deep breath from the diaphragm, loosen your hold, swing your arms back and forth and feel the release of tension, the tingling of the spine, the feeling of ease and peace settling over you. This is the way proper breathing helps. It is especially important to remember this when nerves are forcing you to race through a reading. Pause appropriately, breathe deeply, and then go on.

It is also important to take time to look at your audience; give them a chance to settle down before starting the reading. This extra pause will give you a chance to calm down, too. There are some students who feel they become more nervous when they look at an audience, but it has been our experience that those who remain glued to the manuscript only become more rigid with fear. Often a visible response from an audience will give a reader more confidence. By ignoring the audience, you miss this support; fear builds up inside of you. By looking at them, you share an experience with them, and in sharing you cease being a figure standing alone while a crowd stares at you. Of course, there are some selections which make it difficult to use this direct contact. For instance, in an intimate poem, such as "How Do I Love Thee?", it would not be particularly apt to address the reading directly to individuals in the audience.

It has been the experience of the authors, based on the findings of the survey, that with the right atmosphere in a class, with *conscientious preparation,* over 75 percent of stage fright should be lessened by the end of four to six weeks. We have found that over 90 percent of our students are afflicted with stage fright at the beginning of a semester, but only 10 percent have not effectively learned to control it within six to nine weeks. The reason is more experience and the chance to read before a class often enough to gain some self-confidence. The type of material read also enters into this picture. Many students find drama readings make them less nervous because they become more involved due to the conversational quality of the dialogue. Others find poetry moves them into another world of involvement.

Whatever techniques are used, it is important that students help themselves in the most significant way of preparation. Read your material to your family, to friends, to anyone who will listen so that you become used to reading orally. It is also a good idea to read aloud other class assignments, newspapers, even the comics, for experience. A well prepared student is a confident student.

One last suggestion is to seek out the help offered by the instructor. Most instructors are only too glad to assist students with their problems, and it is the shortsighted person who prefers to try to exist with his problem rather than get the assistance which can make him feel more secure.

It may seem blunt to say it, but you actually have two choices: to continue to build up stage fright and to make the reading process torture or to convince yourself that concentration on nervousness will bring only undesired results. Emphasis on "I can do it" and on the material itself will insure self-satisfaction, pride in accomplishment, and a relaxed feeling which will make reading a pleasure. Believe in yourself. You will find that the end result will be regret that there is not enough time to do more readings before the semester ends.

Stage fright is up to you. What are you afraid of? Class censure? Classmates are your biggest supporters. Making a mistake? You are in class to make mistakes and to learn how to correct them. Attitude of the instructor? It is a rare case indeed when a teacher enjoys seeing a student do a bad job. Fear of doing a bad reading? Prepare—so you won't. You're probably a lot better than you think you are.

One thing is certain—oral interpretation will bring changes in you that will remain with you all of your life. Don't minimize the experience by concentrating on your nerves.

THE PERFORMANCE

Summary

There are methods to help you gain control over stage fright:

1. Concentrate on the material and not on your nerves.
2. Believe in yourself.
3. Don't try to be critic and reader at the same time. What you may think to be a bad reading may be considered your best.
4. Breathe properly to relieve tension.
5. Look at your audience—they are your biggest support.
6. Read only material *you like*.
7. Prepare—long and often.
8. Read to anyone who will listen to you.
9. Remember the class is in "the same boat."
10. Get to know your classmates *early*.
11. Get help from your instructor.
12. Ask yourself: "What will I gain by thinking of fright so much?"
13. Don't be afraid of making a mistake.
14. Don't assume everyone thinks you look nervous.

You *can* control stage fright.

✒ CHAPTER 4

Let yourself go!

THERE IS A REASON for following the chapter on stage fright with this chapter on getting emotionally involved in the material you choose to read. Getting *involved*—concentrating on the material instead of yourself—is the most important single aid in the control of nerves.

Achieving emotional involvement—letting yourself go—is not easily accomplished, however, especially in America, because we are conditioned to keep our emotions under control. Remember when you fell down and scraped your knee when you were seven and you wanted to howl with the pain? What was it that Mom and Dad said? "Don't cry! Big boys (or girls) don't cry!" And the same thing happened when you broke your arm and when your dog was killed. Americans don't really believe in a show of emotions; emotions should be controlled. Perhaps that is why so many need tranquilizers and ulcer diets, or perhaps Americans don't have time to be emotional.

Now, suddenly, you are told in oral interpretation class that you should "let yourself go," become involved in what you read. If you are saying to yourself at this point, "That's going to take some doing," you are right. But say also that it can and *must* be done if you are to be a successful oral interpreter of literature.

To be able to show honest emotion is a significant objective of the course. Sincerity will never be laughed at. Yet, it takes time to learn to display emotion. Think about a movie you've seen that really had you on the edge of your seat. If a movie doesn't come to mind, recall a book you've read that kept you entranced to the end, a book with real people in it who became your friends or enemies because you became so involved in their lives. Remember how you were caught up in them, living their problems or joys. Think how easy it was to move with those people from one situation to another.

What you want to achieve in this course is to bring together the way you feel as you read silently and the way you feel (and guide your audience to feel) as you read orally. Yes, there's the problem: to become sufficiently immersed in the material you are reading that the audience comes to know the characters and "feel with" them as they move through the set of circumstances that you describe. During one semester a young man tried to read *Oedipus Rex*. It was obvious that he liked the play, that he felt it deeply, but he was not projecting any emotion. It was flat, lifeless. It was after this reading that he asked to talk with the instructor. During their conversation, the professor asked him if he were an American Indian.

"Yes, I am," he said.

"And have you been trained to believe that any show of emotion is a sign of weakness?"

After a pause, he replied, "Yes."

So the problem was not with his feeling but with an inherent tendency to draw away from any outward show of emotion.

Three Keys to Emotional Involvement

There are three keys to achieving emotional response: empathy, experience, and finding the meaning. Empathy is feeling *with* someone. If you feel sympathy for someone, you are sorry that he lost his job or that he failed a class. If you share in the loss, suffering as he suffers, what you feel is empathy. Choosing material of worth will help you become empathically involved; empathic involvement in what you read, and how you read it, is essential to effective oral interpretation. We might do well to look at the author, the reader, and the audience as a team in the understanding and appreciation of literature.

If the author has done his work well, you, the reader, can become involved and, in turn, through your understanding of the author's work and effective use of reading techniques, you can involve the audience in the literature.

Let's look further at the idea of emotional techniques. Here, we would do well to borrow a page from the actor's handbook. Because we were taught to play down our emotions, to control them in most of our activities as adult Americans, we must find a way, as the actor does, to synthesize emotion. He learns how to laugh or cry at the drop of a hat; the experienced actor can switch from a death scene to a rollicking comedy bit and back again to a scene in a courtroom drama with only a moment's pause. With experience, so can you! Practice doing so with the exercises at the end of this chapter, and after you've tried all of our suggestions think of some others yourself.

Experience is the second key to effective emotional involvement. There are basically two types of experience—primary, things we learn firsthand, and vicarious, what we learn from secondary knowledge. These are examples of primary experience: if you ever lived in Alaska, you'd be able to answer questions about it much better than if you'd only heard of the place. If you'd been in an accident, you could describe what it was like better than if you'd only heard of someone's being in an accident or merely read about one in a newspaper. The alternative in each case would be a learned or vicarious experience.

The more often you read material orally, the more effectiveness you will find in achieving emotional responses. In short, repeated readings will give you more primary experience, and will make you a better judge of your own involvement. The more you read the easier you will find it to let yourself go. The words used to describe experience—primary or secondary—may not be understood by your listeners as you intend them to be understood. Words have *denotative* meaning to be sure, but they also have *connotative* meanings. The denotations we can get by looking up the word in the dictionary; the connotations we get from experience. Thus the word "pain" will mean a toothache to one, a broken arm to another, a strained muscle to still another and so on. Each of us will immediately associate the word with his own experience. And this is true with all such abstract words. Such words as freedom, loyalty, justice, happiness, and pleasure—the list is endless—all conjure up precise meanings in our thinking, colored by events in our lives. Therefore, when we prepare materials for oral interpretation we attempt to discover the author's meaning, denotative and connotative, and convey that meaning to our audience.

Finding the meaning is the third key to effective emotional response. Read the following essay "Of Studies" by Francis Bacon.

THE PERFORMANCE

OF STUDIES

FRANCIS BACON

Studies serve for delight, for ornament, and for ability. Their chief use for delight is in privateness and retiring; for ornament, is in discourse; and for ability, is in the judgment and disposition of business. For expert men can execute and perhaps judge of particulars, one by one; but the general counsels, and the plots and marshaling of affairs come best from those that are learned. To spend too much time in studies is sloth; to use them too much for ornament is affectation; to make judgment wholly by their rules is the humor of a scholar. They perfect nature, and are perfected by experience; for natural abilities are like natural plants, that need pruning by study; and studies themselves do give forth directions too much at large, except they be bounded in by experience. Crafty men contemn studies; simple men admire them; and wise men use them: for they teach not their own use; but that is a wisdom without them and above them, won by observation. Read not to contradict and confute, nor to believe and take for granted, nor to find talk and discourse, but to weigh and consider. Some books are to be tasted, others to be swallowed, and some few to be chewed and digested: that is, some books are to be read only in parts; others to be read but not curiously, and some few to be read wholly, and with diligence and attention. Some books also may be read by deputy, and extracts made of them by others; but that would be only in the less important arguments and the meaner sort of books; else distilled books are, like common distilled waters, flashy things. Reading maketh a full man; conference a ready man; and writing an exact man. And, therefore, if a man write little, he had need have a great memory; if he confer little, he had need have a present wit; and if he read little, he had need have much cunning, to seem to know that he doth not. Histories make men wise; poets, witty; the mathematics, subtile; natural philosophy, deep; moral, grave; logic and rhetoric, able to contend. "Abeunt studia in mores." Nay, there is no stand or impediment in the wit but may be wrought out by fit studies: like as diseases of the body may have appropriate exercises. Bowling is good for the stone and reins, shooting for the lungs and breast, gentle walking for the stomach, riding for the head and the like. So if a man's wit be wandering, let him study the mathematics; for in demonstrations, if his wit be called away never so little, he must begin again. If his wit be not apt to distinguish or find differences, let him study the schoolmen; for they are "cymini sectores." If he be not apt to beat over matters, and to call up one thing to prove and illustrate another, let him study the lawyers' cases; so every defect of the mind may have a special receipt.

Now that you have read the entire selection, look up any words that you didn't recognize immediately. For example, what does *confute* mean? *meaner? contend? Abeunt studia in mores? stand? impediment? cymini sectores?*

Any good dictionary will help with all but the Latin terms. The first of the two, *Abeunt studia in mores,* means "studies develop into habits." *Cymini sectores* (Bacon's reference to schoolmen) are "hairsplitters." You could look up such terms in the *Dictionary of Foreign Phrases and Abbreviations.* But knowing the dictionary meaning won't help with other words Bacon used: *tasted, swallowed, chewed* and *digested.* In these instances the context helps with the connotations of the words.

After you have read the entire selection and have become sure of the word meanings, both denotative and connotative, you'll want to identify the mood of the selection. Doing so will help you to highlight the author's purpose in writing the piece. Is he merely reporting, or is he presenting a satirical view of the situation he describes? Bacon, for example, has often had his style referred to as "crisp." His mood is light, witty, often tongue-in-cheek, as he chides his reader into discovering his meaning. Read Bacon's essay again

THE PERFORMANCE

and relate it to your own idea of study. How does the philosophy impress you—sympathetically, indifferently, or antagonistically? Do his thoughts relate to your own reactions as a student?

Edgar Allan Poe has long been regarded as the father of the horror story. His mood is almost universally somber, seeking its effect through shock and vivid, bloodcurdling description. Notice how the choice of words in the following story is woven together to produce a single pervading mood. Every word adds to the meaning and the emotion builds gradually in order to heighten the listeners' responses to the final climax.

In this story you can see why instructors regard emotional involvement in the material as the core of oral interpretation. Read "The Tell-Tale Heart" with an eye to the reading problems the story creates. Note that it begins on an expository level—the main character (actually the only speaking character) simply but nervously relating the story. There is a clue to the lack of emotion in the second paragraph by Poe's use of the lines, "Object there was none. Passion there was none." So it is natural to read these beginning paragraphs without emotion. However, it is vital that the character (voice and manner) be established right from the beginning. You will notice that there is a climactic point when the old man cries out, "Who's there?" Then there's a lull in the emotion until it begins to build again, reaching a second climax with the line, "With a loud yell I threw open the lantern and leaped into the room." Following this climax there is another period of calm and still another build to the final climax of the story. By the time you reach that point in the story where the murderer shrieks, "Villains! dissemble no more! I admit the deed!" your own scream will be as natural as his must have been. In fact, anything less than a muffled scream betrays your lack of involvement in the story. Don't read this story for an audience unless you can become sufficiently involved that you go progressively "mad" as you build to the final scream. Suggestions have been inserted directly into the story to guide your emotional involvement and understanding.

THE TELL-TALE HEART

EDGAR ALLAN POE

True!—nervous—very, very dreadfully nervous I had been and am! but why *will* you say that I am mad? The disease had sharpened my senses—not destroyed—not dulled them. Above all was the sense of hearing acute. I heard all things in the heaven and in the earth. I heard many things in hell. How, then, am I mad? Hearken! and observe how healthily—how calmly I can tell you the whole story.

It is impossible to say how first the idea entered my brain; but once conceived, it haunted me day and night. Object there was none. Passion there was none. I loved the old man. He had never wronged me. He had never given me insult. For his gold I had no desire. I think it was his eye! yes, it was this! One of his eyes resembled that of a vulture—a pale blue eye, with a film over it. Whenever it fell upon me, my blood ran cold; and so by degrees—very gradually—I made up my mind to take the life of the old man, and thus rid myself of the eye for ever.

(In these first two paragraphs the mood is unemotional, candid. But there is a clue to the man's psychotic state in the line, "I think it was his eye! yes, it was this!" Your tone of voice (bring wonder into it) and rate of speech (slower) will telegraph the clue to the audience. Use of "eye" as a symbol of horror and exclamation point shows Poe means it to be emphasized.)

Now this is the point. You fancy me mad. Madmen know nothing. But you should have seen *me*. You should have seen how wisely I proceeded—with what caution— with what foresight—with what dissimulation I went to work!

I was never kinder to the old man than during the whole week before I killed him. And every night, about

THE PERFORMANCE

midnight, I turned the latch of his door and opened it—
oh, so gently! And then, when I had made an opening
sufficient for my head, I put in a dark lantern, all closed,
closed, so that no light shone out, and then I thrust in my
head. Oh, you would have laughed to see how cunningly I
thrust it in! I moved it slowly—very, very slowly, so that I
might not disturb the old man's sleep. It took me an hour
to place my whole head within the opening so far that I
could see him as he lay upon his bed. Ha!—would a
madman have been so wise as this?

> (*The lines up to this point have been expository again. Your
> tone and rate should reflect this mood and add his conceit
> with himself and his plan. A straight reading of the lines up to
> this point will convey his conceit and his matter-of-fact atti-
> tude to the audience.*)

And then, when my head was well in the room, I undid
the lantern cautiously—oh so cautiously—cautiously (for
the hinges creaked)—I undid it just so much that a single
thin ray fell upon the vulture eye. And this I did for seven
long nights—every night just at midnight—but I found
the eye always closed; and so it was impossible to do the
work; for it was not the old man who vexed me, but his
Evil Eye.

> (*Again, the clue to the man's psychotic state. Reflect his
> madness by emphasizing the words, "but his Evil Eye."*)

And, every morning, when the day broke, I went boldly
into the chamber, and spoke courageously to him, calling
him by name in a hearty tone, and inquiring how he had
passed the night. So you see he would have been a very
profound old man, indeed, to suspect that every night,
just at twelve, I looked in upon him while he slept.

> (*Notice that the author supplies periods, such as the above
> lines, of momentary relief—a slackening of the emotion. This
> pattern of builds followed by relief continues as the story de-
> velops with gradually diminishing moments of relief. Feel
> them as you read.*)

YOUR ROLE IN ORAL INTERPRETATION

Upon the eighth night I was more than usually cautious in opening the door. A watch's minute hand moves more quickly than did mine. Never before that night had I *felt* the extent of my own powers—of my sagacity. I could scarcely contain my feelings of triumph. To think that there I was, opening the door, little by little, and he not even to dream of my secret deeds or thoughts. I fairly chuckled at the idea; and perhaps he heard me; for he moved on the bed suddenly, as if startled. Now you may think that I drew back—but no. His room was as black as pitch with the thick darkness, (for the shutters were close fastened, through fear of robbers,) and so I knew that he could not see the opening of the door, and I kept pushing it on steadily, steadily.

I had my head in, and was about to open the lantern, when my thumb slipped upon the tin fastening, and the old man sprang up in the bed, crying out—"Who's there?"

(*Did you notice the build in the above paragraph? It begins matter-of-factly; then suspense creeps in as the lantern is opened; the climax of this segment is reached when you read, "Who's there?" If you feel this segment, your rate will gradually get higher, to the cry, "Who's there?" Relief again follows in the coming lines.*)

I kept still and said nothing. For a whole hour I did not move a muscle, and in the meantime I did not hear him lie down. He was still sitting up in the bed listening;—just as I have done, night after night, hearkening to the death watches in the wall.

(*Relief is indeed momentary this time; the emotion begins to build again right here. Build it slowly and subtly because it is some time before another respite comes.*)

Presently I heard a slight groan, and I knew it was the groan of mortal terror. It was not a groan of pain or of grief—oh no!—it was the low stifled sound that arises from the bottom of the soul when overcharged with awe. I knew the sound well. Many a night, just at midnight, when all the world slept, it has welled up from my own

THE PERFORMANCE

bosom, deepening, with its dreadful echo, the terrors that distracted me. I say I knew it well. I knew what the old man felt, and pitied him, although I chuckled at heart. I knew that he had been lying awake ever since the first slight noise, when he had turned in the bed. His fears had been ever since growing upon him. He had been trying to fancy them causeless, but could not. He had been saying to himself—"It is nothing but the wind in the chimney—it is only a mouse crossing the floor," or "it is merely a cricket which has made a single chirp." Yes, he had been trying to comfort himself with these suppositions; but he had found all in vain. *All in vain;* because Death, in approaching him, had stalked with his black shadow before him, and enveloped the victim. And it was the mournful influence of the unperceived shadow that caused him to feel—although he neither saw nor heard—to *feel* the presence of my head within the room.

When I had waited a long time, very patiently, without hearing him lie down, I resolved to open a little—a very, very little crevice in the lantern. So I opened it—you cannot imagine how stealthily, steathily—until, at length, a single dim ray, like the thread of a spider, shot out from the crevice and full upon the vulture eye.

It was open—wide, wide open—and I grew furious as I gazed upon it. I saw it with perfect distinctness—all a dull blue, with a hideous veil over it that chilled the very marrow in my bones; but I could see nothing else of the old man's face or person: for I had directed the ray as if by instinct, precisely upon the damned spot.

(*The voice rate quickens and the pitch increases gradually as his madness again takes over. Feel the growing tension and panic. The paragraph that follows is only slightly relieving. Maintain the pace and let the pitch drop a notch to show it.*)

And now have I not told you that what you mistake for madness is but over-acuteness of the senses?—now, I say, there came to my ears a low, dull, quick sound, such as a watch makes when enveloped in cotton. I knew *that* sound well too. It was the beating of the old man's heart.

YOUR ROLE IN ORAL INTERPRETATION

It increased my fury, as the beating of a drum stimulates the soldier into courage.

But even yet I refrained and kept still. I scarcely breathed. I held the lantern motionless. I tried how steadily I could maintain the ray upon the eye. Meantime the hellish tattoo of the heart increased. It grew quicker and quicker, and louder and louder every instant. The old man's terror *must* have been extreme! It grew louder, I say, louder every moment!—do you mark me well? I have told you that I am nervous: so I am. And now at the dead hour of the night, amid the dreadful silence of the old house, so strange a noise as this excited me to uncontrollable terror. Yet, for some minutes longer I refrained and stood still. But the beating grew louder, louder! I thought the heart must burst. And now a new anxiety seized me— the sound would be heard by a neighbor! The old man's hour had come! With a loud yell, I threw open the lantern and leaped into the room. He shrieked once—once only. In an instant I dragged him to the floor, and pulled the heavy bed over him. I then smiled gaily,

(*This paragraph continues the emotion—the madness—as the man relives the murder. Rate and pitch—feeling—climax again with the line, "I then smiled gaily, to find the deed so far done." Following this line the rate slows and pitch drops. The mood becomes expository again in the following paragraph with the line, "Yes, he was stone, stone dead."*)

to find the deed so far done. But, for many minutes, the heart beat on with a muffled sound. This, however, did not vex me; it would not be heard through the wall. At length it ceased. The old man was dead. I removed the bed and examined the corpse. Yes, he was stone, stone dead. I placed my hand upon the heart and held it there many minutes. There was no pulsation. He was stone dead. His eye would trouble me no more.

If still you think me mad, you will think so no longer when I describe the wise precautions I took for the concealment of the body. The night waned, and I worked hastily, but in silence. First of all I dismembered the corpse. I cut off the head and the arms and the legs.

THE PERFORMANCE

I then took up three planks from the flooring of the chamber, and deposited all between the scantlings. I then replaced the boards so cleverly, so cunningly, that no human eye—not even *his*—could have detected anything wrong. There was nothing to wash out—no stain of any kind—no blood-spot whatever. I had been too wary for that. A tub had caught all—ha! ha!

(*Notice how subtly the author builds toward the amused laugh in this paragraph. The key to the amusement again centers around the idea that no human eye—not even his—could detect anything wrong. Your own laugh will be as natural as his. Feel it!*)

When I had made an end of these labors, it was four o'clock—still dark as midnight. As the bell sounded the hour, there came a knocking at the street door. I went down to open it with a light heart,—for what had I *now* to fear? There entered three men, who introduced themselves, with perfect suavity, as officers of the police. A shriek had been heard by a neighbor during the night: suspicion of foul play had been aroused; information had been lodged at the police office, and they (the officers) had been deputed to search the premises. I smiled,—for what had I to fear? I bade the gentlemen welcome. The shriek, I said, was my own in a dream. The old man, I mentioned, was absent in the country. I took my visitors all over the house. I bade them search—search *well*. I led them, at length, to *his* chamber. I showed them his treasures, secure, undisturbed. In the enthusiasm of my confidence, I brought chairs into the room, and desired them here to rest from their fatigues, while I myself, in the wild audacity of my perfect triumph, placed my own seat upon the very spot beneath which reposed the corpse of the victim.

(*The above paragraphs are reflective of the complete relaxation of the man. They should be read with abandon—relief dominates the reading of them. The sentences which follow gradually move from abandon to concern as again the man relives his deed. Final climax of the story begins building with the line, "But, ere long, I felt myself getting pale and wished them gone." Rate and tone grow faster and higher until in the final lines your own muffled shriek is natural and spontaneous.*)

The officers were satisfied. My *manner* had convinced them. I was singularly at ease. They sat, and while I answered cheerily, they chatted of familiar things. But, ere long, I felt myself getting pale and wished them gone. My head ached, and I fancied a ringing in my ears: but still they sat and still chatted. The ringing became more distinct—it continued and became more distinct: I talked more freely to get rid of the feeling: but it continued and gained definitiveness—until, at length, I found that the noise was *not* within my ears.

No doubt I now grew very pale;—but I talked more fluently, and with a heightened voice. Yet the sound increased—and what could I do? It was a *low, dull, quick sound—much such a sound as a watch makes when enveloped in cotton.* I gasped for breath—and yet the officers heard it not. I talked more quickly—more vehemently; but the noise steadily increased. I arose and argued about trifles, in a high key and with violent gesticulations, but the noise steadily increased. Why would they not be gone? I paced the floor, to and fro with heavy strides, as if excited to fury by the observation of the men—but the noise steadily increased. Oh God! what *could* I do? I foamed—I raved—I swore. I swung the chair upon which I had been sitting, and grated it upon the boards, but the noise arose over all and continually increased. It grew louder—louder—*louder*! And still the men chatted pleasantly, and smiled. Was it possible they heard not? Almighty God!—no, no! They heard!—they suspected!—they *knew*!—they were making a *mockery* of my horror!—this I thought, and this I think. But anything was better than this agony! Anything was more tolerable than this derision! I could bear those hypocritical smiles no longer! I felt that I must scream or die!—and now—again!—hark! louder! louder! *louder*!—

THE PERFORMANCE

"Villains!" I shrieked, "dissemble no more! I admit the deed!—tear up the planks!—here, here!—it is the beating of his hideous heart!"

There are other aspects of getting the meaning, such as literary structure and imagery which will be dealt with in chapters on types of literature. It will suffice here to say that you will want to examine your material for theme as a part of getting the meaning. Too, you will find it helpful, and often necessary, to do some research on the author if the mood, and thus the meaning, of your selection is not readily clear to you on first or second reading. Learning about him—his life and times—will help you to appreciate more fully his point of view. Don't assume, however, that reading about the author will always give you insight into the purpose of a particular piece of his writing. Failure to understand the selection will most certainly result in a faulty interpretation of the author's meaning. This is especially true of satire. Read the following cutting of this essay as though the author, Jonathan Swift, meant every word of it. In reality, Swift used biting satire to make the point that the English were brutally tyrannizing the Irish. At the same time he pointed up faults in many aspects of the life and thinking of the period. Analysis provided by the authors will help to point up Swift's satire.

A MODEST PROPOSAL

JONATHAN SWIFT

It is a melancholy object to those who walk through this great town or travel in the country, when they see the streets, the roads and cabin doors crowded with beggars of the female sex, followed by three, four, or six children, all in rags, and importuning every passenger for an alms. These mothers, instead of being able to work for their honest livelihood, are forced to employ all their time in strolling, to beg sustenance for their helpless infants, who as they grow up, either turn thieves for want of work, or leave their dear native country to fight for the Pretender in Spain, or sell themselves to the Barbadoes.

I think it is agreed by all parties that this prodigious number of children, in the arms, or on the backs, or at the heels of their mothers, and frequently their fathers, is in the present deplorable state of the kingdom a very great additional grievance; and therefore whoever could find out a fair, cheap, and easy method of making these children sound, useful members of the commonwealth, would deserve so well of the public as to have his statue set up for a preserver of the nation.

(In these first two paragraphs Swift appeals to the reader for compassion in the matter to be discussed and introduces the first point of satire, that anyone solving the problem of the Irish poor would deserve such recognition as to have his statue set up—a hollow payment for service. This material must be handled in a straightforward, matter-of-fact reading to be effective. The emotion lies as much in what is not said as in what is presented.)

But my intention is very far from being confined to provide only for the children of professed beggars; it is of a much greater extent, and shall take in the whole number of infants at a certain age, who are born of parents in effect as little able to support them as those who demand our charity in the streets.

As to my own part, having weighted the several schemes of other projectors, I have always found them grossly mistaken in their computation. It is true, a child, just dropped from its dam, may be supported by her milk for a solar year with little other nourishment, at most not above the value of two shillings, which the mother may certainly get, or the value in scraps, by her lawful occupation of begging and it is exactly at one year old that I propose to provide for them in such a manner as instead of being a charge upon their parents or the parish, or wanting food and raiment for the rest of their lives, they shall, on the contrary, contribute to the feeding and partly to the clothing of many thousands.

(Satire in the two paragraphs above includes the reference to the mother as a "dam," reducing the Irish mother and child to an animal state. The plan is more plausible when one thinks in terms of animals rather than humans. Heighten the satire

THE PERFORMANCE

by emphasizing "dam." Reference to "two shillings" is also satirical since it is such a small sum to use in reference to the worth of human life.)

The number of souls in this kingdom being usually reckoned one million and a half, of these I calculate there may be about two hundred thousand couples whose wives are breeders; from which number I subtract thirty thousand couples who are able to maintain their own children . . . there will remain an hundred and seventy thousand breeders. I again subtract fifty thousand for these women who miscarry, or whose children die by accident or disease within the year. There only remain an hundred and twenty thousand children of poor parents annually born. The question therefore is, how this number shall be reared and provided for . . .

I shall now therefore humbly propose my own thoughts, which I hope will not be liable to the least objection.

(These calculations should be handled lightly. They set the stage in numbers for the details of Swift's "plan.")

I have been assured by a very knowing American of my acquaintance in London, that a young healthy child well nursed is at a year old a most delicious, nourishing, and wholesome food, whether stewed, roasted, baked, or boiled, and I make no doubt that it will equally serve in a fricassee or a ragout.

(The obvious reference in this paragraph was to the barbaric American. It was popular at the time to regard the American as little better than the savages with whom he lived in America.)

I do therefore humbly offer it to public consideration that of the hundred and twenty thousand children already computed, twenty thousand may be reserved for breed . . . (and) that the remaining hundred thousand may at a year old be offered in sale to the persons of quality and fortune through the kingdom, always advising the mother to let them suck plentifully in the last month, so as to render them plump and fat for a good table. A child will make two dishes at an entertainment for friends, and when the family dines alone, the fore or hind quarter will make a reasonable dish, and seasoned with a little pepper or salt will be very good boiled on the fourth day, especially in winter.

(The plan is detailed. Satire runs rampant in this paragraph. Reference is again made to Irish animals with the use of the word "breed." Persons of quality and fortune, it will later develop, are landlords, again a satirical play on words. Final satirical reference is made to how far one "suckling" (a term which refers to pigs) will go in feeding the "persons of quality." The subtle points of satire should be brought out in your reading by emphasizing those key words or by tossing off the others in the sentence.)

I grant this food will be somewhat dear, and therefore very proper for landlords, who, as they have already devoured most of the parents, seem to have the best title to the children.

I have already computed the charge of nursing a beggar's child (in which list I reckon all cottagers, labourers, and four-fifths of the farmers) to be about two shillings per annum, rags included, and I believe no gentleman would repine to give ten shillings for the carcass of a good fat child, which, as I have said, will make four dishes of excellent nutritive meat, when he has only some particular friend or his own family to dine with him. Thus the squire will learn to be a good landlord, and grow popular among his tenants, the mother will have eight shillings net profit, and be fit for work till she produces another child.

Those who are more thrifty (as I must confess the times require) may flay the carcass; the skin of which, artificially dressed, will make admirable gloves for ladies, and summer boots for fine gentlemen.

Secondly, the poor tenants will have something valuable of their own, which by law may be made liable to

THE PERFORMANCE

distress, and help to pay their landlord's rent, their corn and cattle being already seized, and money a thing unknown.

(These lines bring in a direct sarcastic note with references to the products to be made from the skin and the fine folks who will wear them, and ending again on the abject poverty of the peasants. Again, the subtlety of the satire will show in your reading the material in a light off-handed manner, as though you were dealing in sheep or pigs instead of humankind.)

Thirdly, whereas the maintenance of a hundred thousand children, from two years old and upward, cannot be computed at less than ten shillings apiece per annum, the nation's stock will be thereby increased fifty thousand pounds per annum, besides the profit of a new dish, introduced to the tables of all gentlemen of fortune in the kingdom who have any refinement in taste, and the money will circulate among ourselves, the goods being entirely of our own growth and manufacture.

Fourthly, the constant breeders, besides the gain of eight shillings sterling per annum, by the sale of their children, will be rid of the charge of maintaining them after the first year . . . This would be a great inducement to marriage, which all wise nations have either encouraged by rewards, or enforced by laws and penalties. It would increase the care and tenderness of mothers toward their children, when they were sure of a settlement for life, to the poor babes, provided in some sort by the public, to their annual profit instead of expense. We should see an honest emulation among the married women, which of them could bring the fattest child to the market. Men would become as fond of their wives, during the time of their pregnancy, as they are now of their mares in foal, their cows in calf, their sows when they are ready to farrow, nor offer to beat or kick them (as is too frequent a practice) for fear of a miscarriage . . .

(The satire branches out in the above paragraph to include the areas of promiscuity, mother love, father love, and the treatment of wives by their husbands.)

YOUR ROLE IN ORAL INTERPRETATION

I can think of no one objection, that will possibly be raised against this proposal, unless it should be urged that the number of people will be thereby much lessened in the kingdom. This I freely own, and it was indeed one principal design in offering it to the world. I desire the reader will observe, that I calculate my remedy for this one individual kingdom of Ireland, and for no other that ever was, is, or, I think, ever can be upon earth. Therefore let no man talk to me of other expedients: Of taxing our absentees at five shillings a pound: Of using neither clothes, nor household furniture, except what is of our own growth and manufacture: Of utterly rejecting the materials and instruments that promote foreign luxury: Of curing the expensiveness of pride, vanity, idleness, and gaming in our women: Of introducing a vein of parsimony, prudence and temperance: Of learning to love our Country, wherein we differ even from Laplanders, and the inhabitants of Topinamboo: Of quitting our animosities and factions: . . . Of being a little cautious not to sell our country and conscience for nothing: Of teaching landlords to have at least one degree of mercy toward their tenants. Lastly of putting a spirit of honesty, industry, and skill into our shopkeepers, who, if a resolution could now be taken to buy only our native goods, would immediately unite to cheat and exact upon us in the price, the measure, and the goodness, nor could ever yet be brought to make one fair proposal of just dealing, though often and earnestly invited to it.

Therefore I repeat, let no man talk to me of these and the like expedients till he hath at least some glimpse of hope that there will ever be some hearty and sincere attempt to put them in practice.

(*Notice in the above lines, the range of grievances that Swift identifies. Nearly every aspect of life comes under his indictment.*)

But as to myself, having been wearied out for many years with offering vain, idle, visionary thoughts, and at

THE PERFORMANCE

length utterly despairing of success, I fortunately fell upon this proposal. . . . I am not so violently bent upon my own opinion as to reject any offer, proposed by wise men, which shall be found equally innocent, cheap, easy and effectual. But before something of that kind shall be advanced in contradiction to my scheme . . . I desire those politicians, who dislike my overture, and may perhaps be so bold as to attempt an answer, that they will first ask the parents of these mortals, whether they would not at this day think it a great happiness to have been sold for food at a year old, in the manner I prescribe, and thereby have avoided such a perpetual scene of misfortunes as they have since gone through by the oppression of landlords, the impossibility of paying rent without money or trade, the want of common sustenance, with neither house nor clothes to cover them from the inclemencies of the weather, and the most inevitable prospect of entailing the like or greater miseries upon their breed forever.

I profess, in the sincerity of my heart, that I have not the least personal interest in endeavouring to promote this necessary work, having no other motive than the public good of my country, by advancing our trade, providing for infants, relieving the poor, and giving some pleasure to the rich. I have no children by which I can propose to get a single penny; the youngest being nine years old, and my wife past child-bearing.

Study the following poems. Use the three keys to emotional involvement in each case. Discuss their meaning in class or with friends. Your own understanding and appreciation will increase as you do.

MY LAST DUCHESS
Ferrara

ROBERT BROWNING

That's my last Duchess painted on the wall,
Looking as if she were alive. I call
That piece a wonder, now: Fra Pandolf's hands
Worked busily a day, and there she stands.
Will't please you sit and look at her? I said
"Frà Pandolf" by design, for never read
Strangers like you that pictured countenance,
The depth and passion of its earnest glance,
But to myself they turned (since none puts by
The curtain I have drawn for you, but I)
And seemed as they would ask me, if they durst,
How such a glance came there; so, not the first
Are you to turn and ask thus. Sir, 'twas not
Her husband's presence only, called that spot
Of joy into the Duchess' cheek: perhaps
Frà Pandolf chanced to say, "Her mantle laps
Over my lady's wrist too much," or "Paint
Must never hope to reproduce the faint
Half-flush that dies along her throat." Such stuff
Was courtesy, she thought, and cause enough
For calling up that spot of joy. She had
A heart—how shall I say?—too soon made glad,
Too easily impressed; she liked whate'er
She looked on, and her looks went everywhere.
Sir, 'twas all one! My favor at her breast,
The dropping of the daylight in the West,
The bough of cherries some officious fool
Broke in the orchard for her, the white mule
She rode with round the terrace—all and each
Would draw from her alike the approving speech,
Or blush, at least. She thanked men,—good! but thanked
Somehow—I know not how—as if she ranked

THE PERFORMANCE

My gift of a nine-hundred-years-old name
With anybody's gift. Who'd stoop to blame
This sort of trifling? Even had you skill
In speech—(Which I have not)—to make your will
Quite clear to such an one, and say, "Just this
Or that in you disgusts me; here you miss,
Or there exceed the mark"—and if she let
Herself be lessoned so, nor plainly set
Her wits to yours, forsooth, and made excuse,
—E'en then would be some stooping: and I choose
Never to stoop. Oh, sir, she smiled, no doubt,
Whene'er I passed her; but who passed without
Much the same smile? This grew; I gave commands;
Then all smiles stopped together. There she stands
As if alive. Will't please you rise? We'll meet
The company below then. I repeat,
The Count your master's known munificence
Is ample warrant that no just pretense
Of mine for dowry will be disallowed;
Though his fair daughter's self, as I avowed
At starting, is my object. Nay, we'll go
Together down, sir. Notice Neptune, though,
Taming a sea-horse, thought a rarity,
Which Claus of Innsbruck cast in bronze for me!

THE LITTLE BLACK BOY

WILLIAM BLAKE

My mother bore me in the southern wild,
And I am black, but O! my soul is white;
White as an angel is the English child,
But I am black, as if bereav'd of light.

My mother taught me underneath a tree,
And sitting down before the heat of day,
She took me on her lap and kissed me,
And pointing to the east began to say:

"Look on the rising sun: there God does live,
And gives his light, and gives his heat away:
And flowers and trees and beasts and men receive
Comfort in morning, joy in the noonday.

"And we are put on earth a little space,
That we may learn to bear the beams of love;
And these black bodies and this sunburnt face
Is but a cloud, and like a shady grove.

"For when our souls have learn'd the heat to bear,
The cloud will vanish; we shall hear his voice,
Saying: 'Come out from the grove, my love and care,
And round my golden tent like lambs rejoice.' "

Thus did my mother say, and kissèd me;
And thus I say to little English boy:
When I from black and he from white cloud free,
Around the tent of God like lambs we joy,

I'll shade him from the heat, till he can bear
To lean in joy upon our Father's knee;
And then I'll stand and stroke his silver hair,
And be like him, and he will then love me.

DOVER BEACH

MATTHEW ARNOLD

The sea is calm tonight.
The tide is full, the moon lies fair
Upon the straits;—on the French coast the light
Gleams and is gone; the cliffs of England stand,
Glimmering and vast, out in the tranquil bay.
Come to the window, sweet is the night air!
Only, from the long line of spray
Where the sea meets the moon-blanch'd land,

Listen! you hear the grating roar
Of pebbles which the waves draw back, and fling,
At their return, up the high strand,
Begin, and cease, and then again begin,
With tremulous cadence slow, and bring
The eternal note of sadness in.
Sophocles long ago
Heard it on the Aegean, and it brought
Into his mind the turbid ebb and flow
Of human misery; we
Find also in the sound a thought,
Hearing it by this distant northern sea.

The Sea of Faith
Was once, too, at the full, and round earth's shore
Lay like the folds of a bright girdle furl'd.
But now I only hear
Its melancholy, long, withdrawing roar,
Retreating, to the breath
Of the night-wind, down the vast edges drear
And naked shingles of the world.

Ah, love, let us be true
To one another! for the world, which seems
To lie before us like a land of dreams,
So various, so beautiful, so new,
Hath really neither joy, nor love, nor light,
Nor certitude, nor peace, nor help for pain;
And we are here as on a darkling plain
Swept with confused alarms of struggle and flight,
Where ignorant armies clash by night.

COME UP FROM THE FIELDS, FATHER

WALT WHITMAN

Come up from the fields, father, here's a letter from our
    Pete,
And come to the front door, mother—here's a letter from
    thy dear son.
Lo, 'tis autumn;

Lo, where the trees, deeper green, yellower and redder,
Cool and sweeten Ohio's villages, with leaves fluttering
    in the moderate wind;
Where apples ripe in the orchards hang, and grapes on the
    trellised vines;
(Smell you the smell of the grapes on the vines?
Smell you the buckwheat, where the bees were lately
    buzzing?)
Above all, lo, the sky, so calm, so transparent after the rain,
    and with wondrous clouds;
Below, too, all calm, all vital and beautiful—and the farm
    prospers well.

Down in the fields all prospers well;
But now from the fields come, father—come at the daugh-
    ter's call;
And come to the entry, mother—to the front door come
    right away.
Fast as she can she hurries—something ominous—her steps
    trembling;
She does not tarry to smooth her hair, nor adjust her cap.
Open the envelope quickly;
O this is not our son's writing, yet his name is signed;
O a strange hand writes for our dear son—O stricken
    mother's soul!
All swims before her eyes—flashes with black—
    she catches the main words only;
Sentences broken—*gun-shot wound in the breast,*
    cavalry skirmish, taken to hospital,
At present low, but will soon be better.

Ah, now the single figure to me,
Amid all teeming and wealthy Ohio, with all its cities and
    farms,
Sickly white in the face, and dull in the head, very faint,
By the jamb of a door leans.
Grieve not so, dear mother, (the just-grown daughter
    speaks through her sobs;
The little sisters huddle around, speechless and dismay'd;)
See, dearest mother, the letter says Pete will soon be better.

THE PERFORMANCE

Alas, poor boy, he will never be better (nor maybe needs
    to be better, that brave and simple soul;)
While they stand at home at the door, he is dead already;
The only son is dead.
But the mother needs to be better;
She, with thin form, presently drest in black;
By day her meals untouch'd—then at night fitfully sleeping,
    often waking,
In the midnight waking, weeping, longing with one deep
    longing,
O that she might withdraw unnoticed—silent from life,
    escape and withdraw,
To follow, to seek, to be with her dear dead son.

THE PARTING

MICHAEL DRAYTON

Since there's no help, come let us kiss and part—
Nay, I have done, you get no more of me;
And I am glad, yea, glad with all my heart,
That thus so cleanly I myself can free.
Shake hands for ever, cancel all our vows,
And when we meet at any time again,
Be it not seen in either of our brows
That we one jot of former love retain.
Now at the last gasp of Love's latest breath,
When, his pulse failing, Passion speechless lies,
When Faith is kneeling by his bed of death,
And Innocence is closing up his eyes,
    —Now if thou wouldst, when all have given him over,
    From death to life thou might'st him yet recover.

YOUR ROLE IN ORAL INTERPRETATION

Summary

At the very center of oral interpretation is emotional involvement in the material you are going to read. There are three keys to letting yourself go—becoming involved:

The first key is *empathy*—feeling with the author and the characters in the selection.

The second key is *experience,* primary and vicarious. Call upon your past experience for help in becoming involved.

The third key is *finding the meaning.* Define unfamiliar words both connotatively and denotatively. Read the entire selection. Discover the author's purpose in writing the piece. Identify the mood. Learn what you can of the life of the author and his times.

Exercises

If you have trouble letting yourself go, role-playing is a device that will help you get involved. Try the exercises below.

The important thing with such exercises is not to feel silly doing them. Also, remember the physiological changes within your body with each emotion. The faster heartbeat, the short breaths, for fear; the exhilarating singing of your nerves, the lightness, when you feel happy; the tenseness, the blood rushing to your face, the feeling of everything inside building to a peak, when you feel anger; the sense of peace and relaxation, the confidence, when you are experiencing a quiet moment of real contentment.

1. Create a feeling of personal injustice. Your professor has just failed you in a course that you felt you had honestly passed. You feel he is putting into play his prejudices against you and you march into his office to protest.

2. A feeling of happiness is also part of our life. Suppose you are going to the airport to meet someone whom you have wanted to see for a long, long time. Perhaps you are in love with this person. He—or she—walks into the airport smiling and rushes to you. What is your feeling?

3. You have probably felt frustrated. Try this situation: it is vitally important that you complete an important assignment before nine o'clock that night. Suddenly, some people drop by your house and you don't wish to be rude by asking them to leave. So you stick it out—and they stay and stay. By 8:30 you know you're not going to make it. How do you feel?

4. Picture anger in your mind. Say the words "I hate it!" over and over until you really experience the feeling. Then try saying "I love you" until you get the right feeling. Or think of a funny story you heard recently and keep thinking of it until it again becomes funny to you. Then start laughing.

5. Now recall a very sad moment in your life. Relive it. Feel the lump coming in your throat, the tears into your eyes. Hold the feeling and soon you'll feel like crying. Let go and cry.

ᚠᚣ CHAPTER 5

What shall I read?

THE MOST consistent problem facing a beginning student in oral interpretation is: What should I read?

While it is usually the custom for professors to allow students to choose their own material, there are some who believe in assigning definite subjects. In the latter case, there is no problem about finding material, but in the former the problem is one that has to be solved.

It is wise to remember that part of the experience in oral interpretation is learning to develop new reading tastes. And the search for material serves to broaden such an experience and to enrich each individual. Still, it is often a monumental task to choose a specific selection from the thousands of books available. Many students, unfortunately, come to college woefully unequipped with sufficient reading background so their difficulties are even more pronounced. Selection then becomes a matter of searching and searching, making several choices, eliminating some, and finally, too often in desperation, choosing just any one. It is hoped that during the course itself, students will learn to begin the search very early and allow themselves enough time to find the one reading that really has meaning for them.

In selecting material for expository prose, the problem may not be as pronounced since many textbooks are replete with examples. This type of literature deals with essays, articles, journals, diaries, letters, persuasive writings, almost any type of prose that does not tell a story—although there can be expository prose incorporated within narrative prose. A description of a setting or of a character would be, for example, expository. A student can therefore begin his search among his own textbooks or those of a friend. Literature texts are of particular value. He may also refer to articles in such magazines as *Saturday Review of Literature, Atlantic, Harper's,* such weekly news magazines as *Time, Newsweek, Life,* and *Look.* The criterion here is the same as that for any kind of literature—the search should always be for writing that has stature.

You may have in mind a certain subject area that interests you—sailing, theatre, fishing, anything. If you are looking for material on this area, it is wise to consult the *Reader's Guide to Periodical Literature,* which indexes by subject articles to be found in magazines and other periodicals. It is an invaluable timesaver and a reference of inestimable value. You can also check the subject card catalog in the library for up-to-date books on the area of interest.

There are many authors who have contributed to expository prose. Among the most prominent are James Thurber, W. Somerset Maugham, Bruce Catton in his books on the Civil War, John Gunther, Jean-Paul Sartre, Mark Twain, and Richard Armour. A more detailed list of expository passages is given at the end of this chapter.

When it comes to narrative prose, the problem is more complex since there are an endless number of novels and short stories. Here the student has more to do than simply find a piece of material. He has to find a selection that can be extracted from a whole novel and still be complete within itself—or that can be cut and still represent with clarity the novel's intent. In many cases, this will necessitate reading a novel with enough thoroughness that the student will know exactly what the story entails. One cannot read a *part* of a novel with any degree of intelligence without knowing the *total* picture. Since it is literally impossible for students to read four or five novels to find one selection for an oral interpretation, they should recall those they have read in the past and liked. If, however, none have been read, the *Masterpieces of World Literature in Digest Form,* published by Harper's, can provide plot summaries. Then—once a book is chosen and a particular selection made, the book should be read in its entirety for a clear picture of the total work.

Another source of information is, of course, book reviews in magazines, particularly in the *New York Times Book Review* and in *Saturday Review of Literature.* Weekly news magazines and *Harper's* and *Atlantic* carry good review sections, as do some of the more reputable newspapers. By reading a review a student can discover the type of novel a book is and the nature of its plot.

YOUR ROLE IN ORAL INTERPRETATION

In addition, there are best seller lists to guide students. These can be found posted in the library, in bookstores, in newspapers. Bookstores can also provide an excellent source of possible material.

As for short stories, there are countless anthologies, many of which are listed at the end of this chapter. Stories by Flannery O'Connor, Eudora Welty, Katherine Anne Porter, Shirley Jackson, and others are reliable sources. Go to your favorite authors for possible selections.

When it comes to finding poetry, there is an equally difficult problem in that there are so many anthologies that the student is lost in a maze of titles. The *Poetry Index* is an excellent choice for locating appropriate material. It not only classifies poetry by type but it also is annotated so as to give one at least an idea of the basic theme of a poem. Often students select for poetry the writings of T. S. Eliot (not always a good choice because of the difficulty in understanding the symbolism in some of his writings), Dylan Thomas (who presents the same problem), Edgar Allan Poe (he did other things besides "The Raven"), W. H. Auden, Karl Shapiro, Matthew Arnold, Keats, Shelley, Browning, Carl Sandburg, Robert Frost, and Amy Lowell. A few suggestions have been made at the close of this chapter but again the *Poetry Index* is your best bet.

In the matter of drama, reviews of current plays on Broadway or of plays in your local community can offer good suggestions. There is also a *Play Index* in the libraries, a Burns Mantle edition of *Best Plays* of each year and other such "Best Play" collections. However, such editions must be used with care because mere summaries of plots are often inadequate in guiding a reader in the characterizations involved in plays. A sketchy summation of plot cannot go into sufficient detail on characterization, the essential concern of the interpreter.

In drama there are also the classics which are too often over-looked—plays by Moliere, Shaw, Shakespeare, Voltaire, Corneille, Sheridan, Oliver Goldsmith, and many more. There are also any number of dramatic anthologies, such as the *Theatre Guild Anthology*, *Masters of Modern Drama* (published by Random House), *Thirty Famous One Act Plays*, *Theater World*, etc.

The library is, of course, the most reliable place to find material. If you have an idea about an author you have liked, you can look up that author in the card catalog for references to his works. Or, if you know the title of a work but are not sure of the author, look in the card catalog under the title. In drama, also, a motion picture is often adapted from a play; so if you happen to have seen a film you liked, check the title to see if it is based on a play. That information is always given in the film's titles at the beginning. Finally, if you do not find the information you want in the catalog, check with your librarian.

All readers should immediately become acquainted with *The Reader's Adviser and Bookman's Manual*. As it states on the cover, it is "A guide to the best in print in Literature, Biographies, Dictionaries, Encyclopedias, Bibles, Classics, Drama, Poetry, Fiction, Science, Philosophy, Travel, and History." It is an endless source of material with clear annotations of contents of all fields of literature. Also it tells exactly what type of material is contained in the anthologies.

So much for suggestions about material, but what about information about the author? It is always desirable to know something about the author of a selection you are to read.

There are, of course, various encyclopedias that can be consulted. On the jackets of most modern novels and on many editions of plays, biographical data is given about the authors. *The Reader's Encyclopedia* provides information on just about every author of importance. And there is also the *Dictionary of National Biography* which gives detailed biographical data on literary figures. Occasionally you may select the work of an obscure writer. If you do, there are definite possibilities that you will not find any information. In such a case, you may also assume that you have chosen a work that is not of the literary quality necessary for a course in oral interpretation.

What is the test then for good literature? For one thing, the fact that it has withstood the test of time—that generations have continued to consider it worthy of study—is a good criterion. But this is not meant to imply that only the so-called classics are of significance. Often works from the past are better designed for silent reading than oral, just as some contemporary literature is best read silently. For example, take such philosophical treatises of today as Erich Fromm's *Art of Loving*. As profound as this book is it does not lend itself to very arresting or compelling oral reading.

If a writing has qualities of good language, and a theme that has an application to most of us, it should be a good choice. The fact that the material relates to our contemporary times is not, however, a sufficient criterion for judgment. Many articles that have been written about LSD are of superficial value. Irresponsible and uninformed columnists and, in some cases, magazine writers have indulged themselves with analysis of Viet Nam. The reader must

YOUR ROLE IN ORAL INTERPRETATION

make every effort to check into the writer's background to make certain that he is qualified to write about a subject.

While the suggestions above refer mainly to expository writings, the same judgment is necessary in choosing contemporary fiction writers and dramatists.

Much of contemporary literature is highly stylized, loosely structured, and consequently needs careful scrutiny. And with much of today's fiction devoted to sexual excursions, it is wise to find out whether such excursions are the stories' only claim to attention. It is not to be inferred that suggestive scenes, if done well, should be avoided, but it is advisable to decide just how well done they are. For instance, Henry Miller is considered by some literary authorities as an excellent writer, but there are others who think him somewhat overrated. Consequently, any reading of his material should undergo critical judgment. Laurence Durrell excels in dramatic imagery; his use of word color and descriptive effects is like words set to music. Much of his writing, therefore, would be acceptable.

Jean Genet, the noted French author, is critically accepted, and yet certain sections from, for instance, *The Balcony* would be questionable for a classroom situation. On the other hand, there is much of Edward Albee's *Who's Afraid of Virginia Woolf* that would be good.

In deciding what is "correct" material to choose, the reader must act as his own censor, although we dislike the word. It is our contention that students in oral interpretation must be exposed to all types of literature. If we ban certain works because they may appear suggestive, then we must ban many of the classics, such as Boccaccio, Balzac, *Song of Solomon,* some of Shakespeare, and Wycherley's *The Country Wife.* We cannot limit the field of oral interpretation by assuming that "acceptable by the majority" is the only rule, because in this case the "majority" is poorly defined, as is "acceptable." Students have an obligation to deal with good literature in all its phases, and usually passages are offensive only when poorly read. For example, some would approach *Who's Afraid of Virginia Woolf* by heavily emphasizing all the profanity, thus obscuring the meaning, the basic theme Albee had in mind. In the same way, J. D. Salinger's *Catcher in the Rye* could be—and has been—distorted by reading with an attitude that all it contains is a teenager's profanity and sexual ideologies. Both of these qualities take on new meaning when one considers the moral concepts behind this story.

THE PERFORMANCE

Censoring is part of the process of choosing material. One must be careful not to approach a selection with the same attitude that existed in one Eastern college where an English instructor was discharged for teaching salacious literature. His assigned topic was *To His Coy Mistress* by Andrew Marvell, a recognized poet and poem of classical value.

Do not settle for insignificant material just because it may seem safe. The shelves are full of pointless writings that are "safe" and not worthy of study—and certainly not worthy of reading aloud. Ask yourself: Does the selection say something? Does it mean something? Is it well written? Do its people come to life? Does its message have clarity and significance? Does the plot deal with real people in a real life situation? Is there imagination in its treatment? Does it provoke the mind as well as the heart? Or—is it mere froth and trivia?

There is one last thought: some students ask to read material they—or their friends—have written. As a rule, this is not too advisable since few students have sufficient training to produce well-written selections. There are, of course, exceptions, and if the instructor decides the work is *worthy* of being read, he should be more than willing to give the student that opportunity—as an honest kind of encouragement. But readers must remember that it is far more difficult to read poorly written material than it is to read good works. Literature with stature has better language, better organization, a better theme, and better characterizations. All of these factors add to the effectiveness of oral reading.

Naturally, in selecting material you must take into account your own personality and interests. We have previously advised you to read what interests you, but in the same way it is unwise to attempt anything that is basically too difficult for you with your background and experience. For instance, if you are the emotional type, very sensitive, the reading of a purely technical, unemotional article would not serve you well. Relate your choice to your own interests. Do not choose anything that does not "speak" to you.

Your audience, of course, must be considered too. While it is advisable to read something that has enough universality of appeal to interest your audience, it is usually possible to captivate listeners with almost any reputable material that is *well read*. So the first obligation should be to prepare the reading carefully.

One cannot always judge what an audience's tastes are since no one can really know each and every member of his audience. Humor is generally a safe bet because laughs from the audience provide an immediate response and everyone enjoys humor. Yet, no reader can successfully broaden himself by reading only one type of literature. Audiences' tastes should be considered, for example, in reading material that is morally offensive or unnecessarily gruesome. A selection which is too juvenile or too poorly written is also a poor choice because it insults your audience and may cause you to lose part of them.

The occasion for which a reading is given also influences choice of material. While we are concerned here primarily with the classroom situation, there are possibilities that students will engage in speech tournaments, in specially arranged concert performances, or in programs where the reading will be the principal entertainment of the evening.

Reading for the class gives a student more chance to experiment with different types of literature. His intention in class is to broaden his reading ability and to be exposed to various forms of writing. With this in mind his choice is highly diversified.

Occasionally students are engaged in concert performances before an invited audience, apart from the classroom. If the audience is sophisticated, as is often the case, more mature types of literature should be read. And certainly reading which has variety and which gives the reader a chance to exploit this versatility is desirable. By the time the reader is ready for such an occasion he will already have passed the embryonic stage as an interpreter and will be expected to read with a good deal of finesse.

For speech tournaments, the choice is extremely important, for only the best in literature is accepted—and more than one form of material often must be used. Here the interpreter is judged for his selection of material as well as his manner of delivery.

If a reading is the primary offering for an evening, if it is being given for a club or some organization, then the type of club will influence to a large extent the kind of material to be used. For instance, if you were to appear before a PTA group or a woman's club, you very likely would avoid anything suggestive or too frank in context.

Choosing material is your first job. Learn to make it also a meaningful experience.

Summary

Finding material is one of the student's primary problems. It is one that should be met early in the course by a conscientious study of the sources available to the interpreter.

THE PERFORMANCE

For readings of expository prose, the *Reader's Guide to Periodical Literature* is perhaps the best source for discovering significant periodical writings on all types of subjects. It is indexed by topic area. Other sources are *Saturday Review of Literature, Atlantic, Harper's, Time, Newsweek, Life, Look, The Reporter.* Textbooks, particularly in English, American and foreign literature courses, provide excellent examples of such prose.

Narrative prose differs from expository prose in that it tells a story, deals with characterization, dialogue, climax, and has more emotional content than expository prose, which emphasizes factual material, and presents ideas and arguments. It is found in journals, diaries, letters, descriptive studies. Novels and short stories make up narrative prose. For summaries of plots of novels, *Masterpieces of World Literature in Digest Form* is one of the best sources. Anthologies which include such short novels as James Hilton's *Lost Horizon* and John Steinbeck's *The Red Pony* are recommended. In addition, book reviews in newspapers and magazines, best seller lists, and book stores also provide good research material.

Short stories are contained in many anthologies, some of which are listed at the end of this chapter. Reputable writers of short stories include Flannery O'Connor, Eudora Welty, Katherine Anne Porter, Shirley Jackson, and such classical examples as Edgar Allan Poe, O. Henry, and Guy de Maupassant.

Poetry is represented in all major literary anthologies. However, the *Poetry Index* provides the most comprehensive source of material. Some popular poets are T. S. Eliot, Dylan Thomas (both of whom present problems to the interpreter because of the complexity of their works), W. H. Auden, Karl Shapiro, Matthew Arnold, John Keats, Percy Shelley, Robert and Elizabeth Browning, Amy Lowell, Edna St. Vincent Millay, Robert Frost, Carl Sandburg, and Ogden Nash.

For ideas in drama, the *Play Index* is highly recommended. In addition, collections of best plays of the year, such as the Burns Mantle editions and *Theatre World,* are a help. There are also many dramatic anthologies, among which are *Elizabethan Plays,* Bertolt Brecht's *Seven Plays, Masters of Modern Drama, Seven Plays of the Modern Theatre, A Treasury of the Theatre,* plus many collections of one-act plays. It is advisable to exercise caution in using readings from any abridged versions of plays, like those found in Burns Mantle, because such condensations do not delve into characterization sufficiently. The entire play should be read before any one scene is taken from it for reading.

YOUR ROLE IN ORAL INTERPRETATION

Students involved in the reading of drama should also consider the works of such classical authors as Shakespeare, Richard Sheridan, Oliver Goldsmith, Ferenc Molnar, Moliere, Corneille, Racine, and others.

For further help on locating material, the *Reader's Adviser and Bookman's Manual* is an excellent source.

The choice of reading is, of course, largely up to the student, and he must act as his own "censor." Oral interpretation involves a consideration of all types of literature, and care should be taken that certain works are not overlooked simply because they may be "suggestive" in some areas. Literature is often distorted by the wrong approach in the oral reading. For example, undue emphasis on profanity in books like the *Catcher in the Rye* distort and detract from the basic theme and purpose of the book. Students must learn to evaluate critically the worth of material, as well as its suitability to audiences' tastes. Always keep in mind that oral interpretation adds to one's cultural background and that unwise censoring limits the experience such a course can provide. A good rule is: If you are in doubt about the "rightness" of some material, check with your professor.

It is necessary, too, to select readings that relate to you, that fit your own interests, experience, and background. Consider your audience, their general tastes, and make certain that what you read will not prove offensive to a number of the listeners. It is not always possible to avoid offending one or two, and you cannot be too concerned about that, but you can take steps not to offend—or unnecessarily bore—the majority.

To offer a guide to students who are in search of material for reading, the following list is presented. It is not to be considered the only list of sources, but will serve as a start in the process of searching for reading materials.

Appropriate Selections for Oral Interpretation

EXPOSITORY PROSE

ARMOUR, RICHARD: *Twisted Tales from Shakespeare.* Satirical plots of Shakespeare's plays.
BENCHLEY, ROBERT: Countless articles of satirical note.

THE PERFORMANCE

Hart, Moss: *Act One*. The autobiography of one of America's greatest playwrights.

Sartre, Jean-Paul: *The Words*. A revealing autobiography. "Republic of Silence." An essay on the meaning of freedom to the French during the Nazi occupation.

Sevareid, Eric: "Dark of the Moon." An essay propounding some worthwhile thoughts for humanity to consider while it rushes to the moon.

Thurber, James: "University Days." An amusing account of Thurber's difficulty with the microscope in biology.

Twain, Mark: *The Innocents Abroad*. Twain's satirical views of Europe.

Woollcott, Alexander: Several fascinating character studies and short stories.

Additional Examples of Expository Prose

(See Hart, Sartre, and Sevareid, above.)

Agee, James: *On Film*. Reviews of films.

Capote, Truman: *In Cold Blood*. A non-fiction account of a murder that reads like a novel. (Has considerable suspense.)

Catton, Bruce: *A Stillness at Appomattox*. One of his many books on the Civil War.

Ciardi, John: "A Way to a Poem." An essay on the structure of a poem. Would need careful reading to make it interesting for oral reading.

Emerson, Ralph Waldo: *Selected Writings* (by Signet-Mentor). Includes 14 essays and 21 poems.

Faulkner, William: Nobel acceptance speech.

Hemingway, Ernest: "Big Two Hearted River." A descriptive account of a fishing trip.

Maugham, W. Somerset: *The Summing Up*. The writer's philosophy of life and writing. Excellent choice of material since it is divided into easily edited sections.

Nabokov, Vladimir: *Speak, Memory*. The autobiography of the Russian writer.

Skinner, Cornelia Otis: *Madame Sarah*. A biography of Sarah Bernhardt that has many good sections.

Steinbeck, John: *Travels with Charley*. Accounts of his trips across the United States.

Thoreau, Henry David: *Selected Journals, Walden*. Both deal with Thoreau's philosophy of living.

Thurber, James: "The Last Flower." Ironic commentary on civilization.

Tynans, Kenneth: *Curtains*. Reviews of Broadway and London plays that offer good reading.

White, Theodore: *The Making of the President, 1960. The Making of the President, 1964*. Both contain segments that lend themselves to oral reading. They also deal with material of current interest.

YOUR ROLE IN ORAL INTERPRETATION

WHITMAN, WALT: *Specimen Days.* Whitman's jottings over twenty years, including his Civil War experiences (Signet-Mentor).

YUTANG, LIN: *The Importance of Living.* Some profound observations on life, culture, and habits.

NARRATIVE PROSE

Humorous

BEMELMANS, LUDWIG: *I Love You—I Love You—I Love You.* Bemelmans is one of contemporary literature's most accomplished humorists.

HEGGENS, THOMAS: *Mister Roberts.* A hilarious and often sentimental account of a group of men on a "wreck of a ship" during World War II.

KERR, JEAN: *Please Don't Eat The Daisies.* Partly expository, but offers a humorous observation of Mrs. Kerr's experiences as a wife and mother.

MAUGHAM, W. SOMERSET: *Of Human Bondage.* The story of the near destruction of a sensitive man by an unprincipled streetwalker.

POE, EDGAR ALLAN: "The Cask of Amontillado," "The Tell-Tale Heart." Both too well-known to need explaining. Both offer problems because of their over-use. As such, of course, they present a challenge to a reader.

THURBER, JAMES: "The Catbird Seat," "The Night the Bed Fell." Thurber's own satirical trursts.

Serious

BENÉT, STEPHEN VINCENT: *The Devil and Daniel Webster.* A classic account of Webster's defense against the Devil.

BIBLE: Any number of passages.

BUCK, PEARL: *The Good Earth.* The prize-winning novel of a humble Chinese farmer and his family.

DAHL, RAOLD: "The Wish." A horror short story, almost entirely descriptive in effect. The vision of terror drawn by a young boy as he crosses a carpet.

BALZAC: *Droll Stories.* Fables of suggestive interest.

FIELDING, HENRY: *Tom Jones.* The bawdy and amusing amorous experiences of Tom Jones. A recognized classic.

HEMINGWAY, ERNEST: *Old Man and the Sea.* A short novel that provides excellent opportunities for oral reading.

JACKSON, SHIRLEY: "The Lottery." A classic of a horror story.

MELVILLE, HERMAN: *Moby Dick.* The memorable novel of a man's conflict with himself in the person of a whale.

THE PERFORMANCE

MITCHELL, MARGARET: *Gone With the Wind.* The ever-popular novel of the Civil War. A modern-day classic.

O'CONNOR, FLANNERY: Reputable short stories.

PORTER, KATHERINE ANNE: *Ship of Fools.* A complex novel of the people aboard a ship before World War II.

SALINGER, J. D.: *Catcher in the Rye.* Salinger's probing, biting, and often amusing story of a teenager with no place to go.

STEINBECK, JOHN: *Grapes of Wrath.* Steinbeck's prize-winning novel about the depression and the lives it influenced.

WELTY, EUDORA: Many famous short stories.

WOLFE, THOMAS: *Look Homeward, Angel, Of Time and the River.* One of the twentieth century's most renowned novelists with two of his most famous novels. Wolfe was a master of descriptive writing.

WRIGHT, RICHARD: *Native Son.* A violent novel of racial prejudice.

Anthologies

Points of View, Kenneth McElheny and James Moffett, eds. (Signet); *Great Modern Short Novels, Great Short Novels, This Is My Best* (Whit Burnett), *Bedside Book of Famous British Stories, The Woollcott Reader, East and West,* and *Mr. Maugham Himself,* edited by W. Somerset Maugham.

DRAMA

Humorous

FRIEL, BRYAN: *Philadelphia, Here I Come.* An amusing modern comedy by a new playwright.

GIBSON, WILLIAM: *Two for the Seesaw.* Comedy drama of the relationship between a good-hearted girl from Brooklyn and a man about to get a divorce. Two characters only.

GOLDSMITH, OLIVER: *She Stoops to Conquer.* A comedy of errors. Restoration period and very funny.

HEGGEN, THOMAS and JOSHUA LOGAN: *Mister Roberts.* Play version of the novel.

KANIN, GARSON: *Born Yesterday.* The long-time hit of a gangster and his seemingly dumb blonde girlfriend.

KERR, JEAN: *Mary, Mary.* A sophisticated comic romp about the complications of a couple getting a divorce.

MANHOFF, BILL: *The Owl and the Pussycat.* A comedy of a lady of easy virtue who moves in on a musician. Two characters only.

PATRICK, JOHN: *Teahouse of the August Moon.* A gentle and very funny play about the American occupation of Okinawa.

YOUR ROLE IN ORAL INTERPRETATION

SCHISGALL, MURRAY: *Luv.* A bawdy, broad farce about two men and a woman and their antics in love. Three people only.

SHAKESPEARE, WILLIAM: *As You Like It, Midsummer Night's Dream.*

SHAW, GEORGE BERNARD: *Pygmalion.* Adapted for *My Fair Lady.*

SHERIDAN, RICHARD: *The School for Scandal.* Another Restoration play, hilarious even today.

SIMON, NEIL: *Barefoot in the Park, The Odd Couple.* Two delightful modern comedies.

VAN DRUTEN, JOHN: *The Voice of the Turtle.* Comedy, drama of a man and two women, of love and commitment.

Serious

ANDERSON, MAXWELL: *Elizabeth the Queen.* In blank verse. Deals with the great queen and her love for Lord Essex. *Mary of Scotland.* The conflict between Mary of Scotland and Queen Elizabeth.

ANOUILH, JEAN: *Becket.* The personal conflict between two former friends, King Henry and Thomas Becket.

ALBEE, EDWARD: *Who's Afraid of Virginia Woolf.* A violent, scathing drama of married life. Two men, two women. Excellent scenes.

BOLT, ROBERT: *A Man for All Seasons.* The prize-winning play of Sir Thomas More's martyrdom. Fine scenes for men.

BRECHT, BERTOLT: *Three Penny Opera, Mother Courage.* Considered two of Brecht's best plays.

CHAYEFSKY, PADDY: *Marty.* Basically a comedy but also contains some moving scenes of a humble Italian who finally, at middle age, falls in love.

CHEKHOV, ANTON: *The Cherry Orchard.* The famous Russian play. (His four major plays are contained in an edition by Signet-Mentor titled *The Major Plays.*)

DELANEY, SHELAGH: *A Taste of Honey.* A sensitive, moving play of a young girl who seems to belong to no one until she finds understanding with a homosexual and a colored seaman. Well-written.

FORESTER, C. S.: *Payment Deferred.* A suspenseful play of an Englishman who commits murder and his slow disintegration.

GIBSON, WILLIAM: *The Miracle Worker.* The story of Helen Keller as a child. Brilliant play with excellent scenes.

GILROY, FRANK: *The Subject was Roses.* A Pulitzer prize play. A son's return from the service forces a man and his wife to look at themselves—and for the son to re-evaluate his life. Excellent scenes.

HANSBERRY, LORRAINE: *A Raisin in the Sun.* A dramatic, moving play of a Negro family who desire to move into a white neighborhood.

HELLMAN, LILLIAN: *The Children's Hour.* Fine play for two women. Subject is accused homosexuality between two women teachers. Beautifully handled theme.

THE PERFORMANCE

HERTZOG, JAN: *The Fourposter*. A play depicting the life of a couple from their wedding night to their old age. Fine choice.

IBSEN, HENRIK: *Ghosts, A Doll's House*.

IONESCO, EUGENE: *The Chairs*. A probing, complex study of two old people and the universe today. Difficult but rewarding.

MILLER, ARTHUR: *Death of a Salesman*. His classic play of a man's refusal to face himself and the world.

O'NEILL, EUGENE: *Long Day's Journey Into Night*. The tragic play that is said to be an autobiography of the author. Two men and two women. *Mourning Becomes Electra*. O'Neill's version of the Greek trilogy. Contains powerful scenes for two people.

OSBORNE, JOHN: *Look Back in Anger*. An angry look at a fading marriage. *Inadmissible Evidence*. A courtroom drama with fine speeches for one reader.

PINTER, HAROLD: *The Caretakers*. An unusual study of a tramp who moves in on two brothers and almost wrecks their lives. Part of the avant-garde movement.

RICE, ELMER: *The Adding Machine*. Good soliloquies. Amusing and yet bitter commentary on society.

ROSTAND, EDMOND: *Cyrano de Bergerac*. Has several notable soliloquies of value, including the "nose" speech and the equally famous "no thank you."

SARTRE, JEAN-PAUL: *No Exit* A remarkable one act of people in hell who look back on life.

SCHARY, DORE: *Sunrise at Campobello*. A dramatic account of Franklin Delano Roosevelt's fight against paralysis.

SCHNITZLER, ARTHUR: *La Ronde*. A delicate treatment of love through several characters' eyes. Good choice.
Leibelei. A drama of a young girl who leaves the security of her father's love to find her own life.

SHAFER, PETER: *Royal Hunt of the Sun*. Almost a poetic play in the confrontation between Pizarro and an Inca chief. Last act contains a superb scene for two men.

WEISS, PETER: *Marat/Sade*. An unusual poetic commentary on the French Revolution. Avant-garde theatre.
The Investigation. More of a testimony than a play dealing with the Nazi war crimes. Good choice for one reader.

WILLIAMS, TENNESSEE: *A Streetcar Named Desire*. Already a classic. The fantasies and tragedy of a woman whose mind leads her into the past and into a distorted view of her life today.
The Night of the Iguana. A derelict priest faces life and influences many people.
The Glass Menagerie. The tender account of a woman who lives in the past and cannot face reality. (Williams has also written several one-act plays that lend themselves to expert reading.)

YOUR ROLE IN ORAL INTERPRETATION

Anthologies

Theatre Guild Anthology; Elizabethan Plays; Masters of Modern Drama; Seven Plays of the Modern Theatre; 24 Favorite One Act Plays; 30 Famous One Act Plays; Complete Book of the American Musical Theatre; All the Plays of Molnar; Consult a *Concise Encyclopedia of Modern Drama* for information.

Also, musical plays often contain good scenes. The following are worth considering: *South Pacific, Oklahoma, King and I, Carousel, Funny Girl, How To Succeed in Business Without Really Trying, Man of La Mancha, Auntie Mame, High Spirits, Hello Dolly, Fanny.*

POETRY

ARNOLD, MATTHEW: "Dover Beach." Perhaps his most noted poem.

BALLADS: Basically lyrics to folk ballads. "Lord Randall" is one example.

BROWNING, ELIZABETH BARRETT: *Sonnets from the Portugese.* Love sonnets to her husband, Robert Browning.

BROWNING, ROBERT: A major poet. "My Last Duchess" and "Porphyria's Lover" are two of his best known.

BYRON, GEORGE GORDON, LORD: A prolific poet. "She Walks in Beauty" is one of his better known.

DICKINSON, EMILY: A contemporary poet. Not all of her poetry is immediately understandable, but she is one of the most popular poets of today.

DONNE, JOHN: One of the greatest of poets. His themes are many and varied. Examples: "Song," "The Good Morrow," "The Funeral."

FROST, ROBERT: A favorite with students. His best are "Mending Wall," "Road Not Taken," "Stopping By Woods on a Snowy Evening."

JOHNSON, JAMES WELDON: "The Creation." A poem of a Negro minister's concept of the creation of the world.

KEATS, JOHN: "Ode on a Grecian Urn," "La Belle Dame Sans Merci," "When I Have Fears that I May Cease To Be" are only a few of his great poems.

LOWELL, AMY: A contemporary poet. "Patterns" is one of her more famous.

MARVELL, ANDREW: "To His Coy Mistress." A satirical poem of seduction.

MILLAY, EDNA ST. VINCENT: A contemporary poet of genuine merit.

NASH, OGDEN: A satirical poet of today. Responsible for most of America's modern light verse.

THE PERFORMANCE

SANDBURG, CARL: A vigorous poet whose themes deal with contemporary problems and with pride in country. "Chicago" and "Prairie" are only two of the many, many poems he has written.

Anthologies

There are endless poetry anthologies, many listed according to the period, in addition to collections of complete works of such poets as Keats, Browning, Shelley, and Sandburg.

YOUR ROLE IN ORAL INTERPRETATION

🎵 CHAPTER 6

Prepare! Prepare!

ONE OF THE most important aspects of the oral reading of literature is also one of the most frequently overlooked—preparation.

It is not at all unusual for students to start work on a selection the night before it is to be given. Such preparation can only lead to disastrous results. A professional reader with much experience would not dream of facing an audience with such little thought given to the preparation of his material. And yet students, who are just beginning a study of interpretation, assume they can "wing it" in class with a fast hour of preparation. This is the biggest mistake you can make.

Preparation begins with the typing of a manuscript, for these reasons: (1) The pages in a book are not printed with oral reading in mind; it is a simple matter for a silent reader to turn the page to find the next word in a sentence, but for an oral reader this will result in a break in the idea. (2) Margins in a book are not set with oral interpretation in mind; you will want to write marginal notes to guide your interpretation. (3) The print in the book is often too small to allow the interpreter to maintain eye contact with his audience and with the printed page at the same time. So—prepare a manuscript!

Here are some general rules to follow in preparing your manuscript for easy oral reading: (1) Choose paper of a quality heavy enough to prevent *rustling* and to stand up under use. (2) Each sentence which begins on a page should end on that page. (3) At least double space your manuscript (triple spacing is even better); doing so allows you space for identifying pauses and emphases. (4) Leave wide margins so that you can write notes to yourself concern-

ing your interpretation. (5) Devise a set of signals such as virgules
(/) which will allow you to signal phrasing, word groupings, and
changes of thought, mood, or idea.

> /—signifies a momentary hesitation, a chance to breathe, to
> help give variety to pace.
>
> //—signifies a longer pause, a change in idea in the selection,
> an introduction of a new mood.
>
> ————————under a word signifies a word to be emphasized or
> "colored."

Along with these markings, you can note in the margins of the
manuscript what mood is involved in each particular section. Is it
anger, love, hate, fear, passion, resentment? Write it out in one or
two words. Then when the mood changes, draw a line to the
margin, and write in "mood changes to . . .," indicating what the
new mood is.

The following selection illustrates the use of such symbols.
Words in the left margin indicate changes in mood; those on the
right indicate changes in pace (rate of reading). Read the selection
closely noting each change of pace and mood, emphasizing the
words which are underlined and pausing as indicated by slant
marks.

LOOK HOMEWARD, ANGEL

THOMAS WOLFE

As darkness came upon the
gray wet day, / the family gathered
in the parlor, / in the last terrible
congress before death, / silent, /
waiting. // Gant rocked petulantly,
/ spitting into the fire, / making a
weak whining moan from time to
time. // One by one, / at intervals, /

*silent-
ominous*

they left the _room_, / _mounting_ the
stairs softly, / and _listening_ outside
the _door_ / of the sick-room. / And
they heard _Ben_, / as, with _incessant_
humming repetition, / like _a_ _child_, /
he _sang_ his _song_,
"There's a mother there at twilight /
Who's glad to know—"//

Eliza sat _stolidly_, / hands
folded, / before the parlor fire. //
Her _dead_ _white_ face had a _curious_
carven look; / the _inflexible_ solidity
/ of _madness_. //

eerie

"_Well_," / she said at length,
slowly, / "you _never_ _know_. / Perhaps this _is_ the _crisis_./Perhaps—"
// her face hardened into granite
again. // She said no more. //

retreat within herself

Coker _came_ in and _went_ at
once, / without _speaking_, / to the
sick-room. // Shortly before nine
o'clock, / _Bessie_ _Gant_ came down.
// "All _right_," / she said quietly.
"You had all better come _up_ now. /
This is the end." //

quiet, resigned

Eliza got up and _marched_ out
of the room with a stolid face. /
Helen followed her: / she was _pant-_

ing with hysteria, / and had begun to wring her big hands. /

frenzied

"Now, get hold of yourself, Helen," / said Bessie Gant warningly. / "This is no time to let yourself go." //

command

Eliza went steadily upstairs, / making no noise. / But as she neared the room, / she paused, / as if listening for sounds within. / Faintly, / in the silence, / they heard Ben's song. // And suddenly, / casting away all pretense, / Eliza staggered, and fell against the wall, / turning her face into her hand, /with a terrible wrenched cry:

apprehension

"O God! If I had known! / If I had known!" /

Then, weeping with bitter unrestraint, / with the contorted and ugly grimace of sorrow, / mother and daughter embraced each other. // In a moment they composed themselves, / and quietly entered the room. //

deep grief

composed

Eugene and Luke pulled Gant to his feet / and supported him up the stairs. // He sprawled upon them, / moaning in long quivering exhalations. /

"Mer-ci-ful God! / That I should have to bear this in my old age. / That I should—"

self pity

"Papa! / For God's sake!" / Eugene cried sharply. / "Pull yourself together! / It's Ben who's dying —not us! / Let's try to behave decently to him for once." //

annoyance

This served to quiet Gant for a moment. / But as he entered the room, / and saw Ben lying in the semi-conscious coma that precedes death, / the fear of his own death overcame him, / and he began to moan again. // They seated him in a chair, at the foot of the bed, / and he rocked back and forth, weeping:

"O Jesus! / I can't bear it! / Why must you put this upon me? / I'm old and sick, / and I don't know where the money's to come from. // How are we ever going to face this fearful and croo-el winter? / It'll cost a thousand dollars before we're through burying him, / and I don't know where the money's to come

selfishness

self pity

from." // He wept affectedly with sniffling sobs. /

"Hush! hush!" cried Helen, / rushing at him. / In her furious anger, / she seized him and shook him. / "You damned old man you, / *anger* I could kill you! / How dare you *contempt* talk like that when your son's dying? // I've wasted six years of my life nursing you, / and you'll be the last one to go!" // In her blazing anger, she turned accusingly on Eliza: /

"You've done this to him. / You're the one that's responsible. / If you hadn't pinched every penny / he'd never have been like this. // Yes, / and Ben would be here, too!" // She panted for breath for a moment. // Eliza made no answer. / She did not hear her. //

almost hysterical "After this, I'm through! / I've been looking for you to die—and *anger—hatred* Ben's the one who has to go." // Her voice rose to a scream of exasperation. / She shook Gant again. / "Never again! / Do you hear that, / you selfish old man? / You've had everything—/Ben's had nothing./

YOUR ROLE IN ORAL INTERPRETATION

And now he's the one to go. / I hate you!" //

"Helen! Helen!" said Bessie Gant quietly. / "Remember where you are." //

"Yes, that means a lot to us," / Eugene muttered bitterly. //

change to silence of death

Then, / over the ugly clamor of their dissension, / over the rasp and snarl of their nerves, / they heard the low mutter of Ben's expiring breath. // The light had been re-shaded: / he lay, / like his own shadow, / in all his fierce gray lonely beauty. // And as they looked and saw his bright eyes already blurred with death, / and saw the feeble beating flutter of his poor thin breast, / the strange wonder, / the dark rich miracle of his life surged over them its enormous love-

awe

liness. // They grew quiet and calm, // they plunged below all the splintered wreckage of their lives, / they drew together in a superb communion of love and valiance, / beyond horror and confusion, / beyond death. //

THE PERFORMANCE

feeling of awe, inspirational

And Eugene's eyes grew <u>blind</u> with <u>love</u> and <u>wonder</u>: / an enor- mous <u>organ-music</u> sounded in his <u>heart</u>, // he <u>possessed</u> them for a moment, / he was a <u>part</u> of their loveliness, // his life <u>soared</u> mag- nificiently out of the <u>slough</u> and pain and <u>ugliness</u>. // He thought:

revelation "That was not <u>all</u>! / That <u>really</u> was not <u>all</u>!" //

Helen turned <u>quietly</u> to Coker, / who was standing in <u>shadow</u> by the <u>window</u>, / <u>chewing</u> upon his long <u>unlighted</u> cigar.//

hopeful "Is there <u>nothing</u> more you can do? / Have you tried <u>everything</u>? / I mean—*everything*?"//

Her voice was <u>prayerful</u> and <u>low</u>. // Coker <u>turned</u> toward her slowly, / taking the cigar between his <u>big</u> <u>stained</u> <u>fingers</u>. / Then, / <u>gently</u>, / with his <u>weary</u> <u>yellow</u> <u>smile</u>, / he answered: "Everything. Not <u>all</u> the king's horses, / not <u>all</u> the <u>doctors</u> and <u>nurses</u> in the world, / can <u>help</u> him <u>now</u>." /

hopelessness "How long have you <u>known</u> this?" she said. //

YOUR ROLE IN ORAL INTERPRETATION

"For two days," he answered. / "From the beginning." // He was silent for a moment. / "For <u>ten</u> years!" he went on with <u>growing</u> energy. // "Since I <u>first</u> saw him, at <u>three</u> in the morning, in the Greasy Spoon, with a <u>doughnut</u> in one hand and a <u>cigarette</u> in the other. // My <u>dear</u>, / <u>dear</u> girl," he said <u>gently</u> / as she tried to speak, / "We can't turn back the days that have <u>gone</u>. // We can't turn <u>life</u> back to the <u>hours</u> when our <u>lungs</u> were sound, / our <u>blood</u> hot, / our bodies <u>young</u>. / We are a <u>flash</u> of fire—/ a <u>brain</u>, / a <u>heart</u>, / a <u>spirit</u>. // And we are <u>three-cents</u>-worth of lime and iron—which we cannot get back." //

resignation

facing reality

regret

He picked up his <u>greasy</u> black slouch hat, / and <u>jammed</u> it carelessly upon his head. / Then he <u>fumbled</u> for a match and <u>lit</u> the chewed cigar. //

wanting to have hope

"Has <u>everything</u> been done?" / she said again. / "I want to <u>know</u>! / Is there <u>anything</u> left worth <u>try</u>ing?" /

THE PERFORMANCE

He made a <u>weary</u> <u>gesture</u> of his arms. /

cold, firm "My dear girl!" he said. / "He's <u>drowning</u>! / <u>Drowning</u>!" //

shock She stood <u>frozen</u> with the <u>hor</u>-ror of his <u>pronouncement</u>. //

Coker looked for a moment at the <u>gray</u> <u>twisted</u> shadow on the bed. / Then, / <u>quietly</u>, / <u>sadly</u>, / *sad* with <u>tenderness</u> and <u>tired</u> wonder, / he said: "Old Ben. / <u>When</u> shall we see <u>*his*</u> like again?" //

Then he went <u>quietly</u> out, / the long <u>cigar</u> <u>clamped</u> <u>firmly</u> in his <u>mouth</u>. //

In a moment, / Bessie Gant, breaking <u>harshly</u> in upon their si-lence / with <u>ugly</u> and <u>triumphant</u> *disgust* <u>matter-of-factness</u>, / said: "<u>Well</u>, / *contempt* it will be a <u>relief</u> to get <u>this</u> over. / I'd rather be called into <u>forty</u> out-<u>side</u> cases / than one in which <u>any</u> of these <u>damn</u> relations are <u>con</u>- <u>cerned</u>. I'm dead for sleep." // *concern for self*

Helen turned <u>quietly</u> upon her. /

"Leave the room!" she said. /

"This is our affair now. / We have the right to be left alone." //

Surprised, / Bessie Gant stared at her for a moment with an angry, / resentful face. / Then she left the room. //

angry

The only sound in the room now / was the low rattling mutter of Ben's breath. / He no longer gasped; / he no longer gave signs of consciousness or struggle. // His eyes were almost closed; / their gray flicker was dulled, / coated with the sheen of insensibility and death. // He lay quietly upon his back, / very straight, / without sign of pain, / and with a curious up-turned thrust of his sharp thin face. // His mouth was firmly shut. // Already, / save for the fee-ble mutter of his breath, / he seemed to be dead—/ he seemed detached, / no part of the ugly mechanism of that sound which came to remind them / of the terrible chemistry of flesh, / to mock at illusion, / at all belief in the strange passage and continuance of life. //

silent
lifeless

sense of unreality

THE PERFORMANCE

finality
emptiness

He was dead, / save for the
slow running down of the worn-out
machine, / save for that dreadful
mutter within him of which he was
no part. // He was dead.

Some students find it hard to read such a marked paper. The signs distract. In that case, use a carbon copy for marking in rehearsal and an unmarked copy for the classroom performance.

It is important to point out two things: (1) The mechanical markings of the selection are not meant to indicate that such an interpretation is the only right one—not at all; each reader will interpret in his own way. (2) The system is devised primarily to aid in analysis of selection, to help teach the value of pauses, of breathing, to discover the changes in ideas and mood, to help in understanding the emotional content, and to understand the value of word coloring and emphasis. Such markings can—and should—be dropped as soon as you are able to conduct such analysis without them. The authors in no way recommend a purely mechanical delivery. What truly matters is that the meaning of the material is conveyed, and each reader will have his own way of meeting that requirement. Yet, it was found that this system of marking is of particular help to the beginning student who is inclined to read everything in a selection with the same pace and inflectional pattern and with little understanding of the material itself.

For a reading that lasts five minutes, it is safe to say that you should rehearse the selection carefully at least ten times. Some students may be more skilled in interpretation than others and can get by with less time but the average reader will need at least that much practice for an effective reading.

It is recommended that rehearsals begin about ten days before you are to give the reading.

You should obviously read the selection in its entirety first. If you are doing a reading from a play, you should read the entire play because a scene taken out of context can often be distorted. One student read the big scene between the Captain and Mr. Roberts from *Mister Roberts*. In his reading the Captain emerged as a sophisticated intellectual. When asked where he got the idea for such an interpretation, he said he'd read a short condensation and this was the impression he had received of the personality of the Captain. It is even more amazing that such a characterization could have been formulated when one considers the type of language the Captain uses in this scene. It is not advisable to read directly in oral performance condensations of plays such as are found in Burns Mantle's *Best Plays*. These are primarily designed for silent reading.

It may be difficult to read an entire novel in preparation for an oral reading; however, if you are going to read a cutting of fiction, it is better to select a scene from a novel you have already read and liked. One student, for instance, had loved *Gone With the Wind*, so she was quickly able to decide on the scene in which Melanie gives birth to her baby. If you have not read many novels—and you should get in the habit of reading good ones—then you should consult a *reliable* condensation of the plot, perhaps *Masterpieces of World Literature in Digest Form*, published by Harper's. However, bear in mind that condensations are never detailed enough, particularly in reference to characterizations, so exercise caution when you use them.

Once you have made your choice of material and have read it to yourself, start again and read it aloud. Silent reading will never produce the results that oral reading does. Too many students think they can get along by reading the selection aloud the first time at the actual reading in class. Forget this idea.

On the first day, spend an hour or possibly more reading the selection aloud—getting the "feel" of it, checking any words you do not understand. It is important that you get in the habit of knowing what each word means. Do not rush over one that is vague to you because it can easily give a different meaning to that part of the selection.

The second day, start to work on the selection again—noticing now how fast you are going. Put the reading on a tape recorder if you have one and then listen to it. Maybe it won't seem too fast to you, but listen to it again and again and you'll begin to pick out the faulty use of voice in rate-pronunciation-inflection, and characterization. Work to correct these faults.

Before continuing rehearsal, you should begin thinking about the introduction to your reading. The introduction has a two-fold purpose: to give the audience any necessary background information about the material and the author and to help set the mood for the reading so the audience will more readily respond. It does not interpret the selection—that is up to the reader himself—and it does

THE PERFORMANCE

not summarize the contents of that material. Nor is it a biography of the author. It prepares the audience for the interpretation you are to give.

For an example, let's say you were going to read Edna St. Vincent Millay's poem, "Interim," the grief-stricken thoughts and emotions of someone whose lover has died. You might begin this way:

Death has many faces to each of us. Yet, to us all it means searing pain, the ache of loneliness, the hollow emptiness inside. We try to recapture memories or to touch physical objects left behind by the one who has died so we can draw closer to that person in our grief. Edna St. Vincent Millay, one of our most prominent contemporary poets, graphically shows us the broken heart of the bereaved in her poem, "Interim."

Introductions should, of course, be in a mood comparable to that of the selection. An amusing satire would not be introduced in a laborious, serious manner—and vice versa.

On the third day, read the selection again, this time making certain that if you have dialogue and characterization, the dialogue is beginning to sound convincing and the characterization to take shape. By now you should start adopting a definitely critical sense.

The fourth and fifth days can be spent in further polishing. You should begin to "feel" the selection; it should come alive.

The sixth day, read it straight through with no stops. Again put it on tape if you have a recorder. This session may not take more than half an hour.

It is quite possible that by now you are getting tired of the whole thing; it may begin to bore you. We can assume that you chose the selection in the first place because you liked it. If you start to lose that interest, you should put it aside at this point for a couple of days. You may not be rehearsing it orally, but you will be thinking about it.

The day before you are to give the reading, go back to it, and this time read it straight through with no stops at least two times. If you make a mistake in the reading, don't stop to correct it, but go on—act just as though you were in the classroom giving the reading. This is a technique similar to the final rehearsal of a play. Many directors have the cast run through the show just as if they were in performance. If mistakes are made, you will have to get over them as well as you can. After all, a mistake may be apparent to you and not at all to the audience, so don't draw attention to it by laboring over corrections. Move on.

Naturally, after you have given the reading twice in this way, it is wise to go back to check over any trouble spots and correct them.

The day of the reading, if possible, read it once more before you give it. By now you should be very well prepared. You should have confidence in your ability to do the reading, and you should feel secure—and less frightened.

ᕗ CHAPTER 7

What do I do with my voice?

You have a voice that is unique to yourself; it is part of the basic equipment that comes with your particular model when you are born. No one has an opportunity to order the deluxe model with ideal resonance and superior quality.

There's no trade-in value either, so a good attitude with which to begin a study of voice is shown in the question, "This is my voice; what can I do to improve it?"

Think of the person—man or woman—who has an ideal voice. What is it about this person's voice that makes you say it is ideal? Is it the pitch, quality, volume, resonance, articulation, or rate that you enjoy? Or is it all of these working in combination?

There is no single *ideal* voice! Be thankful that there is not. Can you imagine the problems that would result if we all had the same type of voice! We'd all sound alike. But the person you think of as having an *ideal* voice probably has done much work to make his voice as effective as possible through manipulation of those variables listed above. Each of the six requires special treatment in this chapter.

It is not necessary that you learn all of the anatomy of voice in order to be able to improve your voice or to use it well, but you should learn, generally, how sound is produced.

Before you can make sound, even noise, a supply of air is necessary, so voice actually begins with breathing. Air from the lungs is forced upward through the vocal cords and out through the mouth and nose. Thus the lungs and diaphragm, working together to supply the air, become the motor of voice. How to breathe correctly is treated fully in the next chapter of this text, so it will suffice for now to say that correct breathing is a necessary first step in making effective use of your voice.

However, you should be aware that no part of the vocal anatomy has the production of voice (or sound) as its primary function. The primary function of breathing, for example, is to supply air for the oxygenation of the cells of the body; the fact is that man has devised a way of using the same supply of air for the production of sound.

What happens to the supply of air, stored in the lungs and controlled in its exhalation by the diaphragm, as it makes its way through the throat and out the mouth and nose determines whether the "voice" that is produced is a whisper or a shout and whether its pitch is high or low, and again what its quality will be. What happens with resonators and articulators determines whether the "speech" produced is deep or shallow, clear or cloudy. But first we must consider how sound is produced from this flow of air. The voice box, or *larynx,* is located in the throat at the point of the Adam's apple. You can locate it by placing your thumb on one side of the Adam's apple and forefinger on the other in a loose "pinching" manner and humming; you can feel the vibration in this way.

Here again, the primary function of the larynx is as a valve, to keep food particles and other foreign objects out of the bronchial tubes and lungs. You know what happens when you swallow something and it "goes down the wrong way"—you cough. And you cough until the object is expelled. The system man devised of vibrating the cords with a flow of air is called *phonation.*

The opening between the two cords is greater when normal breathing is going on, and the cords are stretched tightly when phonation is in process. A whisper shows the cords tightened somewhat but not so tightly as in phonation. The cords do not vibrate during a whisper any more than they do during normal breathing or any more than they do during a sigh; thus the whisper depends on the articulators (lips, teeth, tongue, etc.) rather than on phonation for communication. The tighter the cords are stretched, the higher the note that is produced.

The sound that is produced by the vibration of the vocal cords will differ from person to person according to the length and thickness of the cords. While you should not think of the vocal cords as strings (they are more like lips), they can be compared with the strings of a guitar, in regard to length and thickness, vibrating to produce sound. The thin strings on a guitar produce the higher notes. They have less density and can be stretched more. The

YOUR ROLE IN ORAL INTERPRETATION

strings that produce the lower notes are thicker and have greater density. The order of the strings, in terms of length, also parallels that of the vocal cords. If you place your finger on a string high up on the neck of the instrument and slide it downward toward the body while sound is being produced there will be a rise in the pitch of the sound the string makes. The notes produced will become higher as the string being vibrated becomes shorter. Thus vocal cords or lips that are thicker and longer will produce lower notes; vocal cords that are thinner and shorter will produce higher notes and, therefore, a higher voice. It might be said, then, that a man generally has thicker and longer vocal cords than a woman.

As the sound waves produced by the vibrating vocal folds travel upward through the throat and out the mouth and nose, they are *amplified* by the resonators. Amplified means that the sound waves act on the walls of the throat, mouth, and nose and on the cavities of the throat and head in such a way that there are additional vibrations in each of them and the sound produced is intensified or enlarged. In a sense, the sound is made larger rather than louder.

The final process affecting the sound is articulation. As the enlarged waves enter the mouth and nose and as they leave them, they are acted upon by the tongue, teeth, hard and soft palates, and lips, which divide them into words and shape them into appropriate utterances.

The resultant sound has a unique and distinctive *quality* which is identifiable with the person who originates it. It is this uniqueness that we call vocal quality. Your vocal quality is determined by the modifications that your amplification system works upon the sound wave produced by your vocal cords. One person can affect an approximation of another person's voice by concentrating on his quality. A good mimic can imitate or give an approximation of any number of famous people. President Kennedy was one who was imitated widely because his vocal quality was so interesting. James Cagney, Edward G. Robinson, George Raft, and Humphrey Bogart are other oft-imitated, easily identifiable personalities.

In a recent instance in Los Angeles, a young man was convicted of a crime largely on the basis of his *voice print* taken from a recording of his voice—particularly his vocal quality.

You can't substitute the quality of your voice for another, nor can you alter the quality of your voice tremendously, but you can work to improve it through more effective manipulation of the variables treated in this chapter. You are now ready to analyze and

THE PERFORMANCE

evaluate your voice in terms of some of the common problems or faulty uses of voice.

Problems in the Use of Volume

The most easily identifiable problem of voice in interpretation centers around volume, the force of the air flow over the vocal cords. Beginning students oftentimes use too little force, which results in too little volume. Or they will use too constant a flow of air, thus creating a monotonous volume. In some instances the force of air is consistently too great; the result is a voice that is too loud, that *blasts* the audience.

Problems of volume are as easily solved as they are identified, however. Most often a person who uses too little volume has been told that he has inherited a weak voice, or he has grown up in a family in which any amount of loudness is considered rude. It is usually easy to point out to the first person that his voice is not weak but that he is making weak use of it. For the other person mentioned, it is typically sufficient treatment to point out that when one converses with three or four people at a time volume is not a problem, but when one faces an audience of larger numbers, volume must be increased to meet the demand. Those who cannot hear the presentation certainly can have no appreciation of it.

A good rule of thumb to follow in determining the amount of volume to use in a given situation is to try out your voice in the room before the time of your performance. Test the room for its ability to carry your voice. If possible, have a friend sit in the back of the room and signal to you when your volume is in the right range. Then when you are performing, watch the faces of various members of the audience to see that they are not having to strain to hear.

Faulty Uses of Rate

Certainly as common a problem as use of volume in beginning interpreters is too fast a rate or a choppy rate. Rate is the speed of utterance, the speed of reading. Faulty use of rate is almost always due to a combination of stage fright and too little preparation. The student who is frightened or ill-prepared will read at as fast a rate as he can in order to escape his situation. The result is obvious—instead of sharing conversation and ideas or mirroring characterization, he merely mouths words; in effect he'd have been better off not to read at all. In an earlier chapter the point was made that emotional involvement in the material you read is the core of effective interpretation. This point is the chief clue to controlling too fast a rate. Concentrate in practice sessions on letting the words work their magic. The rate of reading should be determined by the material being read. A good general rule to follow regarding rate is to read the material as you would speak it yourself in a real-life situation. The rate should be natural. A look at the following paragraph, taken from Thoreau's "The Battle of the Ants," will illustrate the point. Read it aloud as though the observations are your own and you are reporting them as they occur to you.

One day when I went out to my wood-pile, or rather my pile of stumps, I observed two large ants, the one red, the other nearly half an inch long, and black, fiercely contending with one another. Having once got hold they never let go, but struggled and wrestled and rolled on the chips incessantly. Looking farther, I was surprised to find that the chips were covered with such combatants, that it was a war between two races of ants, the red always pitted against the black, and frequently two red ones to one black.

Now read it again, as fast as you can pronounce the words. You will notice that when a descriptive passage such as this is read too fast, much of the detail—the color of description—is lost and the listener is left with a few bare facts if he is able to get even that much of the meaning.

One further example should convince you. Read the following letter in each of these two ways: First, read it as fast as you can. You will notice that in doing so, you rob it of its sincerity, its gratitude, its meaning. And, as important, you rob the listener of understanding and appreciation of both Mr. Lincoln and yourself.

THE PERFORMANCE

EXECUTIVE MANSION

Washington, November 21, 1864

Mrs. Bixby, Boston, Massachusetts.

Dear Madam:
    I have been shown in the files of the War Department a statement of the Adjutant-General of Massachusetts that you are the mother of five sons who have died gloriously on the field of battle. I feel how weak and fruitless must be any words of mine which should attempt to beguile you from the grief of a loss so overwhelming. But I cannot refrain from tendering to you the consolation that may be found in the thanks of the republic they died to save. I pray that our Heavenly Father may assuage to the anguish of your bereavement, and leave you only the cherished memory of the loved and lost, and the solemn pride that must be yours to have laid so costly a sacrifice upon the altar of freedom.

Yours very sincerely and respectfully,

Abraham Lincoln

Read it again now, after taking a moment to become involved in its message. Feel what Lincoln must have felt when the loss was brought to his attention.

Reading rate is dictated by the mood of the writing, by the weight of the ideas and by the style of the author. Don't let stage fright or too little preparation force you into too rapid a rate.

Less common than too rapid a rate but also deserving consideration here is the problem of a monotonous rate. A reader who seldom varies the rate of his reading will soon lull his audience to sleep. Most of the time, when a selection is longer than the Lincoln letter, and less tragic, you'll discover that the author has built into his writing, especially if it is suspenseful, some segments of momentary relief. These are designed to give the reader a chance to relax.

YOUR ROLE IN ORAL INTERPRETATION

In an oral reading, these segments give you a chance to vary the rate and eliminate monotony for your audience.

Too ponderous a rate is a third fault. However, it is much less common in beginning readers of literature and the problem is usually solved once the person involved has a chance to hear himself on tape. Typically the person who reads too slowly does so because he is impressed with the weight of the message, or he is lulled by the sound of his own voice, or he lacks the motivation and energy to read.

Problems in the Use of Pitch

How phonation takes place has been discussed. Pitch is determined by the frequency of vibration of the vocal cords. Just as there are habits of dress, there are habits that we fall into regarding pitch. The pitch or tone of voice that you most commonly use is said to be your *habitual pitch*. The highest and lowest note you can reach mark the boundaries of your *pitch range*. The mid-point between the two notes identifies what is known as your most desirable or *optimum pitch*. In order to find your optimum level, try this exercise. Using the "ah" sound in a sharp, staccato manner, say "ah" in a low register and gradually, with slight pauses between notes, go up the scale. The note which seems the most comfortable to you is your optimum pitch; it is usually a note and a half below your habitual pitch. If your optimum pitch is the most suitable or desirable pitch for your voice, then practice should make it possible for you to make your habitual pitch and your optimum pitch the same.

You might notice that your voice is lower when you practice reading a selection than it is when you read in front of a group. We can look at the performance situation for the answer. In practice you are relaxed and alone; your throat and neck are also relaxed. When you are in performance, your throat and neck tighten with the rest of your body, if you have stage fright, and your voice rises in pitch. It takes practice and experience to keep the throat relaxed and open so that the desired pitch is achieved.

To determine whether or not you have a tight throat, tape your voice in several practice sessions and tape it again when you are in performance before an audience. Compare the several practice sessions with the performance and see if you or your friends can detect a rise in pitch. If you have a marked problem your instructor will undoubtedly point it out to you. A tape recorder is indispensable in overcoming pitch faults.

A second fault in the use of pitch and even more common than too high a pitch is a monotonous, unvaried pitch, a monotone. No aspect of voice will rob your reading of vitality and life more quickly than a monotonous repetition of the same pitch. Again, lack of emotional involvement, preparation, and stage fright are the chief culprits.

Can you imagine Patrick Henry standing before the Congress and droning monotonously, "Give me liberty or give me death"? If he had used a dull, lifeless tone, the man would not be remembered as the vigorous, fiery champion of liberty that he was.

Try the following lines by Helen Keller in each of these two ways: First, read them in a monotone; work consciously to give the ideas meaning but keep the pitch constant. You will quickly see that without variety of pitch for emphasis, meaning is lost or at least badly distorted.

Now and then I have tested my seeing friends to discover what they see. Recently I was visited by a very good friend who had just returned from a long walk in the woods, and I asked her what she had observed. "Nothing in particular," she replied. . . . How was it possible, I asked myself, to walk for an hour through the woods and see nothing worthy of note? I who cannot see find hundreds of things to interest me through mere touch. I feel the delicate symmetry of a leaf. I pass my hands lovingly about the smooth skin of a silver birch or the rough shaggy bark of a pine.

Read the lines again and experiment with pitch. Another name for pitch is melody, so this time vary the melody—let it identify Miss Keller's enthusiasm and zest for living. Let your use of pitch reflect a positive, happy attitude toward life and vision. The essay these lines were taken from appears in its entirety in Chapter 10. Read the entire essay for a full appreciation of her ideas on the importance of *seeing* what we see.

One additional fault in the use of pitch needs attention. It is

YOUR ROLE IN ORAL INTERPRETATION

identified in the voice that sends sentence after sentence running down hill like this:

I asked	I feel
her	the delicate
what	symmetry of
she had	a leaf.
observed.	

Again, a tape recorder is necessary in overcoming this reading fault. Interpreters who read in a pitch pattern are not aware of their problem. A tape recording of the voice quickly identifies the habit, and conscientious practice will eliminate it. Practice should include reading in a variety of new patterns until the old one has come under control. One good exercise is to reverse the habit. If you have been allowing all sentences to run down hill, practice reading several lines of any familiar literature in such a way that the sentences run up hill instead of down. Or vary the reading in such a way as to let sentences run up and down in rapid succession. Before long the old habit will disappear, and a voice with more vitality will take its place.

Faulty Use of Resonance

The only common fault that centers around resonance is too little use of the resonators. The fault is often called a tight throat or pinched throat and results in a voice that is thin and weak. The throat and mouth are the primary resonating cavities of the voice with the nasal cavity influencing primarily the *m, n,* and *ng* sounds. If the throat and lower jaw are tense and the mouth is dry, the resonating cavities are reduced in size and effectiveness; the voice produced doesn't get proper amplification. The point was made earlier in the chapter that it isn't the voice that is weak; rather, it is that weak use is being made of the resonators. Practice some isometrics for opening these cavities so that they can work more effectively in their amplifying function. Isometrics is a system of exercises that put strain on particular muscles and then follow the period of strain or tension with a period of relaxation. Remember, in using isometrics that the period of relaxation should be equal in time to the period of tension. To work for more control in relaxation of the throat and neck and mouth try this: While standing in a comfortable, but erect, position with your weight balanced on the balls of both feet, let your lower jaw drop down as far as it will without force; now yawn and you will feel the throat and mouth enlarge. While still in that position sigh quietly several times. Next, close your mouth, grit your teeth, and tighten the neck muscles—even hunching your shoulders if necessary to put tension on the throat and mouth. Make the cavities of throat and mouth as small as you can. Hold the tension for a few seconds, then relax and repeat the yawn and sigh. The purpose of this exercise is to gain sufficient control over the muscles that tense the throat and mouth that you can relax them at will, particularly when you feel them tensing up during a reading.

You will notice that you can't repeat the above exercise more than a couple of times in succession without feeling real tiredness in the throat and lower jaw. This is ready evidence of the need for relaxation of these muscles when you are in a performance situation.

Faulty Use of Articulators

The faults spoken of thus far have centered in one way or another around voice. When we examine the faulty use of the articulators, the lips, teeth, tongue, and soft palate, we are not concerned with voice but with speech. The articulators are used to divide the voice stream into speech sounds and into words—language. Faulty use of these articulators, then, must center around clarity. Any speech sound that draws attention to itself and, therefore, away from the ideas being expressed is faulty in that situation or location. Diction fault, or faulty pronunciation, might mean that you are a northerner performing in the south, or an easterner performing in the west. This fault arises from the regional nature of our American English. It isn't a problem that is limited to America by any means; a Southern Frenchman has difficulty communicating with a Parisian, and a cockney has difficulty with those of other regions of England. But this problem can't be helped without sufficient time to "localize" pronunciation, and other problems—faulty articulation—can be improved immediately with practice and concentration. Of course, the fault referred to here is too casual or slovenly pronunciation of words. *Doin', thinkin', nuttin', sompin', fergit,* are examples of this problem. Good advice is to choose as a standard for effective pronunciation people in your community who are experienced in the use of language—ministers, educators, business leaders—and pattern your pronunciation after them.

Occasionally (rarely) a student will need to work for a less precise pattern of pronunciation than he is used to in order not to have attention drawn to his speech. An affected or too precise diction is distracting to an audience if it is inappropriate to the literature being read.

The tape recorder is of immense value in solving articulation problems.

Faulty Types of Vocal Quality

It is possible that the problems discussed in this section are due to physical difficulties. If it is said that your voice is hoarse, harsh, nasal, or breathy, you would do well to have a physical check-up before starting any comprehensive program of improvement. For the larger number of students, though, problems of vocal quality are a result of improper vocal habits. Or at least the student can improve his vocal quality by first learning what the problems are and then working to reduce or eliminate the problems.

HOARSENESS

The most common cause of hoarseness is overuse of the voice or unusual strain on it at a game or other vocal activity. A cold or sore throat might also be the cause. A neglected throat infection may well lead to permanently damaged vocal folds and thus a husky or hoarse vocal quality. Whatever the cause of the hoarseness, the vocal lips become swollen and irritated from rubbing together, and, therefore, vibrate less rapidly in phonation; hoarseness results in a raspy, unpleasant quality. If illness or throat infection is apparent, complete rest is in order and immediate or continuing medical treatment. Hoarseness characterizes the prize fighter, the hoodlum, and the bum, in literature.

HARSHNESS-STRIDENCY

Voices with a metallic or shrill quality are said to be strident or harsh. The problem in this case is strain on the vocal cords themselves. They are stretched too tightly during phonation and the result is a tone or quality that isn't fully developed. This voice is characteristic of the highly nervous individual who is easily irritated and quick to let everyone know it. He is a whiner as a male; a shrew, a hellion, a nag as a female.

BREATHINESS

If excess air escapes during phonation a breathy quality is the result. It may well be that this is an organic fault which will require professional help, but many cases of breathiness are improved by awareness of the problem and consistent practice. Breathiness is characteristic of the sexpot and the confidence man. It is evident in various readings when a vocal whisper is necessary. Marilyn Monroe was noted for the breathy quality in her speech.

NASALITY

A "nasal twang" or *nasality* is caused from an excess of air escaping through the nose or an excessive nasal resonation. If there are no physical defects, it means simply that you use the nose for resonating other sounds than *m, n,* or *ng.* You can hear the difference between a nasal pronunciation and a normal pronunciation of *ah* by pronouncing it first while keeping open the mouth and the back of the throat (behind the soft palate or *velum*) so that a good portion of the sound goes through the nose. Try it several times that way and then pronounce it again with the mouth open but allow the soft palate and *velum* to close off the nose. You will notice that the second way produces a clearer *ah* and a de-nasalized one.

EFFECTIVE QUALITY

The key to your most effective vocal quality is relaxation. In order for the various parts of the body that work together to produce voice to operate efficiently, you must be relaxed. Unnecessary strain in the use of the breathing, phonating, resonating, and articulating mechanisms will result in a distortion of your most effective quality.

Another important point must be made about vocal quality. The problems identified give useful insight to the interpreter of literature, especially when it becomes necessary or advantageous to characterize people in performance of drama and narrative prose. You can learn to approximate the various qualities discussed in this chapter and by doing so you will create more believable characters

YOUR ROLE IN ORAL INTERPRETATION

in the plays and stories you read. Experiment with quality as you do with rate, volume, resonance, and pitch.

Summary

There is no single ideal voice, but the student can learn to make the most effective use of the voice he has.

Sound is produced by allowing a column of air from the lungs to pass over the vocal folds causing them to vibrate. The sound thus produced is amplified by the resonating chambers of the throat, mouth, and nose and formed into speech sounds by the articulators —the tongue, teeth, and lips.

Problems with voice arise from the faulty use of resonance, volume, pitch, quality, and rate. Such faulty use may be due to physical malfunction or handicap which should have medical attention before the student attempts to eliminate these problems.

The key to making most effective use of the voice is relaxation of the parts of the body that produce voice. A consistent program of practice will insure improvement.

Effective Vocal Exercises

For Projection:

1. Place your hand on your abdomen and say "ah" as you might for a throat examination. Then take a moderately deep but comfortable breath and again, say "ah." This time apply pressure with your hands suddenly. You should note appreciable loudness. Repeat, producing three loud "ahs" without straining. Breathe in if necessary after each "ah."

2. Say the following commands, each on a single breath, without strain and without an increase in pitch level toward the end:

> All aboard!
> He's out!
> Come here!
> Away with you!
> I'll go when ready!
> I mean what I say!
> There you go again!

3. Start an "ah" in a tone which is barely audible, gradually increase the volume to the count of ten, then gradually decrease the volume from the count of ten to twenty. Count from one to twenty *slowly*. This is to be done in one breath.

4. Count from one to five: begin in a barely audible tone at one and end with a five which can really be heard. Count one to seven, increasing loudness to four and then decreasing loudness from five to seven.

5. Say the following, first in a conversational tone, then as if you were trying to reach the back row, and then as if you were talking to someone about a half a block away:

> I'll go in a few minutes.
> The time is now.
> I'll say this for the last time.
> Listen if you wish to understand.

What do I do with my body?

A PERSISTENT question with students as they start a course of oral interpretation is: What do I do with my hands? Too often they answer the question with the customary system of tightly clenching their hands behind them, folding them in front, or casually dipping them into their slacks or coat pockets.

The inability to use gestures—and this is what we are talking about when we refer to hands—is a typical problem. Yet, oral interpretation does not depend just on gestures as such. It depends on the total use of the body—on proper breathing, on posture, on non-verbal communications such as facial expressions. This chapter, then, concerns itself with the various aspects of the body in communication.

Use of the Body

It is therefore important to learn early the importance of the body in the process of communication, for communication is not just a matter of the voice and the ear—the entire body is an expressive medium. The face conveys emotion through a smile, a frown, a look of consternation. The shoulders can "speak"—a shrug of the shoulders can indicate indifference, uncertainty, for example. The posture of the body can show confidence or despair. The posture you use as you walk to the stand for your reading tells much of how you are feeling inside. A slouching attitude, with the shoulders drooped, the spine curved, the chest pulled in, indicates a lack of energy, laziness, or indifference and conveys to the audience that same feeling. In contrast, a brisk walk to the stand, the body erect but not strained, the chest out, indicates confidence, assurance, a positive quality. The posture of the body is of vast importance in creating the right audience response. Carelessly leaning on the reading stand, crossing the legs in an awkward position which puts the weight all on one part of the body are habits that should be changed as soon as possible.

The body is the machine, our physical self. Its muscles, its nervous system regulate our actions. When you are tense or angry, the muscles are taut, tightened. Think of yourself as violently angry now. Feel what is happening to you. Or hang on to an object tightly, purposely straining every muscle. Now relax the muscles; think of contentment, peace, utter and complete relaxation. Take a deep breath; feel the tingling in the spine, a flooding of relief.

For still another example, imagine yourself riding in a car. It is going very fast down a mountain road. You hear the tires whining. Suddenly, a sharp curve looms ahead. The driver attempts to slow down but—can he make it? The sensation you feel at this time is fear. The heart beats faster. There is a shortness of breath. Every nerve seems to be screaming inside. Panic, terror, all these feelings come over you. Muscles grow tighter. The car makes the curve— just barely. The driver sighs heavily; he slows down. You breathe more deeply. The muscles begin to relax. The heart beats more slowly. You feel an aftereffect almost like fainting. The blood seems to drain out of your head. Gradually, the nerves begin to quiet down. You can breathe more normally. A sense of security, of safety comes over you. You return to a more natural state. Such are examples of functions of the body—emotions you can call on for your reading.

Breathing

Let's consider one of the body's primary functions—one of the essential functions to the reader—breathing.

It is a common habit among beginning students to raise the chest when told to "breathe." It is only through experience that you learn that clavicular breathing, or breathing from the chest only, adds no force and does not improve breath control. The mechanism involved in breathing is a complicated one, but we shall simplify it here for purposes of clarity.

The motor controls the breath when sounds are produced and regulates the force and volume of the vocal tone. To use the motor properly, there must be a constant supply of fuel—air. Remember— breath is the fuel used in the production of speech sounds. But at no time should the chest be lowered while sound is being produced. The motor is composed largely of respiratory muscles in the general region of the diaphragm. It provides the power necessary for expulsion, regulation, and control of the air in the production of voice and speech.

One point should be stressed. The average reader breathes only about one-half as often as he should for ease in reading and total effect.

Insufficient and improper breathing robs a selection of all emotional content because there is no time for an expression of feeling. Improper breathing makes reading more difficult, for you find yourself more concerned with getting to the first punctuation mark before your breath runs out than with communicating the meaning of the literature you are reading. Also, faulty breathing adds to tension. Taking a proper breath with sufficient frequency relieves tension and makes it possible for you to phrase more effectively as well as with more ease.

For example, read St. Paul's first Epistle to the Corinthians, Chapter 13. Try it breathing at each place marked with (B). This is the usual reading of a new reader:

Though I speak with the tongues of men and of angels, and have not charity, I am become as sounding brass, or a tinkling cymbal (B) And though I have the gift of prophecy, and understand all mysteries and all knowledge (B) and though I have all faith, so that I could remove mountains, and have not charity, I am nothing. (B)

Now try the selection a second way, taking a breath at the end of each line; the lines are arranged in breath groups to illustrate proper breathing.

THE PERFORMANCE

Though I speak with the tongues
Of men and of angels
And have not charity
I am become as sounding brass
Or a tinkling cymbal.
And though I have the gift of prophecy
And understand all mysteries
And all knowledge
And though I have all faith
So that I could remove mountains
And have not charity
I am nothing.

This second example could produce choppiness in delivery unless breathing is handled properly. Sharp, sudden intakes of breath or overly prolonged pauses do not create a smooth flow, but natural, gentle inhalations of breath add immeasurably to the reader's ease and the beauty of the selection.

Proper breathing is not governed solely by punctuation marks. In the selection above you will note that pauses are made and breath taken often within a phrase which is not set off by punctuation marks. The sense and mood of the material are the determining factors. Punctuation marks are not designed simply to identify breathing places. Their purpose in writing is also grammatical.

Breathing properly can also help students who find certain combinations of words difficult to pronounce. Often the reader will rush through a passage with complex alliterative or consonant sounds for fear that he will stumble over them. Such a "block" is caused by pressure, often by fear of garbling a line. If a breath is taken before that particular line, usually the pressure is relieved, the muscles relax, and the reader can go through it with no difficulty. Often a breath can be taken before a troublesome word within a phrase to relieve the tension and make the reading easier.

One student had a long-standing problem in which he became "terrified" of certain lines in a speech or a reading. It was only when he learned to use sufficient breath, to take in enough fuel, that he found the way to get rid of this fear and to regard words as valuable tools instead of terrifying monsters.

Do not think that a breath must be taken only before or after a phrase. It can be taken for only one word, such as "Ah" or

YOUR ROLE IN ORAL INTERPRETATION

"So!" or "What!" The way you breathe and how often you breathe depend largely on how you feel about a selection. And yet, conversely, the proper breathing increases the emotional response to the material being read.

Gestures

In addition to the matter of breathing, one is also faced with the use of the hands—and the body itself.

Gestures are of two kinds—autistic, those which are a part of our automatic physical mannerisms such as a tic, wink, or grimace—and those that are partly planned and yet come as the result of an inner response.

There is nothing worse than the mechanical, thoroughly planned gesture. In the eighteenth and nineteenth centuries, students were taught how to gesture, how to use the arms and the hands to express an emotion. The result was an effect of windmills, of gestures that had too little relation to the emotion being expressed.

It is safe to say that gestures must be felt—they cannot really be taught. Oh, it is possible to show when one is being badly used; it is possible to define a certain set of typical movements, but a reader will find that gestures will come only when he is so deeply responsive to his material that his body physiologically responds to the reactions of his nervous system. If he is immersed in a selection dealing with deep sorrow he may find it natural to put his hands over his face as if to wipe away tears—or if he is angry he may feel like clenching his fist. But gestures are an intimate part of each person's physical makeup and few people react with the same kind of physical movement to express an emotion.

It is important, though, to realize that gestures add much to a reading. For example, *Mister Roberts:* suppose you were reading the scene in the play where Pulver returns, his uniform in tatters and covered with soap suds, after blowing up the laundry. This scene demands physical action since it is a physically hilarious scene. You could not read it effectively without gestures, without some bodily movement. In another way, James Weldon Johnson's "The Creation" calls for gestures to help make the images come alive. On the other hand, introspective material such as "When I Have Fears That I May Cease To Be" would not call for gestures to add either clarity or beauty. It is a selection that is too "within" the person. Bodily movement would detract.

In some cases bodily movement is so important that interpretative reading is not the proper medium. Let us take Eugene Ionesco's "The Chairs". This avant-garde play depends a great deal on illusion. While the old man and the old woman talk throughout the play to imaginary people, the physical action of bringing on the chairs is an integral part of the play itself. To stand at a rostrum and merely read this play would destroy much of the necessary illusion.

There are some suggestions to be made for gestures and a few examples are given at the end of this chapter, but remember that they are only *suggestions*. The gestures would be mechanical unless accompanied by the proper emotional inner response.

For example, consider a feeling of anger: a direct verbal assault on the object of that anger would ordinarily require a sharp, forceful straight-armed gesture. A feeling of resignation, of indifference, might be identified with a shrug of the shoulders, or a listless moving of the hands ending with the palms upward; a desire to avoid something repugnant would require a gesture of sharpness, the hand and arm perhaps moving up from the face and down across the body to the side; a feeling of disbelief or amazement might be accentuated by raising hands and arms upward past the sides of the head.

But—any gesture which looks right, which does not draw attention to itself and which adds clarity to the material, is a good gesture. Any gesture that draws attention away from the material or to itself is a bad one. Your authors feel that the body must move for complete communication.

Physical Expression in Interpretation

Let us now consider the total involvement of the body. Suppose you are going to read a selection which involves an older man or woman. You must make a distinction between that person and a younger character. Here the body serves the interpreter. A slight slouching of the body, bent spine, and limpness of the body can give the illusion of age. In contrast, a character of strength and vigor would be pictured with a straight, erect posture, shoulders back, head high.

If a man were reading a woman's part, his movements would

be lighter, not as strong. Or if he were reading the part of an old man, his arms and hands might shake visibly, his movements would be slower, more halting. The posture of the body would reflect such characters.

Keep in mind that in using the term "movement," reference is made to gestures and actions that are within the realm of the interpreter only—not those more expansive movements demanded by the stage.

There is also the matter of facial expressions, in the use of the body, for the face, more than any other part of the body, does much to insure total communication. Too many students read with no change of expression. A smile adds much richness to a humorous selection. If the selection calls for anger, a tightness of the facial muscles, a contraction of the eyes, a menacing frown helps. If slyness and subtlety are indicated, a lifting of the eyebrows works. The important thing to remember is that the face can add much to the effect of what you are reading. The face is a reflection of how you feel inside, a part of your emotional response. Let it light up and reveal your feeling.

Gestures and bodily movement will never develop as long as you hang onto a rostrum as you read. Let your body become free and it will begin to support your voice, to talk for you. Once you learn to involve your body in what you read, tension will diminish and you will find yourself more at ease in the reading situation.

Summary

The body is an essential part of communication, for the interpreter speaks with his hands, face, shoulders, his entire body—not just his voice.

The manner in which you walk to the stand and the posture you use at the stand are indicators of how you feel inside. If you are nervous and insecure, bodily posture indicates that you are. If you are prepared, secure, a confident erectness of the body conveys this feeling of security to your audience.

Breathing properly is of first importance in the use of the body. One of the most common faults in oral reading is not breathing often enough and not taking in sufficient fuel. Improper intake of air causes dull, flat, monotonous reading. It also results in increased

THE PERFORMANCE

tension within the reader. To breathe correctly, it is necessary to breathe from the diaphragm. The common practice of raising the shoulders and breathing from the chest is one to be eliminated as quickly as possible.

Learning to use the diaphragm in breathing will also do much to relieve diction "blocks" that occur in some cases.

Gestures are a vital part of the reading process. No one can teach you when to use a gesture. Gestures are best when they come from a physiological reaction within you. They must be a part of the response you have to the literature you read. Nothing is worse than a mechanical display of waving hands. Such excesses draw attention to the reader rather than to the material.

The body can also aid the interpreter in suggesting characters. Stooped shoulders, a bent spine, and frail movements add to the impression of old age. Vigorous, firm, positive movements of the body help to identify a strong character, a dynamic personality.

Facial expressions, too, are of vital importance. When an interpreter reveals, through his facial expressions, how he is reacting "inside" to his material, the material itself takes on new and more meaningful dimensions.

The body is the frame around you; learn to make it a supportive and useful frame.

Exercises

The following exercises are helpful in learning to use the body effectively in oral interpretation.

For Proper Breathing:

1. To insure proper breathing lie flat on your back and note the movement of the middle portion of your body as you breathe. Or— place three or four heavy books on this section of the body, breathe, and note the movement of the books.

2. To further increase the desired activity in the diaphragm, place your hands across the stomach, breathe in and out without raising the shoulders and feel the expansion in front and sides.

3. Read the following selection on one breath, not hurrying the reading and making certain you are articulating properly:

YOUR ROLE IN ORAL INTERPRETATION

Ring out, wild bells, to the wild sky,
The flying cloud, the frosty light;
The year is dying in the night;
Ring out, wild bells, and let him die.

For Breath Control:

1. Inhale normally. Now release the breath while producing the sound "s." Sustain the sound for ten seconds. Repeat with the sound "sh" and then "th" as in "think," and "f" as in "fall."

2. Inhale deeply. Repeat above exercises; see how much longer you can sustain "m" or "ah."

3. Try saying each of the following on a single breath. If you don't make it the first time, try a deeper inhalation later. Do not intentionally whisper.

   a. Harry had heroic inclinations and made energetic accomplishments.
   b. Fido, his friendly dog, shared Harry's inclinations.
   c. Heaven helps those who help themselves and the devil take the hindmost.
   d. What is truth for most of us is not truth for all of us.
   e. The crisp and crackly leaves fell from the tree.
   f. The rushing stream washed the shrubbery along with it.
   g. Double, double, toil and trouble;
     Fire burn and cauldron bubble.
   h. Was this the face that launch'd a thousand ships,
     And burnt the topless towers of Ilium?

4. *Important.* Never raise shoulders or chest in breathing. Stand before a mirror as you inhale and exhale and see if this is a fault you are committing. Also, stand up, lean forward, grasp an object firmly, and breathe. You'll see it is hard to raise your shoulders then.

For Effective Gestures:

The following can be used to help get you into the habit of using gestures. It is important to keep in mind that these are *only* suggestions. You cannot operate as a robot. You must respond to literature with your whole being before any physical reactions can be called forth.

1. Since gestures involve the body, try swinging your arms back and forth loosely by your sides. Then let your arms draw circles at the side. The important thing is to keep them loose, free.

2. Picture yourself in a violent rage. Perhaps you have just found that someone you trusted has told an incredible lie about you and has embroiled you in a very unpleasant situation. Your anger rises higher and higher. You could cheerfully strangle this person. Try slowly moving your hands into clenched fists. Be tense. As your anger increases, you make short, staccato movements with your fists. Suddenly, your hands spring open and you reach out with them to grab the person's throat. The hands touch the throat and tighten their grip around it. And you press hard, harder, harder. The anger subsides at last. Slowly you release the pressure. The hands come away and then—drop limply by your sides.

3. Imagine you are starving and you are begging for something to eat. You hold your hands in front of you in a cupped shape, reaching out only a short distance. You feel shame inside, despair. The hands are held in a curved manner, palms up. Now—no one comes near. Suddenly you see someone about twenty feet away walking towards you. Reach out your hands towards him. Stretch your arms as far as they will go. The hands are now not so cupped but the palms are still up. The person comes nearer and nearer. You reach out more anxiously, more pleadingly. He starts to move away. You stretch your arms and your hands after him, now more urgently. There is a slight strain in the arm. But the figure leaves. You draw back the arms slowly, the hands return to their cupped position for a moment, and then you drop them limply at your side.

4. Take the scene in *Mister Roberts* after Pulver has blown up the laundry. By using gestures, describe how Pulver would act physically in telling of his experience with the fulminate of mercury, how he would react to the entire incident, particularly in describing the explosion itself.

5. Read the following:

ODE TO THE WEST WIND

PERCY BYSSHE SHELLEY

1

O wild West Wind, thou breath of Autumn's being,
Thou, from whose unseen presence the leaves dead
Are driven, like ghosts from an enchanter fleeing,

Yellow, and black, and pale, and hectic red,
Pestilence–stricken multitudes: O thou,
Who chariotest to their dark wintry bed

The winged seeds, where they lie cold and low,
Each like a corpse within its grave, until
Thine azure sister of the Spring shall blow

Her clarion o'er the dreaming earth, and fill
(Driving sweet buds like flocks to feed in air)
With living hues and odours plain and hill:

Wild Spirit, which art moving everywhere;
Destroyer and preserver; hear, oh, hear!

2

Thou on whose stream, 'mid the steep sky's commotion,
Loose clouds like earth's decaying leaves are shed,
Shook from the tangled boughs of Heaven and Ocean,

Angels of rain and lightning: there are spread
On the blue surface of thine aëry surge,
Like the bright hair uplifted from the head

Of some fierce Maenad, even from the dim verge
Of the horizon to the zenith's height,
The locks of the approaching storm. Thou dirge

THE PERFORMANCE

Of the dying year, to which this closing night
Will be the dome of a vast sepulchre,
Vaulted with all thy congregated might

Of vapours, from whose solid atmosphere
Black rain, and fire, and hail will burst: oh, hear!

3

Thou who didst waken from his summer dreams
The blue Mediterranean, where he lay,
Lulled by the coil of his crystalline streams,

Beside a pumice isle in Baiae's bay,
And saw in sleep old palaces and towers
Quivering within the wave's intenser day,

All overgrown with azure moss and flowers
So sweet, the sense faints picturing them! Thou
For whose path the Atlantic's level powers

Cleave themselves into chasms, while far below
The sea-blooms and the oozy woods which wear
The sapless foliage of the ocean, know

Thy voice, and suddenly grow gray with fear,
And tremble and despoil themselves: oh, hear!

4

If I were a dead leaf thou mightest bear;
If I were a swift cloud to fly with thee;
A wave to pant beneath thy power, and share

The impulse of thy strength, only less free
Than thou, O uncontrollable! If even
I were as in my boyhood, and could be

The comrade of thy wanderings over Heaven,
As then, when to outstrip thy skiey speed
Scarce seemed a vision; I would ne'er have striven

YOUR ROLE IN ORAL INTERPRETATION

As thus with thee in prayer in my sore need.
Oh, lift me as a wave, a leaf, a cloud!
I fall upon the thorns of life! I bleed!

A heavy weight of hours has chained and bowed
One too like thee: tameless, and swift, and proud.

5

Make me thy lyre, even as the forest is:
What if my leaves are falling like its own!
The tumult of thy mighty harmonies

Will take from both a deep autumnal tone,
Sweet though in sadness. Be thou, Spirit fierce,
My spirit! Be thou me, impetuous one!

Drive my dead thoughts over the universe
Like withered leaves to quicken a new birth!
And, by the incantation of this verse,

Scatter, as from an unextinguished hearth
Ashes and sparks, my words among mankind!
Be through my lips to unawakened earth

The trumpet of a prophecy! O, Wind,
If Winter comes, can Spring be far behind?

Can you feel the exaltation in the poem, the surge of emotion, the contrast in the images? What do you feel when he says, "O wild West Wind?" What kind of bodily movement seems natural here? Do you get a feeling of utter freedom and elation or perhaps a feeling of supplication? Move on to the line, "the leaves dead are driven, like ghosts from an enchanter fleeing." Feel the lifelessness, the dryness of the dead leaves, and then their floating like ghosts.

Read again the lines, "Angels of rain and lightning: there are spread/On the blue surface of thine aëry surge."

Angels are usually associated with something light, airy, delicate, not with such vigorous actions as rain and lightning. So your

THE PERFORMANCE

bodily responses here should be based on whether you felt that these angels were harbingers of nature's violent actions or whether they were to be used in the accustomed interpretation of the word. Certainly if you took the former interpretation, you would probably want to use a firm, decisive gesture, made sharply and vigorously.

Another possible section for gestures is found in the lines:

> If I were a dead leaf thou mightest bear;
> If I were a swift cloud to fly with thee,
> A wave to pant beneath thy power and share
> The impulse of thy strength . . .

Feel the emptiness of the dead leaf, and notice how your reaction changes in reference to the swift cloud. The cloud would call for fast, light reading—any gesture would be a relaxed one. But in dealing with the wave, which gives a feeling of bigness, of vast energy, of sweeping power, any gesture must be firm and vigorous.

The same feeling of urgency, of supplication would again occur in "Oh, lift me as a wave, a leaf, a cloud! I fall upon the thorns of life! I bleed!"

Let your body react quickly as the references move from "lift me," which has the feeling of giving of one's entire body to the weight of the wave, to the lightness and fragility of the leaf and the cloud. But then the change is abrupt and swift as you feel the heaviness of the body, the draining of exaltation and the drop to despair on "I fall upon the thorns of life! I bleed!" The line ends with a surrender of oneself—a lessening of all tension.

In analyzing this section, read it over quietly and when you feel like making a movement with the arms or hands or head or shoulders, do so. Pantomime it, then go back and read it aloud—and let your body support your voice.

Keep in mind, however, that there is much in poetry that defies the use of gestures. Poetry relates an intimate, personal, deeply emotional experience that would be unjustly invaded by gestures.

6. Let us turn to *Cyrano de Bergerac* by Edmond Rostand, a great romantic play combining comedy and tragedy with equal distinction. It has lived through time because of the beauty of its language and the magnificence of its portrait of Cyrano—a swash-

buckler, a fighter, a sensitive man, a man in love but one who fears to express his love for a woman. Physically, he is noted for a rather prominent nose, and in this famous speech he replies to a man who has been taunting him about its size. Read his speech to yourself and visualize his feelings; then read it aloud again and see how many of the movements you first felt you are able to incorporate in the oral reading:

Excerpt from CYRANO DE BERGERAC

EDMOND ROSTAND

ACT I

. . . Ah . . . your nose . . . hem! . . .
Your nose is . . . rather large!
CYRANO (*gravely*).   Rather.
VALVERT (*simpering*).   Oh well—
CYRANO (*coolly*).   Is that all?
VALVERT (*turns away, with a shrug*).   Well, of course—
CYRANO.   Ah, no, your sir!
You are too simple. Why, you might have said—
Oh, a great many things! Mon dieu, why waste
Your opportunity? For example, thus:
AGGRESSIVE: I, sir, if that nose were mine,
I'd have it amputated—on the spot!
FRIENDLY: How do you drink with such a nose?
You ought to have a cup made specially.
DESCRIPTIVE: 'Tis a rock—a crag—a cape—
A cape? say rather, a peninsula!
INQUISITIVE: What is that receptacle—
A razor-case or a portfolio?
KINDLY: Ah, do you love the little birds
So much that when they come and sing to you,
You give them this to perch on? *INSOLENT:*
Sir, when you smoke, the neighbors must suppose

THE PERFORMANCE

Your chimney is on fire. *CAUTIOUS:* Take care—
A weight like that might make you topheavy.
THOUGHTFUL: Somebody fetch my parasol—
Those delicate colors fade so in the sun!
PEDANTIC: Does not Aristophanes
Mention a mythologic monster called
Hippocampelephantocamelos?
Surely we have here the original!
FAMILIAR: Well, old torchlight! Hang your hat
Over that chandelier—it hurts my eyes.
ELOQUENT: When it blows, the typhoon howls,
And the clouds darken. *DRAMATIC:* When it bleeds—
The Red Sea! *ENTERPRISING:* What a sign
For some perfumer! *LYRIC:* Hark—the horn
Of Roland calls to summon Charlemagne!—
SIMPLE: When do they unveil the monument?
RESPECTFUL: Sir, I recognize in you
A man of parts, a man of prominence—
RUSTIC: Hey? What? Call that a nose? Na, na—
I be no fool like what you think I be—
That there's a blue cucumber! *MILITARY:*
Point against cavalry! *PRACTICAL:* Why not
A lottery with this for the grand prize?
Or—parodying Faustus in the play—
"Was this the nose that launched a thousand ships
And burned the topless towers of Ilium?"
These, my dear sir, are things you might have said
Had you some tinge of letters, or of wit
To color your discourse. But wit,—not so.
You never had an atom—and of letters,
You need but three to write you down—an Ass.
Moreover,—if you had the invention, here
Before these folk to make a jest of me—
Be sure you would not then articulate
The twentieth part of half a syllable
Of the beginning! For I say these things
Lightly enough myself, about myself,
But I allow none else to utter them.

YOUR ROLE IN ORAL INTERPRETATION

First of all, keep in mind the type of man Cyrano was. He was a swashbuckler, a fighter, an expert swordsman, a romanticist, a man who used his body freely and energetically. This speech cannot be read effectively without bodily involvement. Doing so would rob the scene of much of Rostand's meaning.

In analyzing the speech, one clue to physical support is the number of adjectives Cyrano uses to describe the distinctive aspects of his nose, such as aggressive, friendly, respectful, eloquents, etc. Each calls for a different physical reaction. *Aggressive* requires a tightening of the muscles, a more rigid attitude, a firmness. *Friendly* shows the body more at ease, more relaxed, a lighter and happier attitude. And *Kindly* calls for a smoothness in bodily movement, an ease, a gentleness, a relaxation of the muscles.

The line, ". . . if that nose were mine," would very likely call for a gesture to the nose. "A rock—a crag—a cape!" might bring forth an expansive movement, a sweep of the arm to indicate the bigness. In contrast, the reference to "razor-case" could be read without any bodily movement at all. If movement were used, it would have to be a small, rather pinched gesture. In the comment "when you smoke," a sweeping gesture from the nose up might be fitting; and a gesture with the arm sweeping down on "when it bleeds." On the *Rustic* section, "That there's a blue cucumber!" could be read with staccato-like pointings with the index finger. When Cyrano says "military," the body should be erect, tense, rigid, and on "Point against cavalry!" the gesture could be a firm outreaching of the arm in the order of a military command. When Cyrano again returns his comments to the man directly, there is a change in bodily reaction. Now he leaves the dramatic buffoonery and speaks directly to his adversary. He is sarcastic and also threatening.

Again, it is important to bear in mind that the suggestions made above are not to be considered as the only possible gestures or movements. You, as the reader, must respond in your own way. But before you can use your body, you must experience some physiological reaction to the character speaking, to what he is saying, to the changes in his views and emotions. Your reactions should follow naturally and add to the total effect of the reading.

Learn to use the body—but never become a stereotyped robot. The gestures must be part of you—not apart from you.

THE PERFORMANCE

❧ CHAPTER 9

How fast do I read?

IN CHAPTER 6 a diacritical marking of *Look Homeward, Angel* was given to teach you how to analyze according to moods and emotions. It also indicated the use of virgules for proper phrasing and changes of thought. This model will serve as a good guide for the contents of this chapter.

No reading can be effective without the use of the three keys to oral interpretation: pacing, pausing, and emphasis. They can make or destroy interpretative reading.

Rate or Pacing

One of the most common of all faults in the reading of literature is a sameness in rate of reading, or pacing, and the tendency to read in one breath, pausing only for punctuation marks. The beginning reader will read a sentence to a comma, pause momentarily (if at all) and then race quickly on to the period. In the process of this rapid and monotonous pacing, thought and meaning become lost.

Learn quickly that the elements that govern your reading are thought and content. You have to decide what the author is trying to say, what ideas he is bringing forth, how he builds to a climax, what are the characters like which he creates. When such matters are analyzed, you will find that pausing and pacing fall almost into a natural pattern.

Some sections need a slower, more precise pacing; for instance, in the reading of descriptive passages, a slower pace is usually necessary in order to bring out effectively the images used by the author. If he is trying to create a setting of sublimity, of peace and contentment, the pace should be relaxed, languid, slower, to stress the general effect of beauty. If the author is describing a scene of vivid action or vigorous movement, the pacing is more rapid. In Poe's "The Tell-Tale Heart," (see chapter 4), the panic the man feels at the end as he believes he is being discovered requires a faster pace in order to heighten the excitement. In contrast, the irony of Swift's "A Modest Proposal" demands a slower, more emphatic kind of pacing in order to highlight the primary concepts. And a relaxed love scene between two people should be read more slowly to convey the proper mood.

Of course, pacing must be varied. No selection has all the same mood throughout. The analysis of the moods and emotions is vitally important. A rate of speed that varies by degrees of rapidity adds variety and color to a reading. Pacing problems in poetry, prose, and drama are almost identical and all are based on a thorough understanding of the moods.

Poetry probably presents the most complex study of pacing. It is the general tendency of readers to read all poems with the same rate, and yet, incorporated within the poetic structure are images of differing emotions, concepts of different complexities, stories with suspense and action and romance, personal expressions of deep feeling which by their very nature demand a slower pacing and a more total involvement. Pacing in poetry also demands from the reader an awareness of the rhythm without a concentration on the rhythmic pattern, a "dum-de-dum" effect to the end of each line. Make the thought, the emotion, the experience in the poem your first concern and convey these to your audience. Then the amount of rhythm that should be present in your reading will be there.

Let us look at two poems to indicate the contrast.

Alfred Noyes' poem, "The Highwayman" is an example in which contrasting rates are used. The first part is read at a slower rate to help create the illusion of something ghostly and mysterious. Then in the description of the highwayman, to convey his cavalierish attitude, a faster pace is used. Rate again becomes slower in the description of Tom, the caretaker, and in the references to Bess' appearance. Pacing in this segment is important to make the introduction of Bess more meaningful—and to give the sensual illusion of her long black hair falling over the highwayman's chest. The pace quickens with the entrance of the redcoats and in Bess' struggle to free herself, in her panic to try to warn her lover. The same faster pace for purposes of suspense continues until the highwayman's death and then it slows down noticeably after that, particularly with the last two stanzas of the poem where once more the ghostly and eerie setting returns and unreality becomes a part of the poem itself.

Now let's look at "How Do I Love Thee?" by Elizabeth Barrett Browning. This is a lyric poem, reflective, and extremely personal. It deals with her deep love for Robert Browning and, therefore, is highly sensitive in nature. There is nothing in the poem to indicate a need for faster pacing. She is not thinking in excited terms, but in reflective ones. She is not dealing in suspense, but in her inner feeling. So the pace would be slower, more relaxed.

HOW DO I LOVE THEE?

ELIZABETH BARRETT BROWNING

How do I love thee? Let me count the ways.
I love thee to the depth and breadth and height
My soul can reach, when feeling out of sight
For the ends of Being and ideal Grace.
I love thee to the level of every day's
Most quiet need, by sun and candlelight.
I love thee freely, as men strive for Right;
I love thee purely, as they turn from Praise.
I love thee with the passion put to use
In my old griefs, and with my childhood's faith.
I love thee with a love I seemed to lose
With my lost saints—I love thee with the breath,
Smiles, tears, of all my life!—and, if God choose,
I shall but love thee better after death.

Pacing in the reading of expository prose adds to clarity of the author's ideas. Proper pacing of vivid descriptions adds to the fullness of appreciation of what is being described. Pacing is important in the reading of narrative prose to build suspense, to highlight action, and to prepare the audience for the climax. The attitudes of the characters as they are expressed in dialogue form are often

THE PERFORMANCE

different from the attitude of the author in expository writing. The general tendency in the reading of narrative is for a reader to come to life with feeling and proper pacing in the reading of dialogue and then fall back into a routinely consistent pacing in the other sections of the story. And yet, pacing is also vitally important in the reading of the narrative and expository sections that give a reason for the dialogue.

A good example of typical pacing needed for descriptive writing is found in *The Sea of Grass* by Conrad Richter.

That lusty pioneer blood is tamed now, broken and gelded like the wild horse and the frontier settlement. And I think that I shall never see it flowing through human veins again as it did in my Uncle Jim Brewton riding a lathered horse across his shaggy range or standing in his massive ranch house, bare of furniture as a garret, and holding together his empire of grass and cattle by the fire in his eyes. His rude empire is dead and quartered today like a steer on the meat-block, but I still lie in bed at night and see it tossing, pitching, leaping in the golden sunlight of more than fifty years ago, sweeping up to his very door, stretching a hundred and twenty miles north and south along the river, and rolling as far into the sunset as stock could roam—a ranch larger than Massachusetts with Connecticut thrown in, his fabulous herds of Texas cattle sprinkled like grains of cinnamon across the horizons, his name a legend even then, his brand familiar as the ABC's in every packing-house, and his word the law, not dead sentences in a book, but a moving finger writing on a cottonwood tree where all who rode could very plainly read.

I can see his bedroom, just a bunk in the corner, with a fancy horsehair bridle and ropes on the wall, and a brown buckskin partly cut away in strips for whang leather. And I can see his huge parlor, without rugs or furniture, piled to the pine rafters with white sacks of flour and burlapped hills of sugar and green coffee, and wooden buttes of boxed tobacco, dried fruits, and canned tomatoes, just the provisions for his hundred hands and everyone else who passed that way, rancher or cowboy, settler or prospector, Mexican, Indian, or outlaw, all welcome at his table.

But what moves across my eye unforgettably is his spring roundup when six or seven wagons working back from the Arizona line reached the headquarters range with a vast, almost mythical herd the like of which will never be seen in this coutry again.

Farther than the eye could strain through the dust, the grass was colored with milling cattle, while bulls rode and fought, and cows and calves bawled, and countless horns clacked, and sixty or seventy of us kept saddling fresh mounts and galloping here and there in a stirring, daylong excitement.

The free wild life we lived on that shaggy prairie was to me the life of the gods. And that there should be any-one who would not love it as we did, who should even hate it passionately and secretly, and yet the memory of whose delicate presence in that violent land still stirs me with emotion after fifty years, had not occurred to me then. But I was only a boy whose face had never known a razor, in a pair of California britches turned up to let my boots into the stirrups, that early fall day I rode with rebellious young back to Salt Fork to be shipped off to Missouri to school before my uncle would fetch back to the ranch the scarcest article in the territory, a woman, the one we had never seen, who was coming all the way from St. Louis to marry him.

The first paragraph should be read in a slower pace to make clear the author's theme and purpose. The second paragraph con-veys a feeling of lifelessness and needs a still slower pacing until the line, "see it tossing, pitching, leaping in the golden sunlight." The adjectives used here demand a somewhat faster pace but it should change to a slower pace again for emphasis on "sweeping up to his very door, stretching a hundred and twenty miles north and south . . ."

The paragraph beginning with "I can see his bedroom" is

THE PERFORMANCE

reflective in nature and should be handled with a slower pace. Then the mood changes in the next paragraph which deals with the action of the herd and the pacing quickens. There is a change again with the line "The free wild life we lived . . ."

For an example of the pacing of narrative, read the following:

Excerpt from LORD OF THE FLIES

WILLIAM GOLDING

The hunters were looking uneasily at the sky, flinching from the stroke of the drops. A wave of restlessness set the boys swaying and moving aimlessly. The flickering light became brighter and the blows of the thunder were only just bearable. The littluns began to run about, screaming.

Jack leapt on to the sand.

"Do our dance! Come on! Dance!"

He ran stumbling through the thick sand to the open space of rock beyond the fire. Between the flashes of lightning the air was dark and terrible; and the boys followed him, clamorously. Roger became the pig, grunting and charging at Jack, who side-stepped. The hunters took their spears, the cooks took spits, and the rest clubs of firewood. A circling movement developed and a chant. While Roger mimed the terror of the pig, the littluns ran and jumped on the outside of the circle. Piggy and Ralph, under the threat of the sky, found themselves eager to take a place in this demented but partly secure society. They were glad to touch the brown backs of the fence that hemmed in the terror and made it governable.

"Kill the beast! Cut his throat! Spill his blood!"

The movement became regular while the chant lost its first superficial excitement and began to beat like a steady pulse. Roger ceased to be a pig and became a hunter, so that the centre of the ring yawned emptily. Some of the littluns started a ring on their own; and the complementary circles went round and round as though repetition would achieve safety of itself. There was the throb and stamp of a single organism.

YOUR ROLE IN ORAL INTERPRETATION

The dark sky was shattered by a blue-white scar. An instant later the noise was on them like the blow of a gigantic whip. The chant rose a tone in agony.

"Kill the beast! Cut his throat! Spill his blood!"

Now out of the terror rose another desire, thick, urgent, blind.

"Kill the beast! Cut his throat! Spill his blood!"

Again the blue-white scar jagged above them and the sulphurous explosion beat down. The littluns screamed and blundered about, fleeing from the edge of the forest, and one of them broke the ring of biguns in his terror.

"Him! Him!"

The circle became a horseshoe. A thing was crawling out of the forest. It came darkly, uncertainly. The shrill screaming that rose before the beast was like a pain. The beast stumbled into the horseshoe.

"Kill the beast! Cut his throat! Spill his blood!"

The blue-white scar was constant, the noise unendurable. Simon was crying out something about a dead man on a hill.

"Kill the beast! Cut his throat! Spill his blood! Do him in!"

The sticks fell and the mouth of the new circle crunched and screamed. The beast was on its knees in the centre, its arms folded over its face. It was crying out against the abominable noise something about a body on the hill. The beast struggled forward, broke the ring and fell over the steep edge of the rock to the sand by the water. At once the crowd surged after it, poured down the rock, leapt on to the beast, screamed, struck, bit, tore. There were no words, and no movements but the tearing of teeth and claws.

Then the clouds opened and let down the rain like a waterfall. The water bounded from the mountain-top, tore leaves and branches from the trees, poured like a cold shower over the struggling heap on the sand. Presently the heap broke up and figures staggered away. Only the beast lay still, a few yards from the sea. Even in the rain

THE PERFORMANCE

they could see how small a beast it was; and already its blood was staining the sand.

Now a great wind blew the rain sideways, cascading the water from the forest trees. On the mountain-top the parachute filled and moved; the figure slid, rose to its feet, spun, swayed down through a vastness of wet air and trod with ungainly feet the tops of the high trees; falling, still falling, it sank toward the beach and the boys rushed screaming into the darkness. The parachute took the figure forward, furrowed the lagoon, and bumped it over the reef out to sea.

Toward midnight the rain ceased and the clouds drifted away, so that the sky was scattered once more with the incredible lamps of stars. Then the breeze died too and there was no noise save the drip and trickle of water that ran out of clefts and spilled down, leaf by leaf, to the brown earth of the island. The air was cool, moist, and clear; and presently even the sound of the water was still. The beast lay huddled on the pale beach and the stains spread, inch by inch. . . .

The line of his cheek silvered and the turn of his shoulder became sculptured marble. The strange attendant creatures, with their fiery eyes and trailing vapors, busied themselves round his head. The body lifted a fraction of an inch from the sand and a bubble of air escaped from the mouth with a wet plop. Then it turned gently in the water.

Somewhere over the darkened curve of the world the sun and moon were pulling, and the film of water on the earth planet was held, bulging slightly on one side while the solid core turned. The great wave of the tide moved farther along the island and the water lifted. Softly, surrounded by a fringe of inquisitive bright creatures, itself a silver shape beneath the steadfast constellations, Simon's dead body moved out toward the open sea.

The first paragraph requires a slower pacing to set the stage and to identify suspense. But then on "The littluns began to run about, screaming," the pace quickens. The following paragraph should be read at a faster rate and with an increase in intensity. There is a change to a slower pace on "The dark sky was shattered by a blue-white scar," and then an increase in speed with "Kill the beast! Cut his throat! Spill his blood!" Rate gets even faster up to the point of "The sticks fell and the mouth of the new circle crunched and screamed." At "Then the clouds opened and let down the rain like a waterfall" the mood is more relaxed. The action has hit its peak. The author is again concerned with description. A faster pace is needed momentarily on "Now a great wind blew the rain sideways . . ." But the mood changes again to a slower rate on "It sank toward the beach". The slower rate continues with an even more relaxed feeling, an even slower pace on the last paragraph.

In drama, pacing is used to build scenes to their climaxes. If there is a scene of great suspense, the pacing gradually becomes faster until it hits the peak moment. Then there is usually a slowing down, an abrupt change of pace for the aftermath and the climax. A scene which features sophisticated chatter, as in Noel Coward's *Private Lives*, is usually read with fast pacing. A scene in which a man confesses some weaknesses or some great conflict, as in Hamlet's famous speech "To be or not to be," requires a slower pace, a more introspective mood. After all, no one thinks aloud to himself in a meditative mood with a fast rate of speech.

Often authors of plays—and of novels—will punctuate to indicate where a change of pacing is needed. Dots and dashes will be used to specify changes of pace, and always these elements require a slight drop or rise in pitch and typically, a slower pace. In drama, this is a much used form. In the death scene in *King Lear,* given in another chapter, note how the pacing changes. In the first part, "Howl, howl, howl, howl!" the pace is more rapid, conveying urgency and anxiety. Then the pace changes with "She's gone forever" to denote the tragedy of the death. It quickens somewhat with "Lend me a looking glass. If that her breath will moist or stain the stone, Why, then she lives." In these lines Lear's excitement and hope that his daughter is alive must be made apparent to the audience.

This note of hope and expectancy continues until "A plague upon you murderers, traitors all." Here Lear speaks with more anger and the pace quickens, but immediately it slows again to convey his sorrow as he says, "I might have saved her . . ." The conversation that follows moves rather fast with no need for any profound changes in pace. The many interrupted speeches indicate a fluidity

THE PERFORMANCE

of conversation. As Lear becomes more frantic and his failing mind more apparent with "And my poor fool is hang'd," the pace speeds up. But it changes abruptly to a slower pace on "Pray you undo this button," and again on "Thank you, sir." At this point rate quickens to denote his excitement as he says, "Do you see this?" And it gets even faster on "Look there, look there." After that there is a slowing of pace to give emphasis to the tragedy that has taken place.

In Sophocles' *Antigone*, Haemon comes to beg his father's mercy for Antigone, whom he loves and who has been condemned to death for going against Creon's edict. In the beginning of the scene, there is a slower pace as the two men spar and discuss their relationship. Then with "So, my son, do not be led by passing fancy . . ." the pace becomes even slower—for emphasis. Emphasis is the key in these lines and remains so until the end of Creon's speech with "Let no-one call us woman's underlings." Haemon remains calm and tries to reason with his father, so the pace is slower, but it becomes slightly faster on "But I can hear these murmurs in the dark." As he continues to try to reason with his father, the pace remains slower. But as the two men begin to argue, it picks up with "And is a man of my age to be taught . . ." It builds to an even faster peak as they argue and condemn each other to "No, she will never perish at my side." Here Haemon has made his decision; he is firm, definite; his pace slows to his exit.

Excerpt from ANTIGONE

SOPHOCLES

CREON. . . . My son, have you heard that sentence has
    been passed
On your betrothed? Are you here to storm at me?
Or have I your good will, whatever I do?
HAEMON. Father, I am in your hands. You in your wis-
    dom
Lay down for me the paths I am to follow.
There is no marriage in the world
That I would put before my good advisor.
CREON. Yes, keep this always in your heart, my son:
Accept your father's word as law in all things.

YOUR ROLE IN ORAL INTERPRETATION

For that is why men pray to have
Dutiful children growing up at home,
To repay their father's enemies in kind
And honor those he loves no less than he does.
But a man is sowing troubles for himself
And enemies' delight—what else?—when he
Sires sons who bring no profit to their father.
So, my son, do not be led by passing fancy
To lose your head for a woman's sake. You know,
The warmth goes out of such embraces, when
An evil woman shares your home and bed.
False friends are deadlier than a festered wound.
So turn from her with loathing; let her find
A husband for herself among the dead.
For now that I have caught her, the only one
Of all the city to disobey me openly,
My people shall not see me break my word.
I shall kill her. Let her plead the sacred ties
Of kinship! If I bring up my own family
To flout me, there will be no holding others.
A man who sees his family obey him
Will have authority in public matters.
But if anyone offends, or violates the laws,
No word of praise shall he ever have from me.
Whoever the state appoints must be obeyed,
In little things or great things, right or wrong.
I should have confidence that such a man
Would be as good a ruler as a subject
And in a hail of spears would stand his ground
Where he was put, a comrade you could trust.
But disobedience is the worst of evils;
It is this that ruins cities, it is this
That makes homes desolate, turns brothers in arms
To headlong rout. But those who are preserved
Owe their lives, the greater part of them to discipline.
And so we must stand up for law and order,
Not let ourselves be worsted by a woman.
If yield we must, then let us yield to a man.

THE PERFORMANCE

Let no-one call us woman's underlings.

CHORUS.   Unless the years have robbed me of my wits
You seem to have sound sense in what you say.

HAEMON.   Father, the gods endow mankind with reason,
The highest quality that we possess.
It is not for me to criticize your words.
I could not do it, and would hate to try.
And yet, two heads are sometimes better than one;
At least, it is my place to watch, on your behalf,
All that men do and say and criticize.
Fear of your frown prevents the common man
From saying anything that would displease you,
But I can hear these murmurs in the dark,
The feeling in the city for this girl.
"No woman" they say "has ever deserved death less,
Or died so shamefully in a noble cause.
When her brother fell in the slaughter, she would not
Leave him unburied, to provide a meal
For carrion dogs or passing birds of prey.
Is she not, then, deserving golden honors?"
This is what men are whispering to each other.
Father, there is nothing dearer to my heart
Than your continuing prosperity.
What finer ornament could children have
Than a father's proud success—or he, than theirs?
So wear an open mind; do not suppose
That you are right, and everyone else is wrong.
A man who thinks he has monopoly
Of wisdom, no rival in speech or intellect,
Will turn out hollow when you look inside him.
However wise he is, it is no disgrace
To learn, and give way gracefully.
You see how trees that bend to winter floods
Preserve themselves, save every twig unbroken,
But those that stand rigid perish root and branch,
And also how the man who keeps his sails
Stretched taut, and never slackens them, overturns
And finishes his voyage upside down.

YOUR ROLE IN ORAL INTERPRETATION

Let your anger rest; allow us to persuade you.
If a young man may be permitted his opinion
I should say it would be best for everyone
To be born omniscient; but otherwise—
And things have a habit of falling out differently—
It is good to learn from good advice.

CHORUS.   My lord, if he speaks to the point you ought to
    listen,
And Haemon, you to him. There is sense on both sides.

CREON.   And is a man of my age to be taught
What I should think by one so young as this?

HAEMON.   Nothing that is not right; young though I may
    be,
You should judge by my behavior, not my age.

CREON.   What sort of behavior is it to honor rebels?

HAEMON.   I would never suggest that the guilty should be
    honored.

CREON.   And is she not infected with this disease?

HAEMON.   The people of Thebes unanimously deny it.

CREON.   Will the city tell me how I am to rule?

HAEMON.   Listen to that! Who is being childish now?

CREON.   Is the state to listen to any voice but mine?

HAEMON.   There is no state, when one man is its master.

CREON.   Is not the state supposed to be the ruler's?

HAEMON.   You would do well as the monarch of a desert.

CREON.   It seems the woman has a champion here.

HAEMON.   Then you are the woman! It is you I care about!

CREON.   Insolent cub! Will you argue with your father?

HAEMON.   I will, when I see you falling into error.

CREON.   Am I wrong to respect my own prerogatives?

HAEMON.   It is no respect, when you offend the gods.

CREON.   How contemptible, to give way to a woman!

HAEMON.   At least I do not give way to temptation.

CREON.   But every word you say is a plea for her.

HAEMON.   And for you, and for me, and for the gods be-
    low.

CREON.   You will never marry her this side of the grave.

HAEMON.   Then she will die—and take somebody with her.

THE PERFORMANCE

CREON. So! Do you dare to go so far? Are you threatening me?

HAEMON. Is it threatening, to protest a wrong decision?

CREON. You shall pay for this. A fine one to teach wisdom!

HAEMON. If you were not my father, I should call you a fool.

CREON. You woman's slave; do not try to wheedle me!

HAEMON. Would you stop everyone from speaking but yourself?

CREON. Indeed! I tell you, by the gods above us,
You shall pay for using such language to your father.
(to the Attendants)
Bring this abomination out, and let her die
Here, in his presence, at her bridegroom's side.

HAEMON. No, she will never perish at my side,
So do not think it. From this moment on
Your eyes will never see my face again.
So rave away, to those who have more patience!

Variety in pacing is needed not only for clear meaning and more exact emotional expression but to give you, the reader, moments of relaxation. You could never maintain an unvarying, fast pace or a consistently slow pace without finding the reading difficult and monotonous.

Pausing

To many readers, there is one time to pause and that is when a period or a comma is reached. But, as in pacing, pausing is not regulated entirely by punctuation marks—but rather by thought group, thought content. Without pauses, reading becomes mechanical. There is no variety, no clarity, no use of emphasis, no meaning. It is like listening to a record that repeats itself over and over.

Pauses serve four purposes: (1) They clearly define changes in ideas and emotions. (2) They serve to emphasize key words and key thoughts. (3) They provide a basis for an emotional outlet in the reader. (4) They give the reader the necessary opportunity to breathe, to take in the fuel that is his ammunition.

Pauses give life, beauty, intensity to readings. If used properly, they are your best tool. But if omitted or used incorrectly, they can disrupt continuity of thought and intention. To use too few pauses insures monotony. To use too many makes for a choppy reading with vagueness and confusion the result.

The duration of a pause is a vital matter. A pause for the purpose of taking a breath or for emphasizing a word or phrase is usually of short duration. The voice tone flows from the last sound of the previous word to the beginning sound of the next word. For example, "He knew her secret, / her desperate / secret." If there is a complete change of idea or mood, the pause is more abrupt and of longer duration. "He had had it. // His mind went back to the day he first met her, / a grey day. / But he tossed aside such reminiscences at once. // The hurt was too much." At the double slash lines, the pause is definite, of longer duration, to heighten change in thought and idea. Pauses at the points identified in the following segment would introduce choppiness: "He went home // He walked down the street // slowly // He was in a hurry." // Notice that there is no sense of movement in the lines, only a feeling of choppiness.

Pauses are essential in poetry in order to convey mood and meaning through the imagery the lines contain. Read the following poem without any pauses except at the end of each line.

TEARS, IDLE TEARS

ALFRED, LORD TENNYSON

Tears, idle tears, I know not what they mean,
Tears from the depth of some divine despair
Rise in the heart, and gather in the eyes
In looking on the happy autumn-fields,
And thinking of the days that are no more.

Fresh as the first beam glittering on a sail,
That brings forth our friends up from the underworld,
Sad as the last which reddens over one
That sinks with all we love below the verge;
So sad, so fresh, the days that are no more.

Ah, sad and strange as in dark summer dawns
The earliest pipe of half-awakened birds

THE PERFORMANCE

To dying ears, when unto dying eyes
The casement slowly grows a glimmering square;
So sad, so strange, the days that are no more.

Dear as remembered kisses after death,
And sweet as those by hopeless fancy feigned
On lips that are for others, deep as love.
Deep as first love, and wild with all regret;
O Death in Life, the days that are no more.

Now read the poem again with the following markings, pausing slightly and taking a breath when you come to a single virgule; make a more definite pause when you come to double virgules. Notice how the meaning is heightened.

Tears / idle tears / I know not what they mean //
Tears from the depth / of some divine despair
Rise in the heart / and gather in the eyes /
In looking on the happy / autumn fields /
And thinking of the days / that are no more //

Fresh as the first beam / glittering on a sail /
That brings forth our friends up from the underworld//
Sad as the last / which reddens over one
That sinks with all we love / below the verge //
So sad / so fresh / the days that are no more //

Ah / sad and strange / as in dark summer dawns
The earliest pipe / of half-awakened birds
To dying ears / when unto dying eyes /
The casement slowly grows / a glimmering square //
So sad / so strange / the days that are no more //

Dear as remembered kisses after death /
And sweet as those / by hopeless fancy feigned
On lips / that are for others / deep as love //
Deep as first love / and wild with all regret //
O Death in Life / the days / that are no more //

YOUR ROLE IN ORAL INTERPRETATION

John Keats' "Ode To a Nightingale" is an excellent example of how pauses add to the beauty of the imagery and to the meaning. Read the following, noting the effect of the pausings.

ODE TO A NIGHTINGALE

JOHN KEATS

My heart aches, / and a drowsy numbness pains
My sense, / as thought of hemlock I had drunk, //
Or emptied some dull opiate to the drains
One minute past, // and Lethe-wards had sunk: //
'Tis not through envy of thy happy lot, /
But being too happy in thine happiness,— /
That thou, light-wingèd Dryad of the trees, /
In some melodious plot
Of beechen green, / and shadows numberless, /
Singest of summer / in full-throated ease. //

O, for a draught of vintage! / that hath been
Cooled a long age, / in the deep-delvèd earth, //
Tasting of Flora / and the country green, /
Dance, / and Provencal song, / and sunburnt mirth! //
O for a beaker full of the warm South, /
Full of the true, / the blushful Hippocrene, /
With beaded bubbles winking at the brim, /
And purple-stainèd mouth; /
That I might drink, / and leave the world unseen, /
And with thee / fade away / into the forest dim: /

Fade far away, / dissolve, / and quite forget
What thou among the leaves hast never known, /
The weariness, / the fever, and the fret
Here, / where men sit and hear each other groan; //
Where palsy shakes a few, / sad, / last grey hairs, //
Where youth grows pale, / and specter-thin, / and dies; /
Where but to think is to be full of sorrow
And leaden-eyed despairs,/
Where Beauty cannot keep her lustrous eyes, /
Or new Love pine at them / beyond to-morrow. //

THE PERFORMANCE

Knowing when to pause as you read prose is equally important and there are differences in the reading of expository and narrative prose. John Donne's *Quis Homo* is a selection worthy of study since it deals in concepts and not in plot or characterization.

We are all conceived in close prison; in our Mothers' wombs, we are close prisoners all; when we are born, we are born but to the liberty of the house; prisoners still, though within larger walls; and then all our life is but a going out to the place of execution, to death. Now was there ever any man seen to sleep in the cart, between Newgate and Tyburn? Between the prison, and the place of execution, does any man sleep? And we sleep all the way; from the womb to the grave we are never thoroughly awake; but pass on with such dreams, and imaginations as these, I may live as well as another, and why should I die, rather than another? But awake, and tell me, says this text, *Quis Homo?* Who is that other that thou talkest of? *What man is he that liveth, and shall not see death?*

Donne's theory is that we are never entirely free, that we are in a kind of prison all our lives. We are imprisoned from the womb to the grave. Death is inevitable for us all and we tend to sleep through life rather than live life wide-awake. Now re-read this selection, noting the markings. See if the meaning is not clearer.

We are all conceived / in close prison // in our Mothers' wombs / we are close prisoners all // when we are born / we are born but to the liberty / of the house // prisoners still / though within larger walls // and then all our life / is but a going out to the place of execution / to death // Now was there ever any man / seen to sleep in the cart / between Newgate and Tyburn? // Between the prison and the place of execution / does any man sleep? // And we sleep all the way // from the womb to the grave / we are never thoroughly awake / but pass on with such dreams/and imaginations as these//I may live as

well as another // and why should I die / rather than an-
other? // But awake / and tell me / says this text /
Quis homo? // Who is that other that thou talkest of? //
What man is he that liveth / and shall not / see death?

In line one, the pause before "in close prison" is given not only
for smoother phrasing but to emphasize the key concept—prison.
The pause before "when we are born . . ." stresses the idea that we
enter life and live life as prisoners. The change of idea on "and then
all our life . . ." requires a longer pause to emphasize life vs. death
theory. There is another change in idea on "Now was there ever any
man . . ." which brings in a new concept of prison—the actuality of
the prison of Newgate where prisoners were taken in carts to
Tyburn, the place of execution. This is a further extension of the
idea of prison to death. The change before "And we sleep all the
way" is to stress Donne's theory of our living only a half life. The
personal reference comes in "I may live as well as another. . . ."
There is a further distinction and new concept in the reference to
the title, which means "Who is the man?" The pause after "that
liveth" and before "and shall not see death?" is to serve as emphasis
on the contrast between life and death.

It is well to keep in mind that this is part of a sermon that
Donne gave, and since it was meant to be delivered, the use of
pauses becomes even more significant.

Narrative prose, dealing as it does in characterization, mood,
and dialogue makes special demands on the reader in regard to
pauses. In the following selection from *Sons and Lovers* by D. H.
Lawrence, we can see what the correct use of pauses does to make
this section come alive.

Excerpt from SONS AND LOVERS

D. H. LAWRENCE

"You were late," she said.   *pause here to*
"Was I?" he answered. —   *indicate the*
There was silence for a while.   *silence and need for*
"Was it rough riding?" she   *next line*
asked.
"I didn't notice it." —   *another pause here*
                                     to indicate difficulty
                                     in keeping conversation going

THE PERFORMANCE

She continued quickly to lay the table. When she had finished—

"Tea won't be for a few minutes. Will you come and look at the daffodils?" she said.

He rose without answering. They went out into the back garden under the budding damson-trees. *pause / focus of attention here / changes here / to the garden / the pause / emphasize / the change*

Pause here / as focus / changes / again The hills and the sky were clean and cold. Everything looked washed, rather hard. Miriam glanced at Paul. He was pale and impassive. It seemed cruel to her that his eyes and brows, which she loved, could look so hurting.

"Has the wind made you tired?" she asked. She detected an *Pause to / heighten her / concern* underneath feeling of weariness about him.

"No, I think not," he answered.

"It must be rough on the road —the wood moans so."

"You can see by the clouds it's a south-west wind; that helps me here."

"You see, I don't cycle, so I don't understand," she murmured.

"Is there need to cycle to know that!" he said.

pause to / show the / strain / between / the two She thought his sarcasms were unnecessary. They went forward in silence . . . Miriam went on her knees before one cluster, took a wild-looking daffodil between her hands, turned up its face of gold to her, and bowed down, caressing it with her mouth and cheeks and brow. He stood aside, with his hands in his pockets, watching her . . .

"Why must you always be fondling things?" he said irritably.

"But I love to touch them," she replied, hurt.

"Can you never like things without clutching them as if you wanted to pull the heart out of them? Why don't you have a bit more restraint, or reserve, or something?"

Pause to show her hurt

She looked up at him full of pain, then continued slowly to stroke her lips against a ruffled flower. Their scent, as she smelled it, was so much kinder than he; it almost made her cry.

"You wheedle the soul out of things," he said. "I would never wheedle—at any rate, I'd go straight."

He scarcely knew what he was saying. These things came from him mechanically. She looked at him. His body seemed one weapon, firm and hard against her.

Pause to emphasize relation between them

"You're always begging things to love you," he said, "as if you were a beggar for love. Even the flowers, you have to fawn on them . . .

"You don't want to love—your

THE PERFORMANCE

eternal and abnormal craving is to be loved. You aren't positive, you're negative. You absorb, absorb, as if you must fill yourself up with love, because you've got a shortage somewhere."

a pause to heighten the shock she feels

She was stunned by his cruelty, and did not hear. He had not the faintest notion of what he was saying. It was as if his fretted, tortured soul, run hot by thwarted passion, jetted off these sayings like sparks from electricity. She did not grasp anything he said. She only sat crouched beneath his cruelty and his hatred of her. She never realized in a flash. Over everything she brooded and brooded.

Pause to show change of focus

slightly longer pause as a new thought + new characters are introduced

After tea he played with Edgar and the brothers, taking no notice of Miriam. She, extremely unhappy on this looked-for holiday, waited for him. And at last he yielded and came to her. She was determined to track this mood of his to its origin. She counted it not much more than a mood.

Pause to show new attention on his past

"Shall we go through the wood a little way?" she asked him, knowing he never refused a direct request . . . *Pause here to show Paul's unhappiness*

"We will go back to the house," he said. "I don't want to talk out."

Pause — mood changes here

They went past the lilac-tree, whose bronze leaf-buds were com-

YOUR ROLE IN ORAL INTERPRETATION

ing unfastened. Just a fragment remained of the haystack, a monument squared and brown, like a
pillar of stone. There was a little
bed of hay from the last cutting.

"Let us sit here a minute," said
Miriam. . . .

At that moment a big bull-
terrier came rushing up, open-
mouthed, pranced his two paws on
the youth's shoulders, licking his
face. Paul drew back laughing. Bill
was a great relief to him. He pushed
the dog aside, but it came leaping
back.

"Get out," said the lad, "or I'll
dot thee one."

But the dog was not to be
pushed away. So Paul had a little
battle with the creature, pitching
poor Bill away from him, who, however, only floundered tumultuously
back again, wild with joy. The two
fought together, the man laughing
grudgingly, the dog grinning all
over. Miriam watched them. There
was something pathetic about the
man. He wanted so badly to love,
to be tender. The rough way he
bowled the dog over was really
loving. Bill got up, panting with
happiness, his brown eyes rolling
in his white face, and lumbered
back again. He adored Paul. The
lad frowned.

THE PERFORMANCE

"Bill, I've had enough o' thee," he said.

But the dog only stood with two heavy paws, that quivered with love, upon his thigh, and flickered a red tongue at him. He drew back.

"No," he said—"no—I've had enough."

And in a minute the dog trotted off happily, to vary the fun. He remained staring miserably across at the hills, whose still beauty he begrudged. He wanted to go and cycle with Edgar. Yet he had not the courage to leave Miriam.

"Why are you sad?" she asked humbly.

"I'm not sad; why should I be," he answered. "I'm only normal."

She wondered why he always claimed to be normal when he was disagreeable.

"But what is the matter?" she pleaded, coaxing him soothingly.

"Nothing!"

"Nay!" she murmured.

He picked up a stick and began to stab the earth with it.

"You'd far better not talk," he said.

"But I wish to know—" she replied.

He laughed resentfully.

"You always do," he said.

YOUR ROLE IN ORAL INTERPRETATION

"It's not fair to me," she murmured.

He thrust, thrust, thrust at the ground with the pointed stick, digging up little clods of earth as if he were in a fever of irritation. She gently and firmly laid her hand on his wrist.

"Don't!" she said. "Put it away."

He flung the stick into the currant-bushes, and leaned back. Now he was bottled up.

"What is it?" she pleaded softly.

pause to sharpen the effect of what he has to say

He lay perfectly still, only his eyes alive, and they full of torment.

pause to show how hard it is for him

"You know," he said at length, rather wearily—

"you know—we'd better break off."

It was what she dreaded. Swiftly everything seemed to darken before her eyes.

"Why!" she murmured. "What has happened?"

"Nothing has happened. We only realize where we are. It's no good—" *pause to heighten the fact he can't find the words*

She waited in silence, sadly, patiently. It was no good being impatient with him. At any rate, he would tell her now what ailed him.

"We agreed on friendship," he

went on in a dull, monotonous
voice. "How often have we agreed
for friendship! And yet—it neither
stops there, nor gets anywhere
else."——*Pause to sharpen the silence*

He was silent again. She
brooded. What did he mean? He
was so wearying. There was something he would not yield. Yet she
must be patient with him. *slight pause to show difficulty in expressing himself*

"I can only give friendship—
it's all I'm capable of—it's a flaw in
my make-up. The thing overbal-
ances to one side—I hate a toppling
balance. Let us have done."

There was warmth of fury in
his last phrases. He meant she loved
him more than he her. Perhaps he *pause to heighten the reflection*
could not love her. Perhaps she
had not in herself that which he
wanted. It was the deepest motive
of her soul, this self-mistrust. It was
so deep that she dared neither real- *pause to show her reflection*
ize nor acknowledge it. Perhaps she
was deficient. Like an infinitely
subtle shame, it kept her always
back. If it were so, she would do
without him. She would never let
herself want him. She would merely
see.

"But what has happened?" she
asked.

"Nothing—it's all in myself—it
only comes out just now. We're always like this towards Easter-time."

YOUR ROLE IN ORAL INTERPRETATION

He grovelled so helplessly. She pitied him. At least she never floundered in such a pitiable way. After all, it was he who was chiefly humiliated. —*Pause to add emphasis to next line*

"What do you want?" she asked him.

pause—difficulty in expressing self

"Why—I mustn't come often—that's all. Why should I monopolize you when I'm not—You see, I'm deficient in something with regard to you—" —*Pause the words seem to stop*

He was telling her he did not love her, and so ought to leave her a chance with another man. How foolish and blind and shamefully clumsy he was! . . .

Pause—change of thought

"But I don't understand," she said huskily. "Yesterday—" *Pause—words come to an end*

The night was turning jangled and hateful to him as the twilight faded. And she bowed under her suffering.

"I know," he cried, "you never will! You'll never believe that I can't—can't physically, any more than I can fly up like a skylark—"

"What?" she murmured. Now she dreaded.

"Love you."

Note that the mood switches back and forth from the idyllic appreciation of nature to the obvious reluctance of Paul to tell Miriam the news that is so painful to him—and of her naive unawareness of the problem. It is essential for the reader to use pauses effectively to create the atmosphere, the tension, the con-

THE PERFORMANCE

fusion. Without pauses, Miriam's and Paul's reactions would be blurred, indefinite. Without them Paul's final pronouncement would be lost. Note the references made on the marked copy and the reasons for the longer pauses for changes in mood and thought.

It is necessary to remember that these are not the only possible markings. You may feel a different emotional reaction. You may want to pause in places other than those identified. To do so is perfectly all right. Pause where it is best for you but be sure that continuity is smooth.

You will note that the author has used dashes often to indicate the need for an abrupt pause—or a prolonged one.

O'Neill uses the same technique in *More Stately Mansions*. The following excerpt from the play highlights the technique.

Excerpt from MORE STATELY MANSIONS

EUGENE O'NEILL

SIMON.

(*He pauses, then goes on. Gradually his eyes drop from Joel to his desk, and more and more it seems he is talking to himself.*)

I concentrate all my mind and energy to get a thing done. /

I live with it, / think of nothing else, / eat with it, / take it to bed with me, / sleep with it, / dream of it / —and then suddenly / one day / it is accomplished / —finished, / dead! // —and I become empty, // but at the same time restless and aimless, / as if I had lost my meaning to myself. // A vacation would be in order at such times. // But where? / How? / A voyage to France, / say—with Sara— / a second honeymoon. // But Sara would not leave the children, / and to take the children along would mean it would be their vacation with their mother, / not mine with my wife. // Perhaps Sara would even insist on taking Mother with us! / They have grown to be such loving friends, / drawn to each other by their devotion to the children! / I assure you, / I am left entirely out of it now. // That is Mother's doing, of course.

YOUR ROLE IN ORAL INTERPRETATION

// She imagines she has been very subtle, that I have not seen. / But I have promised myself that as soon as I had time, / I would put a stop to her greedy scheming, / and now the railroad deal is completed— //
(*He smiles strangely*)
That may be the change in activity I need. //
(*He pauses*)
If you ever fall in love, Joel, / take my advice and do not marry / Keep your love to your mistress / with no right of ownership except what she earns day by day, / what she can make you pay for possession. // Love should be a deal forever incomplete / never finally settled, / with each party continually raising the bids, / but neither one concluding a final role. //
(*He laughs mockingly at Joel's cold disapproval*)
Yes, / my advice to you would be to shun marriage / and keep a whore instead!
JOEL.   I cannot see why you wish to discuss such matters with me.
SIMON.   No, neither can I—except that I can trust you to listen without hearing much. //
(*With a conciliating manner*)
Why is it you never come to visit Mother?
JOEL.   You know she has as little desire to see me as I have to see her.
SIMON.   You would be astounded at the way she has transformed herself. / It is as though she had slowly taken possession of Sara / in order to make of my wife a second self through which she could live again. // Or, in another aspect, / trick Sara into being an accessory in the murder of that old self, / which was once my mother. // And so leave me motherless. / But at the same time / by becoming Sara, / leave me wifeless, / for naturally I could not regard— //
(*He stops abruptly—then goes on with an increasing brooding strangeness*)
Sometimes the two have appeared to lose their / separate identities / in my mind's eye— / have seemed, / through

THE PERFORMANCE

the subtle power of Mother's fantastic will, / to merge / and become one woman— / a spirit of Woman made flesh / and flesh of her made spirit, / mother and wife in one— / to whom I was never anything more / than a necessary adjunct of a means to motherhood— / a son in one case, / a husband in the other— / but now no longer needed since the mother / by becoming the wife / has my four sons to substitute for me, / and the wife having them, / no longer needs a husband to use in begetting— // And so I am left alone, / an unwanted son, / a discarded lover, / an outcast without meaning or function / in my own home / but pleasantly tolerated in memory of old service / and as a domestic slave whose greed can be used to bring in money to support Woman! //
(*With vindictive calculation*)
Yes / that is what Mother flatters herself she has accomplished. / But she doesn't realize there are fundamental weaknesses in her plan, / that the past is never dead / as long as we live / because all we are is the past. // She is going to discover, / beginning today, / and Sara, too, / that whenever I wish, / I take back what belongs to me, / no matter— //
(*He checks himself with a sudden wary glance at Joel*)
But all these fanciful speculations are nonsense. //
JOEL. (*Gets up from his chair*)
If you have done, may I go back to my work?
SIMON. Yes. Take your idiotic conscience to hell out of here! //
(*Joel turns and goes into the bookkeeper's office at right, closing the door behind him*)
Even that dull fool realized / I was really addressing myself / —because I have no one but myself. // Yes, Mother has left me with no life but this one / which she always despised / —the ambition to be a Napoleon among traders! // I, who once dreamed—! // Rubbish! The possession of power is the only freedom, / and your pretended disgust with it is a lie. // You must allow for your present state of mind— / the reaction of emptiness / after success / —you've always felt it— / but never so

strongly before— // There is a finality in this / —as if some long patient tension had snapped— // as if I no longer had the power / to discipline my will to keep myself united // —another self rebels / —secedes / —as if at last I must become two selves from now on— / division and confusion / —war / —a duel / to the death— //

(*With revengeful bitterness*)

Well, let those who are responsible for the challenge beware, / for I will make it their duel, too! // Yes, Mother and Sara, / henceforth I must demand that each of you / takes upon herself her full responsibility / for what I have become. // Bah! What rubbishy fantasies!— // As if I really desired two damned possessive women / prying and interfering in my private business! // All I know is that on an impulse / I asked Sara to come here— / some confused feeling that if I get her alone away from Mother's influence, / I would desire her again, // Hadn't I better think out more exactly how I shall attack? / —

No, wait until you feel her out / and see how much of old greedy Sara still lies behind her present self— / the ambitious Sara / who used to long to own an Irish-castle-in-Spain, / gentleman's estate!— / who was willing to use any means— / even her beautiful body / —to get what she wanted. // I should have swindled her into giving herself by promising marriage / —and then having had all I wanted of her, / deserted her / —it would have served her right to be beaten / at her own game // —I would have forgotten her and returned to Mother, / waiting for me in her garden— //

But she wasn't waiting / —She was just as ruthless and unscrupulous about discarding you / as Sara was in taking you. // Mother took pains to point it out to me / by implication / that day she deliberately made up the fairy tale about the exiled Prince and the magic door— //

The scene is basically a long monologue by Simon with Joel making only brief responses. In these speeches, O'Neill uses the dashes heavily for sudden changes of thought, for interrupted thoughts. Simon is thinking aloud of the two women in his life and what both have done to him; the pauses heighten the changes of mood and emphasis as Simon considers first his mother and her influence on him and his marriage and then the closeness both women share while he feels left out. His deep bitterness towards them both is prominently stressed. Note how often Simon switches his thought. Study the double slash marks for the introduction of new emotions and new thoughts even before the preceding one has been finished. Try reading these speeches without regarding all the double slashes, as merely slight pauses for breath, and you'll see that Simon's lines make no sense, have no real meaning. While these marks add contrast and variety to the dialogue, the single slash marks serve to emphasize certain words or phrases and to provide momentary stops for the reader to accentuate key concepts.

This excerpt from O'Neill's play provides an excellent example of how often thoughts can change in a single speech—how different moods are heightened by such pauses. Without such pauses, the monologues would be masses of confusion.

To analyze a selection that is more familiar, look at Hamlet's "O, that this too too solid flesh would melt . . ."

HAMLET.   O, that this too too solid flesh would melt,
Thaw, and resolve itself into a dew!
Or that the Everlasting had not fix'd
His canon 'gainst self-slaughter! O God! God!
How weary, stale, flat, and unprofitable,
Seem to me all the uses of this world!
Fie on't! oh fie, fie! 'Tis an unweeded garden,
That grows to seed; things rank and gross in nature
Possess it merely. That it should come to this!
But two months dead! Nay, not so much, not two.
So excellent a king; that was, to this,
Hyperion to a satyr; so loving to my mother
That he might not beteem the winds of heaven
Visit her face too roughly. Heaven and earth!
Must I remember? Why, she would hang on him
As if increase of appetite had grown
By what it fed on; and yet, within a month,—

Let me not think on't!—Frailty, thy name is woman!—
A little month, or e'er those shoes were old
With which she followed my poor father's body,
Like Niobe, all tears,—why she, even she,—
O God! a beast, that wants discourse of reason,
Would have mourn'd longer—married with mine uncle,
My father's brother, but no more like my father
Than I to Hercules; within a month,
Ere yet the salt of most unrighteous tears
Had left the flushing of her galled eyes,
She married. O, most wicked speed, to post
With such dexterity to incestuous sheets!
It is not, nor it cannot come to good.—
But break, my heart, for I must hold my tongue.

Here we have an example of reflection, of a man's debating with himself his own reason for being, his own purpose. When one is in turmoil with himself, he does not think rapidly or freely. There is conflict, concern, uncertainty, and pauses are the chief means of identifying these for an audience.

Stress

Pausing and pacing are only two of the tools necessary for the reader of literature. Emphasis, stress on words and on thoughts, is also vitally necessary. You can read a scene slowly or rapidly, you can pause in the right places, but if the thoughts and words that give meaning to the selection are not properly stressed, there is insufficient emotional involvement.

In poetry, images are heavily stressed. Impressions are compressed into a few words. Adjectives, verbs, nouns, and adverbs get the most stress. Least emphasis is given to the articles, "a" and "the." Rarely is the "a" pronounced with a long sound ($\bar{a}$).

Note how stress on the underlined words in the following selection from John Keats' "Eve of St. Agnes" adds to the richness and color of the imagery—and how, with appropriate pauses and phrasing, the atmosphere, the setting come alive.

THE PERFORMANCE

THE EVE OF ST. AGNES
JOHN KEATS

St. Agnes' Eve—Ah, bitter chill it was!
The owl, for all his feathers, was a-cold;
The hare limped trembling through the frozen grass,
And silent was the flock in wooly fold;
Numb were the Beadsman's fingers, while he told
His rosary, and while his frosted breath,
Like pious incense from a censer old,
Seemed taking flight for heaven, without a death,
  Past the sweet Virgin's picture, while his prayer he
   saith.

His prayer he saith, this patient, holy man;
Then takes his lamp, and riseth from his knees,
And back returneth, meagre, barefoot, wan,
Along the chapel aisle by slow degrees:
The sculptured dead, on each side, seem to freeze,
Emprisoned in black, purgatorial rails:
Knights, ladies, praying in dumb orat'ries,
He passeth by; and his weak spirit fails
  To think how they may ache in icy hoods and mails.

Northward he turneth through a little door,
And scarce three steps, ere Music's golden tongue
Flattered to tears this aged man and poor;
But no—already had his deathbell rung;
The joys of all his life were said and sung:
His was harsh penance on St. Agnes' Eve:
Another way he went, and soon among
Rough ashes sat he for his soul's reprieve,
  And all night kept awake, for sinners' sake to grieve.

That ancient Beadsman heard the prelude soft;
And so it chanced, for many a door was wide,
From hurry to and fro. Soon, up aloft,
The silver, snarling trumpets 'gan to chide:
The level chambers, ready with their pride,
Were glowing to receive a thousand guests:
The carvèd angels, ever eager-eyed,
Stared, where upon their heads the cornice rests,
  With hair blown back and wings put crosswise on
   their breasts.

YOUR ROLE IN ORAL INTERPRETATION

At length burst in the urgent revelry,
With plume, tiara, and all rich array,
Numerous as shadows, haunting fairily
The brain, new stuffed, in youth, with triumphs gay
Of old romance. These let us wish away,
And turn, sole-thoughted, to one Lady there,
Whose heart had brooded, all that wintry day,
On love, and winged St. Agnes' saintly care,
　　As she had heard old dames full many times declare.
They told her how, upon St. Agnes' Eve,
Young virgins might have visions of delight,
And soft adorings from their loves receive
Upon the honeyed middle of the night,
If ceremonies due they did aright;
As supperless to bed they must retire,
And couch supine their beauties, lily white;
Nor look behind, nor sideways, but require
　　Of Heaven with upward eyes for all that they desire.

For an even more graphic illustration, let us take "The Cry of the Children" by Elizabeth Barrett Browning. Note how the underlined words add richness to the specific meaning.

THE CRY OF THE CHILDREN
ELIZABETH BARRETT BROWNING

Do ye hear the children weeping, O my brothers,
Ere the sorrow comes with years?
They are leaning their young heads against their mothers,
And that cannot stop their tears.
The young lambs are bleating in the meadows,
The young birds are chirping in the nest,
The young fawns are playing with the shadows,
The young flowers are blowing toward the west—
But the young, young children, O my brothers,
They are weeping bitterly!
They are weeping in the playtime of the others,
In the country of the free.
Do you question the young children in the sorrow,
Why their tears are falling so?

THE PERFORMANCE

The old man may weep for his to-morrow
Which is lost in Long Ago;
The old tree is leafless in the forest,
The old year is ending in the frost,
The old wound, if stricken, is the sorest,
The old hope is hardest to be lost.
But the young, young children, O my brothers,
Do you ask them why they stand
Weeping sore before the bosoms of their mothers,
In our happy Fatherland?
They look with their pale and sunken faces,
And their looks are sad to see,
For the man's hoary anguish draws and presses
Down the cheeks of infancy.
"Your old earth," they say, "is very dreary;
"Our young feet," they say, "are very weak!
Few paces have we taken, yet are weary—
Our grave-rest is very far to seek.
Ask the aged why they weep, and not the children;
For the outside earth is cold;
And we young ones stand without, in our bewildering,
And the graves are for the old."
"True," say the children, "it may happen
That we die before our time;
Little Alice died last year—her grave is shapen
Like a snowball, in the rime.
We looked into the pit prepared to take her:
Was no room for any work in the close clay!
From the sleep wherein she lieth none will wake her,
Crying, 'Get up, little Alice! it is day.'
If you listen by that grave, in sun and shower,
With your ear down, little Alice never cries;
Could we see her face, be sure we should not know her,
For the smile has time for growing in her eyes:
And merry go her moments, lulled and stilled in
The shroud by the kirk-chime!
It is good when it happens," say the children,
"That we die before our time."

YOUR ROLE IN ORAL INTERPRETATION

Without the necessary stress on these words, the effect the author is trying to create would be lost. It would be a jumble of words—with no emotion. For example, when you tell of a violent storm, you don't discuss it in the same way as you do a sunny day. If you describe a fat woman, you don't describe her as you would a slender, beautifully proportioned woman. When you say a thing is ugly, you don't treat it in terms you would use if you were talking of something beautiful and fragile. Remember—words are your tools, your equipment as an interpreter. Use them wisely.

For a simple exercise, see how stress changes the meanings in the following sentence: "I am going to see my uncle." "I am going to see my uncle"; this means "I" am and no one else. "I am going to see my uncle," a positive assertion. "I am going to see my uncle"; emphasis on "going" indicates definiteness of action. "I am going to see my uncle"; the stress here is on the direction the action is taking. "I am going to see my uncle"; now the emphasis is on the act of seeing. "I am going to see my uncle—" "my" uncle and nobody else's. "I am going to see my uncle—" not "my" aunt or brother but my uncle.

Proper use of stress also adds clarity of thought and meaning and both are vital in the reading of expository prose.

This selection has been set up by your authors in a structural form to indicate, at the same time, where pauses and stress should occur. As you read the following excerpt, pause at the end of each line for breath or emphasis.

Excerpt from LES MISERABLES

VICTOR HUGO

At Jourdain's
The common room was full of customers,
as the great yard was full of vehicles of every sort—
carts,
cabriolets,
chars-a-bancs,
tilburys,
unnamable carriages,
shapeless,

THE PERFORMANCE

patched,
with their shafts reaching heavenward like arms,
or with their noses in the ground
and their tails in the air.

The vast fireplace,
full of clear flame,
cast an intense heat against the backs of the row
on the right of the table.
Three spits were revolving,
laden with chickens,
pigeons, and legs of mutton;
and a delectable odor of roast meat,
and of gravy dripping from the browned skin,
came forth from the hearth,
stirred the guests to merriment
and made their mouths water.

All the aristocracy of the plough ate there,
at Mast' Jourdain's,
the innkeeper and horse trader—
a shrewd rascal who had money.

The dishes passed
and were soon emptied,
like the jugs of yellow cider.
Everyone told of his affairs,
his sales and his purchases.
They inquired about the crops.
The weather was good for green stuffs,
But a little wet for wheat.

The excerpt from Hugo is highly descriptive, with images demanding proper emphasis and coloring. In the second section, such images as "cast an intense heat," "delectable odor of roast meat," "gravy dripping from the browned skin" need to be stressed because the author is trying to create an atmosphere of a feast and the use of stress on adjectives helps convey the atmosphere.

YOUR ROLE IN ORAL INTERPRETATION

In drama, stress plays a big part. Often one word will receive primary emphasis for effect, as in "You are nothing but—but—a murderer!" Or as in Yank's final speech in Eugene O'Neill's *The Hairy Ape,* where he says, "So you're what she seen when she looked at me—de white faced tart." Or in Hamlet's "To be or not to be," when Hamlet says, "To die, to sleep—no more." In each case the final words in the lines are stressed for emphasis of thought and for dramatic impact.

But emphasis is not used merely for dramatic effect. It can be used to heighten comedy lines. For example, two men are discussing a lady of questionable virtue. The line: "You mean she's a—a— lady?" The emphasis on the last word should convey the double meaning to the word.

In the following selection from Oliver Goldsmith's *She Stoops to Conquer,* stress is used effectively to heighten the comedy effects.

Excerpt from SHE STOOPS TO CONQUER

OLIVER GOLDSMITH

Scene: A Chamber in an old-fashioned House.
Enter Mrs. Hardcastle and Mr. Hardcastle.
MRS. HARDCASTLE. I vow, Mr. Hardcastle, you're very particular. Is there a creature in the whole country, but ourselves, that does not take a trip to town now and then, to rub off the rust a little? There's the two Miss Hoggs, and our neighbour, Mrs. Grigsby, go to take a month's polishing every winter.
HARDCASTLE. Ay, and bring back vanity and affectation to last them the whole year. I wonder why London cannot keep its own fools at home. In my time, the follies of the town crept slowly among us, but now they travel faster than a stage-coach. Its fopperies come down, not only as inside passengers, but in the very basket.
MRS. HARDCASTLE. Ay, your times were fine times, indeed; you have been telling us of them for many a long year. Here we live in an old rumbling mansion, that looks for all the world like an inn, but that we never see company. Our best visitors are old Mrs. Oddfish, the curate's

wife, and little Cripplegate, the lame dancing-master; and all our entertainment your old stories of Prince Eugene and the Duke of Marlborough. I hate such old-fashioned trumpery.

HARDCASTLE.   And I love it. I love everything that's old: old friends, old times, old manners, old books, old wine; and, I believe, Dorothy, (*taking her hand*) you'll own I have been pretty fond of an old wife.

MRS. HARDCASTLE.   Lord, Mr. Hardcastle, you're for ever at your Dorothy's and your old wife's. You may be a Darby, but I'll be no Joan, I promise you. I'm not so old as you'd make me, by more than one good year. Add twenty to twenty, and make money of that.

HARDCASTLE.   Let me see; twenty added to twenty, makes just fifty and seven.

MRS. HARDCASTLE.   It's false, Mr. Hardcastle: I was but twenty when I was brought to bed of Tony, that I had by Mr. Lumpkin, my first husband; and he's not come to years of discretion yet.

HARDCASTLE.   Nor ever will, I dare answer for him. Ay, you have taught him finely!

MRS. HARDCASTLE.   No matter. Tony Lumpkin has a good fortune. My son is not to live by his learning. I don't think a boy wants much learning to spend fifteen hundred a year.

HARDCASTLE.   By learning, quotha! A mere composition of tricks and mischief.

MRS. HARDCASTLE.   Humour, my dear: nothing but humour. Come, Mr. Hardcastle, you must allow the boy a little humour.

HARDCASTLE.   I'd sooner allow him an horse-pond! If burning the footmen's shoes, frighting the maids, and worrying the kittens, be humour, he has it. It was but yesterday he fastened my wig to the back of my chair, and when I went to make a bow, I popt my bald head in Mrs. Frizzle's face.

MRS. HARDCASTLE.   And am I to blame? The poor boy was always too sickly to do any good. A school would be his death. When he comes to be a little stronger, who knows what a year or two's Latin may do for him?

HARDCASTLE. Latin for him! A cat and fiddle. No, no, the alehouse and the stable are the only schools he'll ever go to.

MRS. HARDCASTLE. Well, we must not snub the poor boy, now, for I believe we shan't have him long among us. Any body that looks in his face may see he's consumptive.

HARDCASTLE. Ay, if growing too fat be one of the symptoms.

MRS. HARDCASTLE. He coughs sometimes.

HARDCASTLE. Yes, when his liquor goes the wrong way.

MRS. HARDCASTLE. I'm actually afraid of his lungs.

HARDCASTLE. And truly, so am I; for he sometimes whoops like a speaking trumpet—(*Tony hallooing behind the scenes.*)—O, there he goes—A very consumptive figure, truly!

(*Enter Tony, crossing the stage*)

MRS. HARDCASTLE. Tony, where are you going, my charmer? Won't you give Papa and I a little of your company, lovee?

TONY. I'm in haste, Mother, I cannot stay.

MRS. HARDCASTLE. You shan't venture out this raw evening, my dear. You look most shockingly.

TONY. I can't stay, I tell you. The Three Pigeons expect me down every moment. There's some fun going forward.

HARDCASTLE. Ay; the ale-house, the old place: I thought so.

MRS. HARDCASTLE. A low, paltry set of fellows.

TONY. Not so low neither. There's Dick Muggins the exciseman, Jack Slang the horse doctor, Little Aminadab that grinds the music box, and Tom Twist that spins the pewter platter.

MRS. HARDCASTLE. Pray, my dear, disappoint them for one night at least.

TONY. As for disappointing them, I should not so much mind; but I can't abide to disappoint myself.

MRS. HARDCASTLE. (*detaining him*) You shan't go.

THE PERFORMANCE

TONY. I will, I tell you.

MRS. HARDCASTLE. I say you shan't.

TONY. We'll see which is strongest, you or I.

(*Exits, hauling her out*)

HARDCASTLE. Ay, there goes a pair that only spoil each other. But is not the whole age in combination to drive sense and discretion out of doors? There's my pretty darling, Kate. The fashions of the times have almost infected her too. By living a year or two in town, she is as fond of gauze, and French frippery, as the best of them.

This particular play is a light-hearted farce of the eighteenth century in England. It depends for its effect on a lighter treatment, a generally faster pace. The scene is mainly idle chit-chat but it serves also to introduce the two main characters. Stress, in this instance, is not used for heavily dramatic purposes, but for comedy. And, as such, there are fewer instances of stress than would be found in a more serious play.

Summary

Pacing, pausing, and stress or emphasis are vital elements of interpretative reading. No one speaks at the same rate of speed day in and day out and no one speaks without wide use of pauses. Few speak without any regard for emphasis on certain words for effect. Yet, the average beginning reader in oral interpretation makes the mistake of using one rate, few pauses, and too little emphasis. Thought and content govern the use of pacing, pausing, and emphasis. All these problems are corrected if there is sufficient involvement on the part of the reader.

More exciting sections, those replete with action, need a faster pace. More relaxed, more languid moments take slower pacing. Poetry especially presents problems in pacing because of the tendency readers have to read all material at one pace to the end of each line without regard for the thought or mood involved. The essential consideration in pacing is variety.

The use of pauses is a vital consideration in reading. Pauses add clarity, meaning, dramatic effect, emphasis, emotional values, and also give a reader the necessary chance to breathe and to present the contrasting moods in selections. Without pauses, with the system of reading only from one punctuation mark to the next one, there is monotony and disruption of thought. Pauses heighten the dramatic effects in drama and clarify concepts in prose. If pauses are used incorrectly or if their duration is too long or too abrupt, choppy reading is the result. If pauses are not used often enough, a fast pace and monotony are the results.

Stress and emphasis bring richness and meaning to words. They emphasize primary thoughts or emotions. They help make ideas in prose explicit; through the use of descriptive words, they add atmosphere and color and excitement to narrative; and they are the key to a reading of drama in that they supply importance to the emotions being expressed.

Exercises

1. Read "How Do I Love Thee?" as given in this chapter in a fast pace. Notice how difficult it is to read. Then go back and read it again at a slower pace, with more pauses, reflecting a better understanding of the meaning. You should see that when you read slower you are more able to present the full meaning of the poem.

2. Say "Peter Piper picked a peck of pickled peppers." Read it fast. Then go back and do it slower and see the difference in reading.

3. Read the following in a faster manner than you would ordinarily: "The day was warm, lazy, the kind you stretch out in, the kind the birds liked and the dogs found right for curling up under the shade of a tree." Now read the line to convey the laziness of the setting—at a slower pace.

4. Read this in a slow pace:

The tension mounted in him; his nerves were taut as steel; he was sure he'd have to scream out in anguish. And yet the thing kept coming closer and closer to him, its long arms reaching out for him, reaching for his throat. His heart beat loudly, he looked round for an escape. There was none. He had to get out! He had to get out!

THE PERFORMANCE

You probably found a slower pace too difficult. Now read it in a faster way and see the result.

5. Take an article in your newspaper or magazine. Mark it for pauses to indicate momentary hesitation and complete changes of thought. Read it first without the markings and then read it with the markings. Note the difference.

6. Read the following: "I hate you, you contemptible cad." Read it with no pause. Now read it with a pause before "you contemptible cad."

7. Read the following passage with no particular emphasis and then go back and mark the words that seem to need emphasis. Note the difference.

> "To be or not to be, that is the question.
> Whether 'tis nobler in the mind to suffer
> The slings and arrows of outrageous fortune,
> Or to take arms against a sea of troubles
> And by opposing end them."

8. Repeat the "I am going to see my uncle" exercise in this chapter and then rephrase it to say anything else you wish, such as "I love the lady you saw."

PART THREE

UNDERSTANDING
LITERATURE

How do I read prose?

MORE OF our literature lies in the realm of prose than in either poetry or drama. Prose is the term we apply to any literature which is not poetry or drama. Even that statement is not entirely clear, however, because we have prose which is poetic and poems which, except for name, could be considered prose. The Gettysburg Address has been called "poetic" in its beauty. Some poetry of Whitman and Corso and others lacks much of the structure that we call *poetry* but retains enough of poetry's characteristics that we still call the works *poems*—in effect, they are prose poems.

Prose is generally divided into two categories, fiction and nonfiction. Several editors of collections of literature separate prose into three divisions—expository, narrative, and descriptive. However it is divided, there is much pleasure to be gained from reading it aloud. But let's look at each of these ways of categorizing prose and see what can be learned that will be beneficial to us as interpreters.

Nonfiction as a general category of prose concerns itself primarily with explanation and persuasion. It finds its outlet through essays, editorials, diaries, histories, and letters. Any prose which seeks to inform the reader or persuade him to behave in a certain fashion, treating the ideas directly, is nonfiction.

Biography and autobiography are forms of nonfiction which often bridge between nonfiction and fiction. They are nonfiction to the extent that they are true representations of the lives they describe. On more than one occasion the form has been used to the detriment of the real person about whom the story is dealing. George Washington and the cherry tree is a classic example of such a fabrication. The idea struck the fancy of an author writing about Washington and he used it. And it *became* the most well-known part of George's life.

Moving into fiction, we first run into the historical novel which is part truth, part fiction. *Johnny Tremain, Anne Boleyn,* and *Mutiny on the Bounty* are all examples of the historical novel. This form of prose centers on a historical event or character with a mixture of real and fictional characters moving about together through real and imaginary events. *Johnny Tremain* is a story about a young boy in Boston in pre-Revolutionary War times. He moves about with Paul Revere, the Sons of Liberty, and many of our *real* political figures of the time. He participates in the Boston Tea Party and is present in Boston when the Revolutionary War starts. Through this young man, the author, Esther Forbes, not only tells a fascinating story but gives the reader some additional insight into the influences of that period of history and into the personalities of some of our important historical figures.

That type of prose called fiction, then, finds its outlet in short stories, novels, fables, and tales. Fiction writing, whether it be short story or novel or one of the other forms listed, relieves the author of a need to stay within particular boundaries of truth in order to make his point. He creates the story and all its trappings and may manipulate characters and action according to his desire. He is not encumbered by what has happened in history; he may extend himself to make things happen in his story as he envisions them happening.

In looking at prose in another way as descriptive, expository, persuasive, or narrative, we can draw some further distinctions. Let's begin with descriptive prose because it is most often found as part of the other two divisions rather than as a totally separate one.

Descriptive Prose

The chief characteristic of descriptive prose is its reliance on imagery to put it over. The author of descriptive prose works in the same way as an artist. The difference is in the medium he uses. While the artist might choose among pastels, water colors, oils, or charcoal, the creator of descriptive prose paints with words. In so doing he hopes to give his reader an empathic experience. Such imagery appeals directly to the reader's sense of smell, touch, taste, hearing, and sight. As you read the following sentences, concentrate on the appeal to your senses and watch for your own empathic reactions. Real concentration will make your own senses react in the way each sentence suggests.

1. Jack's mouth watered as he watched the boy squeeze and suck the lemon. The lad sat for fully ten minutes, squeezing and sucking and puckering, his face reflecting the sourness. (What does your mouth feel like?)

2. Jim had never seen the sky so red before; he felt as though he were dropping headlong into Dante's *Inferno*. The reds and oranges were so intense he had to wing over and head the plane north in order to avoid the searing pain the colors brought to his eyes. (Do *your* eyes burn?)

3. He touched her gently and immediately drew back in terror; he was certain now that she was dead. She was cold and clammy and, well, sort of mushy—like a piece of fat that has been soaked in water overnight. (Do you feel a revulsion?)

4. What was that smell? Dan searched his memory for a moment. He knew he had smelled it before; it was a dry, acrid, musty smell—like books left too long in the attic. (Can you smell them?)

5. Oh, what torture! He sat there in front of me and burped; it was a long, low, deep-throated belch that rattled lazily and resonantly out of his mouth and nose. (Can you hear it?)

Imagery—appeal to the senses. These are the clues to effective description. Edgar Allan Poe's *The Sphinx* is an excellent example. Read this excerpt from the story and notice how deftly he uses words to describe. To test his effectiveness try your hand at drawing the sphinx after you read the story, or close your eyes and see if you can picture the sphinx.

THE SPHINX

EDGAR ALLAN POE

During the dread reign of cholera in New York, I had accepted the invitation of a relative to spend a fortnight with him in the retirement of his cottage Ornee on the banks of the Hudson. We had here around us all the ordinary means of summer amusement; and what with rambling in the woods, sketching, boating, fishing, bathing, music, and books, we should have passed the time pleasantly enough, but for the fearful intelligence which reached us every morning from the populous city. Not a day elapsed which did not bring us news of the decease of some acquaintance. Then, as the fatality increased, we learned to expect daily the loss of some friend. At length we trembled at the approach of every messenger. The very air from the South seemed to us redolent with death. That palsying thought, indeed, took entire possession of my soul. I could neither speak, think, nor dream of anything else. My host was of a less excitable temperament, and, although greatly depressed in spirits, exerted himself to sustain my own. . . .

His endeavors to arouse me from the condition of abnormal gloom into which I had fallen, were frustrated, in great measure, by certain volumes which I had found in his library. These were of a character to force into germination whatever seeds of hereditary superstition lay latent in my bosom. I had been reading these books without his knowledge, and thus he was often at a loss to account for the forcible impressions which had been made upon my fancy. . . .

The fact is, that soon after my arrival at the cottage there had occurred to myself an incident so entirely inexplicable, and which had in it so much of the portentous character, that I might well have been excused for regarding it as an omen. It appalled, and at the same time so confounded and bewildered me, that many days elapsed before I could make up my mind to communicate the circumstances to my friend.

Near the close of an exceedingly warm day, I was sitting, book in hand, at an open window, commanding, through a long vista of the river banks, a view of a distant hill, the face of which nearest my position had been denuded by what is termed a landslide, of the principal

portion of its trees. My thoughts had been long wandering
from the volume before me to the gloom and desolation of
the neighboring city. Uplifting my eyes from the page,
they fell upon the naked face of the hill, and upon an
object—upon some living monster of hideous conforma-
tion, which very rapidly made its way from the summit to
the bottom, disappearing finally in the dense forest below.
As this creature first came in sight, I doubted my own
sanity—or at least the evidence of my own eyes; and
many minutes passed before I succeeded in convincing
myself that I was neither mad nor in a dream. Yet when I
described the monster (which I distinctly saw, and calmly
surveyed through the whole period of its progress), my
readers, I fear, will feel more difficulty in being convinced
of these points than even I did myself.

Estimating the size of the creature by comparison
with the diameter of the large trees near which it passed
—the few giants of the forest which had escaped the fury
of the land-slide—I concluded it to be far larger than any
ship of the line in existence. I say ship of the line, because
the shape of the monster suggested the idea—the hull of
one of our seventy-four might convey a very tolerable
conception of the general outline. The mouth of the
animal was situated at the extremity of a proboscis some
sixty or seventy feet in length, and about as thick as the
body of an ordinary elephant. Near the root of this trunk
was an immense quantity of black shaggy hair—more
than could have been supplied by the coats of a score of
buffaloes; and projecting from this hair downwardly and
laterally, sprang two gleaming tusks not unlike those of
the wild boar but of infinitely greater dimensions. Extend-
ing forward, parallel with the proboscis, and on each side
of it was a gigantic staff, thirty or forty feet in length,
formed seemingly of pure crystal, and in shape a perfect
prism,—it reflected in the most gorgeous manner the rays
of the declining sun. The trunk was fashioned like a
wedge with the apex to the earth. From it there were
outspread two pairs of wings—each wing nearly one hun-

dred yards in length—one pair being placed above the other, and all covered with metal scales; each scale apparently some ten or twelve feet in diameter. I observed the upper and lower tiers of wings were connected by a strong chain. But the chief peculiarity of this horrible thing was the representation of a *Death's Head*, which covered nearly the whole surface of its breast, and which was as accurately traced in glaring white, upon the dark ground of the body, as if it had been there carefully designed by an artist. While I regarded the terrific animal, and more especially the appearance on its breast, with a feeling of horror and awe—with a sentiment of forthcoming evil, which I found it impossible to quell by any effort of the reason, I perceived the huge jaws at the extremity of the proboscis suddenly expand themselves, and from them there proceeded a sound so loud and so expressive of woe, that it struck upon my nerves like a knell, and as the monster disappeared at the foot of the hill, I fell at once, fainting, to the floor.

Upon recovering, my first impulse, of course, was to inform my friend of what I had seen and heard—and I can scarcely explain what feeling of repugnance it was which, in the end, operated to prevent me.

At length, one evening, some three or four days after the occurrence, we were sitting together in the room in which I had seen the apparition—I occupying the same seat at the same window, and he lounging on a sofa near at hand. The association of the place and time impelled me to give him an account of the phenomenon. He heard me to the end—at first laughed heartily—and then lapsed into an excessively grave demeanor, as if my insanity was a thing beyond suspicion. At this instant I again had a distinct view of the monster—to which, with a shout of absolute terror, I now directed his attention. He looked eagerly—but maintained that he saw nothing—although I designated minutely the course of the creature, as it made its way down the naked face of the hill.

I was now immeasurably alarmed, for I considered

the vision either as an omen of my death, or, worse, as the forerunner of an attack of mania. I threw myself passionately back in my chair, and for some moments buried my face in my hands. When I uncovered my eyes, the apparition was no longer visible.

You probably noted that about fifty percent of the story is a description of the sphinx and the other fifty percent, a narrative (the story of the retreat from New York and cholera). Without the vivid, detailed, artistic description, however, there'd have been no story.

A further example of description is in order. This time the artist is Antoine de Saint-Exupéry, known around the world for his ability to share his experiences through vivid description. The two excerpts included here are from his book *Wind, Sand and Stars.*

Excerpt from WIND, SAND AND STARS

ANTOINE DE SAINT-EXUPÉRY

One thing that I had loved in Paraguay was the ironic grass that showed the tip of its nose between the pavements of the capital, that slipped in on behalf of the invisible but ever-present virgin forest to see if man still held the town, if the hour had not come to send all these stones tumbling.

I liked the particular kind of dilapidation which in Paraguay was the expression of an excess of wealth. But here, in Concordia, I was filled with wonder. Here everything was in a state of decay, but adorably so, like an old oak covered with moss and split in places with age, like a wooden bench on which generations of lovers had come to sit and which had grown sacred. The wainscoting was worn, the hinges rusted, the chairs rickety. And yet, though nothing had ever been repaired, everything had been scoured with zeal. Everything was clean, waxed, gleaming.

The drawing-room had about it something extraordinarily intense, like the face of a wrinkled old lady. The walls were cracked, the ceiling stripped; and most bewildering of all in this bewildering house was the floor: it had simply caved in. Waxed, varnished and polished though it was, it swayed like a ship's gangway. A strange house, evoking no neglect, no slackness, but rather an extraordinary respect. Each passing year had added something to its charm, to the complexity of its visage and its friendly atmosphere, . . .

It is fascinating that with so few lines of description, the author can give the reader such a full appreciation and clear vision of the state of "bewildering" but "adorable" decay.

In the second segment Exupéry describes one of several nights he and his mechanic spent in the Libyan desert after their plane crashed on a flight from Paris to Saigon. The excerpt included here took place a few nights before they were rescued.

"PRISONER OF THE SAND"

ANTOINE DE SAINT-EXUPÉRY

In this air devoid of moisture the soil is swift to give off its temperature. It was already very cold. I stood up and stamped about. But soon a violent fit of trembling came over me. My dehydrated blood was moving sluggishly and I was pierced by a freezing chill which was not merely the chill of night. My teeth were chattering and my whole body had begun to twitch. My hand shook so that I could not hold an electric torch. I who had never been sensitive to cold was about to die of cold. What a strange effect thirst can have!

Somewhere, tired of carrying it in the sun, I had let my waterproof drop. Now the wind was growing bitter and I was learning that in the desert there is no place of refuge. The desert is as smooth as marble. By day it

YOUR ROLE IN ORAL INTERPRETATION

throws no shadow; by night it hands you over naked to the wind. Not a tree, not a hedge, not a rock behind which I could seek shelter. The wind was charging me like a troop of cavalry across open country. I turned and twisted to escape it: I lay down, stood up, lay down again, and still I was exposed to its freezing lash. I had no strength to run from the assassin and under the sabre-stroke I tumbled to my knees, my head between my hands.

A little later, I pieced these bits together and remembered that I had struggled to my feet and had started to walk on, shivering as I went. I had started forward wondering where I was and then I had heard Prevot. His shouting had jolted me into consciousness.

I went back towards him, still trembling from head to foot—quivering with the attack of hiccups that was convulsing my whole body. To myself I said: "It isn't the cold. It's something else. It's the end." The simple fact was that I hadn't enough water in me. I had tramped too far yesterday and the day before when I was off by myself, and I was dehydrated.

The thought of dying of the cold hurt me. I preferred the phantoms of my mind, the cross, the trees, the lamps. At least they would have killed me by enchantment. But to be whipped to death like a slave! . . .

Confound it! Down on my knees again! We had with us a little store of medicines—a hundred grammes of ninety per cent alcohol, the same of pure ether, and a small bottle of iodine. I tried to swallow a little of the ether: it was like swallowing a knife. Then I tried the alcohol: it contracted my gullet. I dug a pit in the sand, lay down in it, and flung handfuls of sand over me until all but my face was buried in it.

Prévot was able to collect a few twigs, and he lit a fire which soon burnt itself out. He wouldn't bury himself in the sand, but preferred to stamp round and round in a circle. That was foolish.

My throat stayed shut, and though I knew that was a bad sign, I felt better. I felt calm. I felt a peace that was beyond all hope. Once more, despite myself, I was journeying, trussed up on the deck of my slave-ship under the stars. It seemed to me that I was perhaps not in such a bad pass after all.

So long as I lay absolutely motionless, I no longer felt the cold. This allowed me to forget my body buried in the sand. I said to myself that I would not budge an inch, and would therefore never suffer again. As a matter of fact, we really suffer very little. Back of all these torments there is the orchestration of fatigue or of delirium, and we live on in a kind of picture-book, a slightly cruel fairy-tale.

A little while ago the wind had been after me with whip and spur, and I was running in circles like a frightened fox. After that came a time when I couldn't breathe. A great knee was crushing in my chest. A knee. I was writhing in vain to free myself from the weight of the angel who had overthrown me. There had not been a moment when I was alone in this desert. But now I have ceased to believe in my surroundings; I have withdrawn into myself, have shut my eyes, have not so much as batted an eyelid. I have the feeling that this torrent of visions is sweeping me away to a tranquil dream: so rivers cease their turbulence in the embrace of the sea.

Farewell, eyes that I loved! Do not blame me if the human body cannot go three days without water. I should never have believed that man was so truly the prisoner of the springs and freshets. I had no notion that our self-sufficiency was so circumscribed. We take it for granted that a man is able to stride straight out into the world. We believe that man is free. We never see the cord that binds him to wells and fountains, that umbilical cord by which he is tied to the womb of the world. Let men take but one step too many . . . and the cord snaps.

Did you experience the cold, the weight, the defeat with him? Such responses would be essential for effective reading of Exupéry's work.

Mark Twain is also well known for vivid description. Often he is wildly funny and his descriptive prose is effective because he exaggerates so graphically. The following excerpt from his book *Roughing It* needs no explanation; in it he describes an incident that occurred on his trip out west. It seems that the stage-coach broke down and the passengers joined a buffalo hunt while they were waiting for it to be repaired. It is typical of Mark Twain.

Excerpt from ROUGHING IT

MARK TWAIN

Next morning just before dawn, when about five hundred and fifty miles from St. Joseph, our mud-wagon broke down. We were to be delayed five or six hours, and therefore we took horses, by invitation, and joined a party who were just starting on a buffalo hunt. It was noble sport galloping over the plain in the dewy freshness of the morning, but our part of the hunt ended in disaster and disgrace, for a wounded buffalo bull chased the passenger Bemis nearly two miles, and then he forsook his horse and took to a lone tree. He was very sullen about the matter for some twenty-four hours, but at last he began to soften little by little, and finally he said:

"Well, it was not funny, and there was no sense in those gawks making themselves so facetious over it. I tell you I was angry in earnest for awhile. I should have shot that long gangly lubber they called Hank, if I could have done it without crippling six or seven other people—but of course I couldn't, the old 'Allen's' [a revolver] so confounded comprehensive. I wish those loafers had been up in the tree; they wouldn't have wanted to laugh so. If I had had a horse worth a cent—but no, the minute he saw that buffalo bull wheel on him and give a bellow, he raised straight up in the air and stood on his heels. The saddle began to slip, and I took him round the neck and laid close to him, and began to pray. Then he came down and stood up on the other end awhile, and the bull actually stopped pawing sand and bellowing to contemplate the inhuman spectacle. Then the bull made a pass at him and uttered a bellow that sounded perfectly frightful, it was so close to me, and that seemed to literally prostrate my horse's reason, and make a raving distracted maniac of him, and I wish I may die if he didn't stand on his head for a quarter of a minute and shed tears. He was absolutely out of his mind—he was, as sure as truth itself, and he really didn't know what he was doing. Then the bull came charging at us, and my horse dropped down on all fours and took a fresh start—and then for the next ten minutes he would actually throw one handspring after another so fast that the bull began to get unsettled, too, and didn't know where to start in—and so he stood there sneezing, and shoveling dust over his back, and bellowing every now and then, and thinking he had got a fifteen-hundred dollar circus horse for breakfast, certain. Well, I was first out on his neck—the horse's, not the bull's—and then underneath, and next on his rump, and sometimes head up, and sometimes heels—but I tell you it seemed solemn and awful to be ripping and tearing and carrying on so in the presence of death, as you might say. Pretty soon the bull made a snatch for us and brought away some of my horse's tail (I suppose, but do not know, being pretty busy at the time), but *something* made him hungry for solitude and suggested to him to get up and hunt for it. And then you ought to have seen that spider-legged old skeleton go! and you ought to have seen the bull cut out after him, too—head down, tongue out, tail up, bellowing like everything, and actually mowing down the weeds, and tearing up the earth, and boosting up the sand like a whirlwind! By George, it was a hot race! I and the saddle were back on the rump, and I had the bridle in my teeth and holding on to the pommel with both hands. First we left the dogs behind; then we passed a jack rabbit; then we overtook a coyote, and were gaining on an antelope when the rotten girths let go and threw me about thirty yards off to the left, and as the saddle went down over the horse's rump he gave it a lift with his heels that sent it more than four hundred yards up in the air, I wish

I may die in a minute if he didn't. I fell at the foot of the only solitary tree there was in nine counties adjacent (as any creature could see with the naked eye), and the next second I had hold of the bark with four sets of nails and my teeth, and the next second after that I was astraddle of the main limb and blaspheming my luck in a way that made my breath smell of brimstone. I *had* the bull, now, if he did not think of *one* thing. But that one thing I dreaded. I dreaded it very seriously. There was a possibility that the bull might not think of it, but there were greater chances that he would. I made up my mind what I would do in case he did. It was a little over forty feet to the ground from where I sat. I cautiously unwound the lariat from the pommel of my saddle—"

"Your saddle? Did you take your saddle up in the tree with you?"

"Take it up in the tree with me? Why, how you talk. Of course I didn't. No man could do that. It *fell* in the tree when it came down."

"Oh—exactly."

"Certainly. I unwound the lariat, and fastened one end of it to the limb. It was the very best green rawhide, and capable of sustaining tons. I made a slip-noose in the other end, and then hung it down to see the length. It reached down twenty-two feet—half way to the ground. I then loaded every barrel of the Allen with a double charge. I felt satisfied. I said to myself, if he never thinks of that one thing that I dread, all right—but if he does, all right anyhow—I am fixed for him. But don't you know that the very thing a man dreads is the thing that always happens? Indeed it is so. I watched the bull, now, with anxiety—anxiety which no one can conceive of who has not been in such a situation and felt that at any moment death might come. Presently a thought came into the bull's eye. I knew it! said I—if my nerve fails now, I am lost. Sure enough, it was just as I had dreaded, he started in to climb the tree—"

"What, the bull?"

"Of course—who else?"

"But a bull can't climb a tree."

"He can't, can't he? Since you know so much about it, did you ever see a bull try?"

"No, I never dreamt of such a thing."

"Well, then, what is the use of your talking that way, then? Because you never saw a thing done, is that any reason why it can't be done?"

"Well, all right—go on. What did you do?"

"The bull started up, and got along well for about ten feet, then slipped and slid back. I breathed easier. He tried it again—got up a little higher—slipped again. But he came at it once more, and this time he was careful. He got gradually higher and higher, and my spirits went down more and more. Up he came—an inch at a time— with his eyes hot, and his tongue hanging out. Higher and higher—hitched his foot over the stump of a limb, and looked up, as much as to say, 'you are my meat, friend.' Up again—higher and higher, and getting more excited the closer he got. He was within ten feet of me! I had the coil of the lariat all ready; I paid it out slowly, and till it hung right over his head; all of a sudden I let go of the slack, and the slip-noose fell fairly round his neck! Quicker than lightning I out with the Allen and let him have it in the face. It was an awful roar, and must have scared the bull out of his senses. When the smoke cleared away, there he was, dangling in the air, twenty foot from the ground, and going out of one convulsion into another faster than you could count! I didn't stop to count, any- how—I shinned down the tree and shot for home."

"Bemis, is all that true, just as you have stated it?"

"I wish I may rot in my tracks and die the death of a dog if it isn't."

"Well, we can't refuse to believe it, and we don't. But if there were some proofs—"

"Proofs! Did I bring back my lariat?"

"No."

"Did you ever see the bull again?"

YOUR ROLE IN ORAL INTERPRETATION

"No."

"Well, then, what more do you want? I never saw anybody as particular as you are about a little thing like that."

I made up my mind that if this man was not a liar he only missed it by the skin of his teeth.

Vivid? Descriptive? Exaggerated? Well, if it isn't, it just misses being so by the skin of *its* teeth.

Read the whole book. You'll find one wild adventure following another.

The primary reason for cutting literature for interpretation is to make it conform to time limits imposed by the audience or the occasion. It isn't possible to read *most* prose selections in their entirety to an audience because there isn't enough time to do so; therefore, it is necessary to learn some principles of effective cutting.

CUTTING DESCRIPTIVE PROSE

A word of caution is in order in cutting prose which is highly descriptive. It would seem on the surface that descriptive prose is easy to cut because it is so wordy. It is true that description moves slowly; it must do so in order to give the reader a full visual appreciation of the picture the author is painting. But if this kind of writing is cut without care, the picture will be distorted.

A general rule for cutting descriptive prose is that you can cut down but not out. Decide first what descriptive elements are most important in giving the audience a clear and vivid picture; then look for those elements which are least important and cut them down in length. Perhaps you will discover that some segments can be eliminated entirely. If so, cut them out. But preserve fully those important elements of the description that give the audience the author's focus and style. The excerpt which follows has been cut from Mark Twain's *Life on the Mississippi* to sharpen the focus on the two men involved in the fracas, on the abruptness of the final outcome, and to preserve Mark Twain's literary style. Read it first as it has been cut; then go back over it again to see what has been eliminated.

Excerpt *from* LIFE ON THE MISSISSIPPI

MARK TWAIN

They was all about to make a break for him, but the biggest man there jumped up and says:

"Set whar you are, gentlemen. Leave him to me; he's my meat."

Then he jumped up in the air three times, and cracked his heels together every time. ~~He flung off a buckskin coat that was all hung with fringes, and says, "You lay thar till the chewin up's done;" he flung his hat down, which was all over ribbons, and says, "You lay thar till his sufferin's over."~~

~~Then he jumped up in the air and cracked his heels together again~~, and shouted out:

"Whoo-oo-p. I'm the old original iron-jawed, brass-mounted, copper-bellied corpse-maker from the wilds of Arkansaw! Look at me! I'm the man they call Sudden Death and General Desolation! Sired by a hurricane, dam'd by an earthquake, half-brother to the cholera, nearly related to the smallpox on the mother's side! Look at me! I take nineteen alligators and a bar'l of whiskey for breakfast when I'm in robust health, and a bushel of rattlesnakes and a dead body when I'm ailing. ~~I split the everlasting rocks with my glance, and I squench the thunder when I speak! Whoo-oop~~! Stand back and give me room according to my strength! Blood's my natural drink, and the wails of the dying is music to my ear. Cast your eye on me, gentlemen! and lay low and hold your breath, for I'm 'bout to turn myself loose!"

All the time he was getting this off, he was shaking his head and looking fierce, and kind of swelling around in a little circle, tucking up his wristbands, and now and then straightening up and beating his breast with his fist, saying "Look at me, gentlemen!" When he got through, he jumped up and cracked his heels together three times, and let off a roaring "Whoo-oop! I'm the bloodiest son of a wildcat that lives!"

The man that had started the row tilted his old slouch hat down over his right eye; then he bent stooping forward, with his back sagged and his south end sticking out far, and his fists a-shoving out and drawing in in front of him, and so went around in a little circle about three times, swelling himself up and breathing hard. Then he straightened, and jumped up and cracked his heels together three times before he lit again (that made them cheer), and he began to shout like this:

"Whoo-oop! bow your neck and spread, for the kingdom of sorrow's a-coming! Hold me down to the earth, for I feel my powers a-working! ~~Whoo-oop! I'm a child of sin, don't let me get a start!~~ Smoked glass, here, for all! Don't attempt to look at me with the naked eye, gentlemen! ~~When I'm playful I use the meridians of longitude and parallels of latitude for a seine, and drag the Atlantic Ocean for whales!~~ I scratch my head with the lightning and purr myself to sleep with the thunder! When I'm cold, I bile the Gulf of Mexico and bathe in it; when I'm hot, I fan myself with an equinoctial storm; when I'm thirsty I reach up and suck a cloud dry like a sponge; when I range the earth hungry, famine follows in my tracks! Whoo-oop! ~~Bow your neck and spread!~~ I put my hand on the sun's face and make it night in the earth; I bite a piece out of the moon and hurry the seasons; I shake myself and crumble the mountains! ~~Contemplate me through leather—don't use the naked eye! I'm the man with a petrified heart and biler-iron bowels!~~ The massacre of isolated communities is the pastime of my ideal moments, the destruction of nationalities the serious business of my life! The boundless vastness of the great American desert is my inclosed property, and I bury my dead on my own premises!" He jumped up and cracked his heels together three times before he lit (they cheered him again), and as he came down he shouted out: "Whoo-oop!

bow your neck and spread, for the Pet Child of Calamity's a-coming!"

Then the other one went to swelling around and blowing again—the first one—the one they called Bob; next, the Child of Calamity chipped in again, bigger than ever; then they both got at it at the same time, swelling round and round each other and punching their fists most into each other's faces, and whooping and jawing like Injuns; then Bob called the Child names, and the Child called him names back again; Bob called him a heap of rougher names, and the Child come back at him with the very worst kind of language; next, Bob knocked the Child's hat off, and the Child picked it up and kicked Bob's ribbony hat about six foot; ~~Bob went and got it and said never mind, this warn't going to be the last of the thing, because he was a man that never forgot and never forgive, and so the Child better look out, for there was a time a-coming, just as sure as he was a living man, that he would have to answer to him with the best blood in his body. The Child said no man was willinger than he for that time to come, and he would give Bob fair warning, now, never to cross his path again, for he could never rest till he had waded in his blood, for such was his nature, though he was sparing him now on account of his family, if he had one.~~

Both of them was edging away in different directions, growling and shaking their heads and going on about what they was going to do; but a little black-whiskered chap skipped up and says:

"Come back here, you couple of chicken-livered cowards, and I'll thrash the two of ye!"

And he done it too.

Undoubtedly you would have cut some of the segments that were left in, and you'd have left intact some of the lines that were cut. You, in large part, pick and choose the elements to be cut when you are going to read a selection, keeping in mind that, generally,

YOUR ROLE IN ORAL INTERPRETATION

your audience will accept what you give them and that, if you've done your cutting well, they will be unaware that segments of the original are missing. Be careful that the segments—words, phrases, lines, paragraphs or pages—you cut do not distort the author's picture or his style and then be your own master. Cut to make a better oral performance.

Expository Prose

The term "expository" is often a confusing one to beginning interpreters. Your authors regard it as prose which concerns itself directly, by way of explanation or persuasion, with ideas or principles. This textbook is an example. It presents a succession of explanations and arguments, with a series of direct illustrations aimed at giving you an understanding of, an appreciation for, and skill in oral interpretation.

Essays, editorials, reports, diaries, journals, letters, and news stories are all examples of prose which seeks to inform the reader about something or persuade him to accept a particular point of view on matters important to the author of the material.

In the reading of expository prose, which is often material without a heavy emotional content, the responsibility of the reader is to understand fully and present clearly the primary arguments advanced by the writer. The entire essay or article must be read in order to determine what is the essential theme, the primary argument. After that, a study of the thoughts embodied in each paragraph—and each topical sentence—will tell you the author's main points. In the same way, you will discover illustrations and examples used by the author to add support or reading interest to the arguments advanced.

Let us take, for example, Charles Lamb's "Valentine's Day" from *Essays of Elia*. It is a simply conceived, clearly defined essay. Its theme is clearly identified in the title. It is an enthusiastic praise of Valentine's Day and its message of love. It extols romance in flowery terms, to match the theme of the article. And the reference it makes to E. B.'s case is a graphic one to exemplify the theme— that love is one of the world's most exciting emotions. Long may romance live.

VALENTINE'S DAY

CHARLES LAMB

Hail to thy returning festival, old Bishop Valentine! Great
is thy name in the rubric, thou venerable Arch-flamen of
Hymen! Immortal Go-between! who and what manner of
person art thou? Art thou but a name, typifying the
restless principle which impels poor humans to seek per-
fection in union? or wert thou indeed a mortal prelate,
with thy tippet and thy rochet, thy apron on, and decent
lawn sleeves? Mysterious personage! Like unto thee,
assuredly, there is no other mitred father in the calendar;
not Jerome, nor Ambrose, nor Cyril; nor the consigner of
undipt infants to eternal torments, Austin, whom all
mothers hate; nor he who hated all mothers, Origen; not
Bishop Bull, nor Archbishop Parker, nor Whitgift. Thou
comest attended with thousands and ten thousands of
little Loves, and the air is

Brush'd with the hiss of rustling wings.

Singing Cupids are thy choristers and thy precentors; and
instead of the crosier, the mystical arrow is borne before
thee.

In other words, this is the day on which those charm-
ing little missives, ycleped Valentines, cross and intercross
each other at every street and turning. The weary and all
forspent twopenny postman sinks beneath a load of delicate embarrassments, not his own. It is scarcely credible
to what an extent this ephemeral courtship is carried on in
this loving town, to the great enrichment of porters, and
detriment of knockers and bell-wires. In these little visual
interpretations, no emblem is so common as the heart,—
that little three-cornered exponent of all our hopes and
fears,—the bestuck and bleeding heart; it is twisted and
tortured into more allegories and affections than an opera
hat. What authority we have in history or mythology for
placing the headquarters and metropolis of god Cupid in

this anatomical seat rather than in any other, is not very clear; but we have got it, and it will serve as well as any other. Else we might easily imagine, upon some other system which might have prevailed for anything which our pathology knows to the contrary, a lover addressing his mistress, in perfect simplicity of feeling, "Madam, my liver and fortune are entirely at your disposal"; or putting a delicate question, "Amanda, have you a midriff to bestow?" But custom has settled these things, and awarded the seat of sentiment to the aforesaid triangle, while its less fortunate neighbours wait at animal and anatomical distance.

Not many sounds in life, and I include all urban and all rural sounds, exceed in interest a knock at the door. It "gives a very echo to the throne where Hope is seated." But its issues seldom answer to this oracle within. It is so seldom that just the person we want to see comes. But of all the clamorous visitations the welcomest in expectation is the sound that ushers in, or seems to usher in, a Valentine. As the raven himself was hoarse that announced the fatal entrance of Duncan, so the knock of the postman on this day is light, airy, confident, and befitting one that bringeth good tidings. It is less mechanical than on other days; you will say, "That is not the post, I am sure." Visions of Love, of Cupids, of Hymens!—delightful eternal commonplaces, which "having been will always be"; which no schoolboy nor schoolman can write away; having your irreversible throne in the fancy and affections —what are your transports, when the happy maiden, opening with a careful finger, careful not to break the emblematic seal, bursts upon the sight of some well-designed allegory, some type, some youthful fancy, not without verses—

Lovers all, a madrigal

or some such device, not over-abundant in sense—young Love disclaims it,—and not quite silly—something between wind and water, a chorus where the sheep might almost join the shepherd, as they did, or as I apprehend they did, in Arcadia.

All Valentines are not foolish; and I shall not easily forget thine, my kind friend (if I may have leave to call you so) E. B.—E. B. lived opposite a young maiden whom he had often seen, unseen, from his parlour window in C_____e Street. She was all joyousness and innocence, and just of an age to enjoy receiving a Valentine, and just of a temper to bear the disappointment of missing one with good humour. E. B. is an artist of no common powers; in the fancy parts of designing, perhaps inferior to none; his name is known at the bottom of many a well-executed vignette in the way of his profession, but no further; for E. B. is modest, and the world meets nobody half way. E. B. meditated how he could repay this young maiden for many a favour which she had done him unknown; for when a kindly face greets us, though but passing by, and never knows us again, nor we it, we should feel it as an obligation: and E. B. did. This good artist set himself at work to please the damsel. It was just before Valentine's Day three years since. He wrought, unseen and unsuspected, a wondrous work. We need not say it was on the finest gilt paper with borders—full, not of common hearts and heartless allegory, but all the prettiest stories of love from Ovid, and older poets than Ovid (for E.B. is a scholar). There was Pyramus and Thisbe, and be sure Dido was not forgot, nor Hero and Leander, and swans more than sang Cayster, with mottoes and fanciful devices, such as beseemed—a work, in short, of magic. Iris dipt the woof. This on Valentine's eve he commended to the all-swallowing indiscriminate orifice (O ignoble trust!) of the common post; but the humble medium did its duty, and from his watchful stand the next morning he saw the cheerful messenger knock, and by-and-by the precious charge delivered. He saw, unseen, the happy girl unfold the Valentine, dance about, clap her hands, as one after one the pretty emblems unfolded themselves. She danced about, not with light love, or foolish expectations, for she had no lover; or, if she had, none she knew that could have created those bright images which delighted her. It was more like some fairy present; a God-send, as our familiarly pious ancestors termed a benefit received where the benefactor was unknown. It would do her no harm. It would do her good for ever after. It is good to love the unknown. I only give this as a specimen of E. B. and his modest way of doing a concealed kindness.

Good morrow to my Valentine, sings poor Ophelia; and no better wish, but with better auspices, we wish to all faithful lovers, who are not too wise to despise old legends, but are content to rank themselves humble diocesans of Old Bishop Valentine and his true church.

Analyze the essay; you find the opening line sets the key. It is a paean of praise. The reader knows exactly what Lamb is going to prove by that opening statement. And to prove Lamb considers it important, note the use of the exclamation mark at the end of the first sentence. He then asks what the name means—and he lists various personalities in a satirical vein in attempting to define the name. He defines it by:

Thou comest attended with thousands and tens of thousands of little Loves, and the air is
"Brushed with the hiss of rustling wings."
Singing Cupids are thy choristers and thy precentors; and instead of the crosier, the mystical arrow is borne before thee.

Lamb has even used a line of poetry to indicate his feeling that Valentine's Day is a poetic day, a romantic day.

His next thought is what the Day means to such people as the postman. He puts the romantic on the practical side. But he quickly returns to his romantic theme with:

In these little visual interpretations, no emblem is so common as the heart—that little three-cornered exponent of all our hopes and fears—the bestuck and bleeding heart; it is twisted and tortured into more allegories and affections than an opera hat.

His following observation is an attempt to analyze why god Cupid was placed in this anatomical section—the heart—instead of somewhere else. To decide why, Lamb uses irony and sarcasm in his lines: "Madame, my liver and fortune are entirely at your disposal." This line marks the entrance of humor into the article— humor to emphasize a point.

Lamb's reference to the "knock on the door" symbolizes the hope most people feel that someone will enter their lives and bring joy. It is also the symbol of the hopeful heart who waits for love to be returned to it. He contrasts this knock with the raven in Poe's poem and Duncan in Macbeth—and then shows the contrast with the knock of the postman bringing tidings from a loved one.

To show the full meaning of Valentine's Day, the joy and the quickening of the heart that it brings, Lamb then gives a case as a conclusive point—a man's sending a collection of love stories to a woman who had unknowingly been kind to him. Then he ends with a further praise of Valentine and his message.

The central mood is exaltation, joy, happiness. The language is ornate, flowery, often replete with classical allusions. The sentence structure is involved, complex, with thoughts rambling from one idea to another with apparently few smooth transitions. But the language also serves, in its way, as an uninhibited expression of Lamb's own theory—that love is a feeling of elation, of joy, not restricted by any forms. So why should his language or his arrangements of sentences be restricted by a rigidly formal structure? As a reader you must have Lamb's enthusiasm for love and Valentine's Day if you are to read this essay effectively.

Letters involve the personal element in writing. Robert Browning did not write his letters to Elizabeth Barrett without having a great feeling for her. And she did not respond in an indifferent manner either. Consequently, the reader must incorporate the feeling of love these two had for each other in any reading of the letters that passed between them. And to read the letters of Michelangelo, you would have to know the background of them, why they were written, in order to understand what they reveal about him.

YOUR ROLE IN ORAL INTERPRETATION

The letters of Michelangelo reveal much of the turmoil, the frustrations, the problems he met in his life as he tried to help his family. To understand Michelangelo's impatience, you must know about his life, his family obligations, the incessant demand on him for financial help as he tried to carve his career in Florence. Throughout the letters you can sense a feeling of irritation that he is called upon by his family for so many different things, of his own intense desire to make them understand the difficulty of his own financial problem. The letters clearly reveal the torment in Michelangelo as he deals with a family which is singularly unconcerned with his problems. You would not be able to read this letter with the proper irritation without knowing the background. Nor would you be able to read it well without knowing who some of the people mentioned are. For example, the reference to Buonarroto refers to his younger brother. Consiglio was a merchant. Piero de' Medici was the son of Lorenzo de' Medici, the ruling family in Florence. His reference to the image he is sculpturing for his own pleasure is to a Cupid he was working on.

Excerpt from I, MICHELANGELO, SCULPTOR

IRVING STONE

Dearest father—I wish to tell you that last Friday Buonarroto arrived here. As soon as I found out, I went to call on him at the inn. He informed me about how you are getting along, and he told me that Consiglio, the mercer, vexes you a great deal, that he is unwilling to settle on any sort of agreement, and that he wants to have you arrested. I suggest that you try to come to an understanding with him, and give him a few ducats at once; then let me know what you agree that you should give him. I shall send it to you. Although, as I told you, I have little money, I shall try to borrow some to avoid taking it from the bank.

Do not be surprised if occasionally I write you in an angry tone; at times I am quite upset by things that befall one who is away from home.

I agreed to make a statue for Piero de' Medici, and I bought a piece of marble. I never began it, however, because he never kept his promise to me. For this reason I keep to myself, and I am sculpturing an image for my own pleasure. I bought a piece of marble for five ducats, but it wasn't any good. I just threw that money away. Later I bought another piece, also for five ducats. So that you must realize that I too spend money and have my own troubles. In spite of all this, I shall send you what you may ask me, even if I should have to sell myself as a slave.

Buonarroto has a room and he is comfortable, and as long as he will want to stay here he will never lack for anything. I do not have the facilities of keeping him with me, for I am living in someone else's home. The important thing is that I shall see to it that he never lacks what he needs.

(August 19, 1497)

In articles dealing with current problems, tone is important—what seems to concern the author. In the mid-1960's the emphasis was on civil rights and the conflict over Viet Nam. Many articles have been written about both. Some authors argue vehemently for civil rights, and to read such works the interpreter must share the author's indignation and fighting spirit. A great deal of emotion is involved. The same applies to Viet Nam. There are contrasting ideas about Viet Nam, but the reader must read the article in line with the author's own emotional viewpoint.

Since expository prose also concerns itself with biography and autobiography, these are significant matters for you to consider. In the reading of an autobiography, the essential requirement is to know the attitude, the feelings, the personality of the author telling his story. For example, in *Act One* by Moss Hart, you must consider that the playwright underwent many struggles and disillusionments before hitting the top—and that he was also influenced by a great many people. Supposing you were to read the section in which Moss and George Kaufman are working so strenuously on their first co-authored play. To read it with any semblance of feeling, you'd have to know what Moss Hart had gone through before this. In this instance, the selection is almost narrative even though it falls into the expository category. Autobiography is, by its essence, much more personal than biography since it is the author's own innermost feelings guiding the telling of the story.

As for biography, a second person is writing the story of some-one else's life. To be sure, the author has had a close association

YOUR ROLE IN ORAL INTERPRETATION

with the person about whom he is writing. He seeks to know that individual's every thought, idea, concept, mood, temperament— before he starts to write. To be successful he must be an astute observer. You as the reader are then committed to a realistic and conscientious reproduction of both the author's concept and its relation to the subject itself. This is a case where further research into the life of a person being treated in a biography would be of help. Let us say, for example, you were to read *O'Neill* by Arthur and Barbara Gelb. It would be wise to combine the reading of this biography with a study of O'Neill's autobiographical plays, such as *Long Day's Journey Into Night*, plus biographies by other authors.

In the reading of humor, which is often a part of expository prose, Richard Armour's writings are excellent examples, as are those of Robert Benchley and James Thurber. Armour's treatment of the plots of Shakespeare's plays in *Twisted Tales From Shakespeare* is replete with biting satire and irony, so much so, in fact, that it is difficult to take the Shakespearean plot seriously after reading one of Armour's accounts. Yet, one must realize that the author is someone who has great love for Shakespeare. He is a professor and an authority on the Bard's writings, so his satire is even more potent. Here, the reader would have to share in Armour's enjoyment of the satire and give the reading a sense of exaggeration, always keeping in mind that the satire is gentle, not savage and biting.

In James Thurber's "University Days," Thurber pokes fun at himself—and also at the academic system. In reading this selection, you, as the reader, must put yourself into Thurber's shoes, keeping in mind that in his later years he was almost totally blind and yet could still view his handicap as something humorous. You must be aware of the weakness of Thurber's eyes in order to convey the humor in the article with its true significance. And yet, you cannot empathize too deeply with Thurber's problem since he looked upon it lightly enough to write of it in humorous terms.

In all expository prose, it is vital to decide what is the central theme of the article, letter, or journal. Without knowing the theme, you cannot interpret meaningfully. Then you must associate the one isolated segment you choose to read with the total picture, keeping in mind the author's style of writing, his use of language, his sentence structure, his own background, and his own feelings about the subject he has chosen to discuss.

It is best to remember that much expository material is not suited to oral reading. A textbook on technical matters is an example. As previously mentioned in another chapter, Erich Fromm's philosophical treatises often do not lend themselves to oral reading because of the complexity of the theories advanced and because of the involved structure. Also, some expository material has limited audience appeal, so it should be approached with a good deal of care when being used in the field of oral interpretation.

CUTTING EXPOSITORY PROSE

Expository prose is the easiest of the three divisions of prose to cut. It is vital in cutting to read the entire selection and decide on the important points in the writing. Preserve the writer's central idea and his style; minor points or interesting side issues can be most easily cut. Of course you must be careful that what is left after you've finished cutting is more than an encyclopedic account; leave some meat on the bones of the ideas.

The following essay by Helen Keller, called "Three Days To See," lends itself well to oral interpretation because it makes its expository point in an interesting and vivid way. Read the selection as it has been cut first, omitting from your reading the words lined out. Then re-read the essay in its entirety and see if you agree with the cutting that has been done.

THREE DAYS TO SEE

HELEN KELLER

All of us have read thrilling stories in which the hero had only a limited and specified time to live. Sometimes it was as long as a year; sometimes as short as twenty-four hours. But always we were interested in discovering just how the doomed man chose to spend his last days or his last hours. I speak, of course, of free men who have a choice, not condemned criminals whose sphere of activities is strictly delimited.

Such stories set us thinking, wondering what we should do under similar circumstances. What events, what experiences, what associations should we crowd into those last hours as mortal beings? What happiness should we find in reviewing the past, what regrets?

Sometimes I have thought it would be an excellent rule to live each day as if we should die tomorrow. Such an attitude would emphasize sharply the values of life. ~~We should live each day with a gentleness, a vigor, and a keenness of appreciation which are often lost when time stretches before us in the constant panorama of more days and months and years to come. There are those, of course, who would adopt the epicurean motto of "eat, drink, and be merry," but most people would be chastened by the certainty of impending death.~~

~~In stories, the doomed hero is usually saved at the last minute by some stroke of fortune, but almost always his sense of values is changed. He becomes more appreciative of the meaning of life and its permanent spiritual values. It has often been noted that those who live, or have lived, in the shadow of death bring a mellow sweetness to everything they do.~~

Most of us, however, take life for granted. We know that one day we must die, but usually we picture that day as far in the future. When we are in buoyant health, death is all but unimaginable. ~~We seldom think of it. The days stretch out in an endless vista. So we go about our petty tasks, hardly aware of our listless attitude toward life.~~

~~The same lethargy, I am afraid, characterizes the use of all our faculties and senses.~~ Only the deaf appreciate hearing, only the blind realize the manifold blessings that lie in sight. ~~Particularly does this observation apply to those who have lost sight and hearing in adult life. But those who have never suffered impairment of sight or hearing seldom make the fullest use of these blessed faculties. Their eyes and ears take in all sights and sounds hazily, without concentration, and with little appreciation. It is the same old story of not being grateful for what we have until we lost it, of not being conscious of health until we are ill.~~

I have often thought it would be a blessing if each human being were stricken blind and deaf for a few days at sometime during his early adult life. Darkness would make him more appreciative of sight; silence would teach him the joys of sound.

Now and then I have tested my seeing friends to discover what they see. Recently I was visited by a good friend who had just returned from a long walk in the woods, and I asked her what she had observed. "Nothing in particular," she replied. I might have been incredulous had I not been accustomed to such responses, for long ago I became convinced that the seeing see little.

How was it possible, I asked myself, to walk for an hour through the woods and see nothing worthy of note? I who cannot see find hundreds of things to interest me through mere touch. I feel the delicate symmetry of a leaf. I pass my hands lovingly about the smooth skin of a silver birch, or the rough shaggy bark of a pine. In spring I touch the branches of trees hopefully in search of a bud, the first sign of awakening Nature after her winter's sleep. I feel the delightful, velvety texture of a flower, and discover its remarkable convolutions; and something of the miracle of Nature is revealed to me. Occasionally, if I am very fortunate, I place my hand gently on a small tree and feel the happy quiver of a bird in full song. I am delighted to have the cool waters of a brook rush through my open fingers. To me a lush carpet of pine needles or spongy grass is more welcome than the most luxurious Persian rug. To me the pageant of seasons is a thrilling and unending drama, the action of which streams through my finger tips.

~~At times my heart cries out with longing to see all these things. If I can get so much pleasure from mere touch, how much more beauty must be revealed by sight. Yet, those who have eyes apparently see little. The panorama of color and action which fills the world is taken for granted.~~ It is human, perhaps, to appreciate little that which we have and to long for that which we have not, but it is a great pity that in the world of light the gift of sight is used only as a mere convenience, rather than as a means of adding fullness to life.

YOUR ROLE IN ORAL INTERPRETATION

If I were the president of a university I should establish a compulsory course in "How to Use Your Eyes." The professor would try to show his pupils how they could add joy to their lives by really seeing what passes unnoticed before them. He would try to awake their dormant and sluggish faculties.

Perhaps I can best illustrate by imagining what I should most like to see if I were given the use of my eyes, say, for just three days. And while I am imagining, suppose you, too, set your mind to work on the problem of how you would use your own eyes if you had only three more days to see. If with the oncoming darkness of the third night you knew that the sun would never rise for you again, how would you spend those precious intervening days? What would you most want to let your gaze rest upon?

I, naturally, should want most to see the things which have become dear to me through my years of darkness. You, too, would want to let your eyes rest long on the things that have become dear to you so that you could take the memory of them with you into the night that loomed before you.

If, by some miracle, I were granted three seeing days, to be followed by a relapse into darkness, I should divide the period into three parts.

On the first day, I should want to see the people whose kindness and gentleness and companionship have made my life worth living. First I should like to gaze long upon the face of my dear teacher, Mrs. Anne Sullivan Macy, who came to me when I was a child and opened the outer world to me. I should want not merely to see the outline of her face, so that I could cherish it in my memory, but to study that face and find in it the living evidence of the sympathetic tenderness and patience with which she accomplished the difficult task of my education. I should like to see in her eyes that strength of character which has enabled her to stand firm in the face of difficulties, and

that compassion for all humanity which she has revealed
to me so often.

I do not know what it is to see into the heart of a
friend through that "window of the soul," the eye. I can
only "see" through my finger tips the outline of a face. I
can detect laughter, sorrow, and many other obvious
emotions. I know my friends from the feel of their faces.
But I cannot really picture their personalities by touch. I
know their personalities, of course, through other means,
through the thoughts they express to me, through whatever of their actions are revealed to me. But I am denied
that deeper understanding of them which I am sure
would come through sight of them, through watching
their reactions to various expressed thoughts and circumstances, through noting the immediate and fleeting
reactions of their eyes and countenance.

Friends who are near to me I know well, because
through the months and years they reveal themselves to
me in all their phases; but of casual friends I have only an
incomplete impression, an impression gained from a hand-
clasp, from spoken words which I take from their lips
with my finger tips, or which they tap into the palm of my
hand.

How much easier, how much more satisfying it is for
you who can see to grasp quickly the essential qualities of
another person by watching the subtleties of expression,
the quiver of a muscle, the flutter of a hand. But does it
ever occur to you to use your sight to see into the inner
nature of a friend or acquaintance? Do not most of you
seeing people grasp casually the outward features of a
face and let it go at that?

For instance, can you describe accurately the faces of
five good friends? Some of you can, but many cannot. As
an experiment, I have questioned husbands of long standing about the color of their wives' eyes, and often they
express embarrassed confusion and admit that they do not
know. And, incidentally, it is a chronic complaint of wives

~~that their husbands do not notice new dresses, new hats, and changes in household arrangements.~~

~~The eyes of seeing persons soon become accustomed to the routine of their surroundings, and they actually see only the startling and spectacular. But even in viewing the most spectacular sights the eyes are lazy. Court records reveal every day how inaccurately "eyewitnesses" see. A given event will be "seen" in several different ways by as many witnesses. Some see more than others, but few see everything that is within the range of their vision.~~

~~Oh, the things that I should see if I had the power of sight for just three days!~~

The first day would be a busy one. I should call to me all my dear friends and look long into their faces, imprinting upon my mind the outward evidences of the beauty that is within them. I should let my eyes rest, too, on the face of a baby, so that I could catch a vision of the eager, innocent beauty which precedes the individual's consciousness of the conflicts which life develops.

And I should like to look into the loyal, trusting eyes of my dogs—the grave, canny little Scottie, Darkie, and the stalwart understanding great Dane, Helga, whose warm, tender, and playful friendships are so comforting to me.

On that busy first day I should also view the small simple things of my home. I want to see the warm colors in the rugs under my feet, the pictures on the walls, the intimate trifles that transform a house into home. My eyes would rest respectfully on the books in raised type which I have read, but they would be more eagerly interested in the printed books which seeing people can read, for during the long night of my life the books I have read and those which have been read to me have built themselves into a great shining lighthouse, revealing to me the deepest channels of human life and the human spirit.

In the afternoon of that first seeing day, I should take a long walk in the woods and intoxicate my eyes on the beauties of the world of Nature, trying desperately to absorb in a few hours the vast splendor which is constantly unfolding itself to those who can see. On the way home from my woodland jaunt my path would lie near a farm so that I might see the patient horses plowing in the fields (perhaps I should see only a tractor!) and the serene content of men living close to the soil. And I should pray for the glory of a colorful sunset.

When dusk had fallen, I should experience the double delight of being able to see by artificial light, which the genius of man has created to extend the power of his sight when Nature decrees darkness.

~~In the night of that first day of sight, I should not be able to sleep, so full would be my mind of the memories of the day.~~

The next day—the second day of sight—I should arise with the dawn and see the thrilling miracle by which night is transformed into day. I should behold with awe the magnificent panorama of light with which the sun awakens the sleeping earth.

This day I should devote to a hasty glimpse of the world, past and present. I should want to see the pageant of man's progress, the kaleidoscope of the ages. How can so much be compressed into one day? Through the museums, of course. ~~Often I have visited the New York Museum of Natural History to touch with my hands many of the objects there exhibited, but~~ I have longed to see with my eyes the condensed history of the earth and its inhabitants displayed there—animals and the races of men pictured in their native environment; gigantic carcasses of dinosaurs and mastodons which roamed the earth long before man appeared, with his tiny stature and powerful brain, to conquer the animal kingdom; ~~realistic presentations of the processes of evolution in animals, in man, and in the implements which man has used to fashion for himself a secure home on this planet~~; and a thousand and one other aspects of natural history.

~~I wonder how many readers of this article have~~

viewed the panorama of the face of living things as
pictured in that inspiring museum. Many, of course, have
not had the opportunity, but I am sure that many who
have had the opportunity have not made use of it. There,
indeed, is a place to use your eyes. You who see can spend
many fruitful days there, but I, with my imaginary three
days of sight, could only take a hasty glimpse, and pass
on.

My next stop would be the Metropolitan Museum of
Art, for just as the Museum of Natural History reveals the
material aspects of the world, so does the Metropolitan
show the myriad facets of the human spirit. Throughout
the history of humanity the urge to artistic expression has
been almost as powerful as the urge for food, shelter, and
procreation. And here, in the vast chambers of the Metropolitan Museum, is unfolded before me the spirit of
Egypt, Greece, and Rome, as expressed in their art. I
know well through my hands the sculptured gods and
goddesses of the ancient Nile-land. I have felt copies of
Parthenon friezes, and I have sensed the rhythmic beauty
of charging Athenian warriors. Apollos and Venuses and
the Winged Victory of Samothrace are friends of my
finger tips. The gnarled, bearded features of Homer are
dear to me, for he, too, knew blindness.

My hands have lingered upon the living marble of
Roman sculpture as well as that of later generations. I
have passed my hands over a plaster cast of Michelangelo's inspiring and heroic Moses; I have sensed the
power of Rodin; I have been awed by the devoted spirit of
Gothic wood carving. These arts which can be touched
have meaning for me, but even they were meant to be
seen rather than felt, and I can only guess at the beauty
which remains hidden from me. I can admire the simple
lines of a Greek vase, but its figured decorations are lost to
me.

So on this, my second day of sight, I should try to
probe into the soul of man through his art. The things I
knew through touch I should now see. More splendid still,

the whole magnificent world of painting would be opened to me, from the Italian Primitives, with their serene religious devotion, to the Moderns, with their feverish visions. I should look deep into the canvases of Raphael, Leonardo da Vinci, Titian, Rembrandt. I should want to feast my eyes upon the warm colors of Veronese, study the mysteries of El Greco, catch a new vision of Nature from Corot. ~~Oh, there is so much rich meaning and beauty in the art of the ages for you who have eyes to see!~~

~~Upon my short visit to this temple of art I should not be able to review a fraction of that great world of art which is open to you. I should be able to get only a superficial impression. Artists tell me that for a deep and true appreciation of art one must educate the eye. One must learn through experience to weigh the merits of line, of composition, of form and color. If I had eyes, how happily would I embark upon so fascinating a study! Yet I am told that, to many of you who have eyes to see, the world of art is a dark night, unexplored and unillumi-nated~~.

It would be with extreme reluctance that I should leave the Metropolitan Museum, ~~which contains the key to beauty—a beauty so neglected. Seeing persons, how-ever, do not need a Metropolitan to find this key to beauty. The same key lies waiting in smaller museums, and in books on the shelves of even small libraries. But naturally, in my limited time of imaginary sight, I should choose the place where the key unlocks the greatest treasures in the shortest time~~.

The evening of my second day of sight I should spend at a theater or at the movies. Even now I often attend theatrical performances of all sorts, but the action of the play must be spelled into my hand by a companion. But how I should like to see with my own eyes the fascinating figure of Hamlet, or the gusty Falstaff amid colorful Elizabethan trappings! ~~How I should like to fol-low each movement of the graceful Hamlet, each strut of~~

~~the hearty Falstaff!~~ And since I could see only one play, I should be confronted by a many-horned dilemma, for there are scores of plays I should want to see. ~~You who have eyes can see any you like. How many of you, I wonder, when you gaze at a play, or any spectacle, realize and give thanks for the miracle of sight which enables you to enjoy its color, grace, and movement?~~

~~I cannot enjoy the beauty of rhythmic movement except in a sphere restricted to the touch of my hands. I can vision only dimly the grace of a Pavlova, although I know something of the delight of rhythm, for often I can sense the beat of music as it vibrates through the floor, I can well imagine that cadenced motion must be one of the most pleasing sights in the world. I have been able to gather something of this by tracing with my fingers the lines in sculptured marble; if this static grace can be so lovely, how much more acute must be the thrill of seeing grace in motion.~~

~~One of my dearest memories is of the time when Joseph Jefferson allowed me to touch his face and hands as he went through some of the gestures and speeches of his beloved Rip Van Winkle. I was able to catch thus a meager glimpse of the world of drama, and I shall never forget the delight of that moment. But, oh, how much I miss, and how much pleasure you seeing ones can derive from watching and hearing the interplay of speech and movement in the unfolding of a dramatic performance! If I could see only one play, I should know how to picture in my mind the action of a hundred plays which I have read or had transferred to me through the medium of the manual alphabet.~~

So, through the evening of my second imaginary day of sight, the great figures of dramatic literature would crowd sleep from my eyes.

The following morning, I should again greet the dawn, anxious to discover new delights, for I am sure that, for those who have eyes which really see, the dawn of each day must be a perpetually new revelation of beauty.

UNDERSTANDING LITERATURE

This, according to the terms of my imagined miracle, is to be my third and last day of light. I shall have no time to waste in regrets or longings; there is too much to see. The first day I devoted to my friends, animate and inanimate. The second revealed to me the history of man and Nature. Today I shall spend in the workaday world of the present, amid the haunts of men going about the business of life. And where can one find so many activities and conditions of men as in New York? So the city becomes my destination.

I start from my home in the quiet little suburb of Forest Hills, Long Island. Here, surrounded by green lawns, trees, and flowers, are neat little houses, happy with the voices and movements of wives and children, havens of peaceful rest for men who toil in the city. I drive across the lacy structure of steel which spans the East River, and I get a new and startling vision of the power and ingenuity of the mind of man. Busy boats chug and scurry about the river—racy speed boats, stolid, snorting tugs. If I had long days of sight ahead, I should spend many of them watching the delightful activity upon the river.

I look ahead, and before me rise the fantastic towers of New York, a city that seems to have stepped from the pages of a fairy story. What an awe-inspiring sight, these glittering spires, these vast banks of stone and steel— structures such as the gods might build for themselves! This animated picture is a part of the lives of millions of people every day. How many, I wonder, give it so much as a second glance? Very few, I fear. Their eyes are blind to this magnificent sight because it is so familiar to them.

I hurry to the top of one of those gigantic structures, the Empire State Building, for there, a short time ago, I "saw" the city below through the eyes of my secretary. I am anxious to compare my fancy with reality. I am sure I should not be disappointed in the panorama spread out before me, for to me it would be a vision of another world.

Now I begin my rounds of the city. First, I stand at a

busy corner, merely looking at people, trying by sight of them to understand something of their lives. I see smiles and I am happy. I see serious determination, and I am proud. I see suffering, and I am compassionate.

I stroll down Fifth Avenue. I throw my eyes out of focus so that I see no particular object but only a seething kaleidoscope of color. I am certain that the colors of women's dresses moving in a throng must be a gorgeous spectacle of which I should never tire. ~~But perhaps if I had sight I should be like most other women—too interested in styles and the cut of individual dresses to give much attention to the splendor of the color in the mass.~~ And I am convinced, too, that I should become an inveterate window shopper, for it must be a delight to the eye to view the myriad articles of beauty on display.

From Fifth Avenue I make a tour of the city—to Park Avenue, to the slums, to factories, to parks where children play. I take a stay-at-home trip abroad by visiting the foreign quarters. Always my eyes are open wide to all the sights of both happiness and misery so that I may probe deep and add to my understanding of how people work and live. My heart is full of the images of people and things. My eye passes lightly over no single trifle; it strives to touch and hold closely each thing its gaze rests upon. Some sights are pleasant, filling the heart with happiness; but some are miserably pathetic. To these latter I do not shut my eyes, for they, too, are part of life. To close the eye on them is to close the heart and mind.

My third day of sight is drawing to an end. Perhaps there are many serious pursuits to which I should devote the few remaining hours, but I am afraid that on the evening of that last day I should again run away to the theater, to a hilariously funny play, so that I might appreciate the overtones of comedy in the human spirit.

At midnight my temporary respite from blindness would cease, and permanent night would close in on me again. Naturally in those three short days I should not have seen all I wanted to see. Only when darkness had again descended upon me should I realize how much I had left unseen. But my mind would be so crowded with glorious memories that I should have little time for regrets. Thereafter the touch of every object would bring a glowing memory of how that object looked.

~~Perhaps this short outline of how I should spend three days of sight does not agree with the program you would set for yourself if you knew that you were about to be stricken blind. I am, however, sure that if you actually faced that fate, your eyes would open to things you had never seen before, storing up memories for the long night ahead. You would use your eyes as never before. Everything you saw would become dear to you. Your eyes would touch and embrace every object that came within your range of vision. Then, at last, you would really see, and a new world of beauty would open itself before you.~~

I who am blind can give one hint to those who see— one admonition to those who would make full use of the gift of sight: Use your eyes as if tomorrow you would be stricken blind. And the same method can be applied to the other senses. Hear the music of voices, the song of a bird, the mighty strains of an orchestra, as if you would be stricken deaf tomorrow. Touch each object you want to touch as if tomorrow your tactile sense would fail. Smell the perfume of flowers, taste with relish each morsel, as if tomorrow you could never smell and taste again. Make the most of every sense; glory in all the facets of pleasure and beauty which the world reveals to you through the several means of contact which Nature provides. But of all the senses, I am sure that sight must be the most delightful.

You can see in this cutting that the concentration is on Helen's own delight in seeing. There is also another focus in the essay, however, centering around those who can see. Read the essay again and discover this other focus.

What would *you* cut if you were to prepare this essay for an oral performance? Be willing to experiment! Try different ways of

YOUR ROLE IN ORAL INTERPRETATION

getting her main idea across. Be willing to spend the time necessary for effective cutting.

Narrative Prose

Narrative prose tells a story. It has setting, plot, and characters, and moves through one or more climaxes. It is characterized by action. It combines suspense, romance, excitement, tragedy, and comedy all at once in one selection and treats any one of them alone in another. It finds its outlet in short stories and novels primarily, but these terms refuse to be pinned down to any clear-cut definition. Where a short story ends (in length) and a novel begins is difficult to say. So we have short-short stories, short stories, short novels (some as short as a long short story) and novels. A short story, generally, picks up a situation as it moves toward its final climax and records events through that single climax to final resolution. A novel, on the other hand, generally (we can only talk in general terms), might pick up the action at the birth of the main character and record events all through his life, ending when his life ends. A look at a range of novels, however, would show a great deal of variation from this general identification. Sherwood Anderson's *Winesburg, Ohio,* for example, is the story of a town and recounts many situations in the lives of a variety of the townspeople.

You can see that narrative prose is a tremendously dynamic form; as quickly as someone tries to "fence it in," it breaks out in another direction. Narration seldom exists without description; the simple plot wouldn't hold interest without the author's finesse in making the events and characters real, and this is accomplished by adding descriptive elements.

The chief purpose of narrative prose is to entertain; however, it may also be used to point up a problem that the author feels should be corrected or it may be used to instruct the reader in the author's point of view.

When you decide to read narrative prose to an audience, you must first read the selection in its entirety and establish the purpose of writing this piece of literature. Take, for example, the suspenseful short story, "The Monkey's Paw" by W. W. Jacobs. Is its purpose entertainment only? Or does the author wish his readers to think about man's foolishness in wishing for things that he doesn't have? Read the story and think about the author's purpose.

UNDERSTANDING LITERATURE

Consider another example: Shirley Jackson's "The Lottery." Read it in its entirety. Then ask yourself why she wrote it. Was it to record the action of the lottery? Did such a lottery as she describes really ever exist? Were people ever foolish enough to conduct themselves in the manner she describes?

After you've read it, think back over the story and you'll see that little details, such as the children picking up stones, take on great meaning when the end of the story is considered. The references the author makes to the decision made by other towns to do away with the lottery become more meaningful. The hints she gives that the lottery isn't one that people are anxious to win add to the suspense.

No, it was not written just to record the action of a real lottery held each June, but rather to highlight the fact that men have done things even more foolish and inhuman. Compare the fictional lottery with the real Salem witch trials. Which was most inhuman? Salem? Do we still, even today, carry on our own varieties of the lottery? Yes, we do. Perhaps we don't stone members of our communities literally but the influences are still with us.

If you were to read the story for an audience, you would have to be careful not to telegraph, too soon, the final overwhelming climax. Play down the gathering of the stones; don't labor the sections that talk of abandoning the lottery. Treat Mrs. Hutchinson's statement that her husband didn't have time to choose as an incident; play it down. In doing so you heighten the climax.

James Thurber conveys to his readers an understanding of very ordinary people in very ordinary circumstances. In his story "The Secret Life of Walter Mitty," we see Walter, a henpecked husband, retreat into his own world of daydreams where he is the hero. In a series of incidents, Thurber deftly transforms Mitty into a world renowned doctor, an aviator, a spy, an expert shot, and a hydroplane commander, and all the while he is on an errand in the city for his wife. The contrast between the real Mitty and the hero of his daydreams is most entertaining and probably serves also to remind us that we have our own daydreams.

Each of the examples of narrative discussed thus far in the chapter has contained dialogue. In this respect, narrative prose moves a step closer to drama because you, as reader, must characterize the people in the stories you read aloud in order to make them *believable*. This means that you must visualize them clearly and fully and then work with voice and manner to breathe life into them. Naturally this brings us back to emotional response again.

YOUR ROLE IN ORAL INTERPRETATION

The best way to get your audience to respond to the characters in your story is to establish and maintain images of them in the audience's minds. Work with vocal quality, rate, volume, and pitch to create the voice of each character (try to work with only two or three); then support the vocal representation with believable physical involvement. Your audience will have no difficulty telling who it is that says what. However, if you try to characterize too many people, you will confuse the audience. Choose two or three main characters and let the dialogue move through them. Other, less important people can be handled with your narrator's voice (your own) and your reading will be much more effective. Also, it's often possible to put comments that are actually made by additional characters into the mouths of the two or three that you decide to characterize.

Concentrate on becoming emotionally involved with your characters instead of trying to locate them physically in space. Such location is very difficult unless you have rehearsed thoroughly. And even with much rehearsal your audience may become confused or feel that they are watching a ping-pong game.

CUTTING NARRATIVE PROSE

Several general rules for effective cutting of narrative prose should be considered.

1. Choose a selection that is suited to you, to your audience, and to the occasion, especially in terms of time. Then any cutting you have to do will be minimal.

2. If you choose a longer piece, make sure that it can stand alone without what comes before or follows after. Then make sure that your introduction fills in the gap.

3. Cut minor characters if they don't advance the plot or exercise some influence in the segment you are going to read.

4. Where it's possible, cut in large segments.

5. Paraphrase as necessary in order not to leave gaps in the meaning. Paraphrasing is often demanded when you cut large segments so that transition between the remaining elements is smooth.

UNDERSTANDING LITERATURE

6. Cut "he saids" wherever possible. Nothing is more disturbing to an audience than to hear a reader read as though he had no energy at all. For example: " 'We've got to get out and fight,' he shouted angrily." Cut the "he shouted angrily" and shout "We've got to get out and fight!"

A reader is justified in retaining the speaker identification only when the speaker is first introduced. The "he said" is necessary there so that the audience can get acquainted with this new person. Thereafter, the "he said's" should be cut for that character and your voice identify him.

7. Be certain that neither the author's purpose nor his style is distorted or misdirected by your cutting.

Beyond the limits of these rules for cutting you are free to cut. Your guiding light should be: How would James Thurber have cut "The Secret Life of Walter Mitty" if he only had ten minutes for a reading of it? Then, cut!

Study the story that follows. Read it as it has been cut first, noting the flow of the action. Then reread it, adding those segments that have been lined out. Decide what you would do if you were to cut the story for an oral reading. This particular story is a classic of American humor; the author, O. Henry, is noted for his surprise endings. Chances are Johnny will remind you of someone you know.

THE RANSOM OF RED CHIEF

O. HENRY

It looked like a good thing: but wait till I tell you. We were down South, in Alabama—Bill Driscoll and myself—when this kidnapping idea struck us. It was, as Bill afterward expressed it, "during a moment of temporary mental apparition"; but we didn't find that out till later.

There was a town down there, as flat as a flannelcake,

and called Summit, of course. It contained inhabitants of an undeleterious and self-satisfied a class of peasantry as ever clustered around a Maypole.

Bill and me had a joint capital of about six hundred dollars, and we needed just two thousand dollars more to pull off a fraudulent town-lot scheme in Western Illinois with. We talked it over on the front steps of the hotel. ~~Philoprogenitiveness, says we, is strong in semi-rural communities; therefore, and for other reasons, a kidnapping project ought to do better there than in the radius of newspapers that send reporters out in plain clothes to stir up talk about such things.~~ We knew that Summit couldn't get after us with anything stronger than constables and, maybe, some lackadaisical bloodhounds and a diatribe or two in the *Weekly Farmers' Budget*. So, it looked good.

We selected for our victim the only child of a prominent citizen named Ebenezer Dorset. ~~The father was respectable and tight, a mortgage fancier and a stern, upright collection-plate passer and forecloser.~~ The kid was a boy of ten, with bas-relief freckles and hair the color of the cover of the magazine you buy at the news stand when you want to catch a train. Bill and me figured that Ebenezer would melt down for a ransom of two thousand dollars to a cent. But wait till I tell you.

About two miles from Summit was a little mountain, covered with a dense cedar brake. On the rear elevation of this mountain was a cave. There we stored provisions.

One evening after sundown we drove in a buggy past old Dorset's house. The kid was in the street, throwing rocks at a kitten on the opposite fence.

"Hey, little boy!" says Bill, "would you like to have a bag of candy and a nice ride?"

The boy catches Bill neatly in the eye with a piece of brick.

"That will cost the old man an extra five hundred dollars," says Bill, climbing over the wheel.

That boy put up a fight like a welterweight cinnamon bear; but at last we got him down in the bottom of the buggy and drove away. We took him up to the cave, and I hitched the horse in the cedar brake. After dark I drove the buggy to the little village three miles away, where we had hired it, and walked back to the mountain.

~~Bill was pasting court plaster over the scratches and bruises on his features.~~ There was a fire burning behind the big rock at the entrance of the cave, and the boy was watching a pot of boiling coffee, with two buzzard tail-feathers stuck in his red hair. He points a stick at me when I come up and says:

"Ha! cursed paleface, do you dare to enter the camp of Red Chief, the terror of the plains?"

"He's all right now," ~~says Bill, rolling up his trousers and examining some bruises on his shins. "We're playing Indian. We're making Buffalo Bill's show look like magic-lantern views of Palestine in the town hall.~~ I'm Old Hank, the Trapper, Red Chief's captive, and I'm to be scalped at daybreak. By Geronimo! that kid can kick hard."

Yes sir, that boy seemed to be having the time of his life. ~~The fun of camping out in a cave had made him forget that he was a captive himself.~~ He immediately christened me Snake-eye, the Spy, and announced that, when his braves returned from the warpath, I was to be broiled at the stake at the rising of the sun.

Then we had supper; ~~and he filled his mouth full of bacon and bread and gravy, and began to talk. He made a during-dinner speech something like this~~:

~~"I like this fine. I never camped out before; but I had a pet 'possum once, and I was nine last birthday. I hate to go to school. Rats ate up sixteen of Jimmy Talbot's aunt's speckled hen's eggs. Are there any real Indians in these woods? I want some more gravy. Does the trees moving make the wind blow? We had five puppies. What makes your nose so red, Hank? My father has lots of money. Are the stars hot? I whipped Ed Walker twice, Saturday. I don't like girls. You dassent catch toads unless with a~~

string. Do oxen make any noise? Why are oranges round? Have you got beds to sleep on in this cave? Amos Murry has got six toes. A parrot can talk, but a monkey or a fish can't. How many does it take to make twelve?"

Every few minutes he would remember that he was a pesky redskin and pick up his stick rifle and tip toe to the mouth of the cave to rubber for the scouts of the hated paleface. Now and then he would let out a war whoop that made Old Hank, the Trapper, shiver. That boy had Bill terrorized from the start.

"Red Chief," says I to the kid, "would you like to go home?"

"Awe, what for?" says he. "I don't have any fun at home. I hate to go to school. I like to camp out. You won't take me back home again, Snake-eye, will you?"

"Not right away," says I. "We'll stay here in the cave awhile."

"All right!" says he. "That'll be fine. I never had such fun in all my life."

We went to bed about eleven o'clock. We spread down some wide blankets and quilts and put Red Chief between us. We weren't afraid he'd run away. He kept us awake for three hours, jumping up and reaching for his rifle and screeching, "Hist! pard," in mine and Bill's ears, as the fancied crackle of a twig or the rustle of a leaf revealed to his young imagination the stealthy approach of the outlaw band. At last I fell into a troubled sleep and dreamed that I had been kidnapped and chained to a tree by a ferocious pirate with red hair.

Just at daybreak I was awakened by a series of awful screams from Bill. They weren't yells, or howls, or shouts, or whoops, or yawps, such as you'd expect from a manly set of vocal organs—they were simply indecent, terrifying, humiliating screams, such as women emit when they see ghosts or caterpillars. It's an awful thing to hear a strong, desperate, fat man scream incontinently in a cave at daybreak.

I jumped up to see what the matter was. Red Chief was sitting on Bill's chest, with one hand twined in Bill's hair. In the other he had the sharp case-knife we used for slicing bacon; and he was industriously and realistically trying to take Bill's scalp, according to the sentence that had been pronounced upon him the evening before.

I got the knife away from the kid and made him lie down again. But from that moment Bill's spirit was broken. He laid down on his side of the bed, but he never closed an eye again in sleep as long as that boy was with us. I dozed off for a while, but along toward sunup I remembered that Red Chief had said I was to be burned at the stake at the rising of the sun. I wasn't nervous or afraid; but I sat up and lit my pipe and leaned against a rock.

"What are you getting up so soon for, Sam?" ~~asked Bill~~.

"Me?" ~~says~~ I. "Oh, I got a kind of a pain in my shoulder. I thought sitting up would rest it."

"You're a liar!" ~~says Bill~~. "You're afraid. You was to be burned at sunrise, and you was afraid he'd do it. And he would, too, if he could find a match. Ain't it awful, Sam? Do you think anybody will pay out money to get a little imp like that back home?"

~~"Sure," said I. "A rowdy kid like that is just the kind the parents dote on. Now, you and the Chief get up and cook breakfast, while I go up on the top of this mountain and reconnoitre."~~

~~I went up on the peak on the little mountain and ran my eye over the contiguous vicinity. Over toward Summit I expected to see the sturdy yeomanry of the village armed with scythes and pitchforks beating the countryside for the dastardly kidnappers. But what I saw was a peaceful landscape dotted with one man plowing with a dun mule. Nobody was dragging the creek; no couriers dashed hither and yon, bringing tidings of no news to the distracted parents. There was a sylvan attitude of somnolent~~

YOUR ROLE IN ORAL INTERPRETATION

sleepiness pervading that section of the external outward surface of Alabama that lay exposed to my view. "Perhaps," says I to myself, "it has not yet been discovered that the wolves have borne away the tender lambkin from the fold. Heaven help the wolves!" says I, and I went down the mountain to get breakfast.

When I got to the cave I found Bill backed up against the side of it, breathing hard, and the boy threatening to smash him with a rock half as big as a cocoanut.

"He put a red-hot boiled potato down my back," explained Bill, and then mashed it with his foot; "and I boxed his ears. Have you got a gun about you, Sam?"

I took the rock away from the boy and kind of patched up the argument. "I'll fix you," says the kid to Bill. "No man ever struck the Red Chief but what he got paid for it. You better beware!"

After breakfast the kid takes a piece of leather with strings wrapped around it out of his pocket and goes outside the cave unwinding it.

"What's he up to now?" says Bill anxiously. "You don't think he'll run away, do you, Sam?"

"No fear of it," says I. "He don't seem to be much of a home body. But we've got to fix up some plan about the ransom. There don't seem to be much excitement around Summit on account of his disappearance; but maybe they haven't realized yet that he's gone. His folks may think he's spending the night with Aunt Jane or one of the neighbors. Anyhow he'll be missed today. Tonight we must get a message to his father demanding the two thousand dollars for his return."

Just then we heard a kind of war whoop, such as David might have emitted when he knocked out the champion Goliath. It was a sling that Red Chief had pulled out of his pocket, and he was whirling it around his head.

I dodged and heard a heavy thud and a kind of sigh from Bill, like a horse gives out when you take his saddle off. A rock the size of an egg had caught Bill just behind his left ear. He loosened himself all over and fell in the fire across the frying pan of hot water for washing the dishes. I dragged him out and poured cold water on his head for half an hour.

~~By and by Bill sits up and feels behind his ear and says, "Sam, do you know who my favorite Biblical character is?"~~

~~"Take it easy," says I. "You'll come to your senses presently."~~

~~"King Herod," says he. "You won't go away and leave me here alone, will you, Sam?"~~

I went out and caught that boy and shook him until his freckles rattled.

"If you don't behave," ~~says I,~~ "I'll take you straight home. Now, are you going to be good, or not?"

"I was only funning," ~~says he sullenly~~. "I didn't mean to hurt Old Hank. But what did he hit me for? I'll behave, Snake-eye, if you won't send me home, and if you'll let me play the Black Scout today."

"I don't know the game," ~~says I~~. "That's for you and Mr. Bill to decide. He's your playmate for the day. I'm going away for a while on business. Now, you come in and make friends with him and say you are sorry for hurting him, or home you go at once."

I made him and Bill shake hands, and then I took Bill aside and told him I was going to Poplar Cove, a little village three miles from the cave, and find out what I could about how the kidnapping had been regarded in Summit. Also, I thought it best to send a peremptory letter to old man Dorset that day, demanding the ransom and dictating how it should be paid.

~~"You know, Sam," says Bill, "I've stood by you without batting an eye in earthquakes, fire, and flood—in poker games, dynamite outrages, police raids, train robberies, and cyclones. I never lost my nerve yet till we kidnapped that two-legged skyrocket of a kid. He's got me going. You won't leave me long with him, will you, Sam?"~~

YOUR ROLE IN ORAL INTERPRETATION

"I'll be back some time this afternoon," says I. "You must keep the boy amused and quiet till I return. And now we'll write the letter to old Dorset."

Bill and I got paper and pencil and worked on the letter while Red Chief, with a blanket wrapped around him, strutted up and down, guarding the mouth of the cave. Bill begged me tearfully to make the ransom fifteen hundred dollars instead of two thousand. "~~I ain't attempting,~~" ~~says he, "to decry the celebrated moral aspect of parental affection, but we're dealing with humans, and it ain't human for anybody to give up two thousand dollars for that forty-pound chunk of freckled wildcat. I'm willing to take a chance at fifteen hundred dollars. You can charge the difference up to me.~~"

So, to relieve Bill, I acceded, and we collaborated a letter that ran this way:

Ebenezer Dorset, Esq.:

We have your boy concealed in a place far from Summit. It is useless for you or the most skillful detectives to attempt to find him. Absolutely the only terms on which you can have him restored to you are these: We demand fifteen hundred dollars in large bills for his return; the money to be left at midnight tonight at the same spot and in the same box as your reply—as hereinafter described. If you agree to these terms, send your answer in writing by a solitary messenger tonight at half-past eight o'clock. After crossing Owl Creek on the road to Poplar Cove, there are three large trees about a hundred yards apart close to the fence of the wheat field on the right-hand side. At the bottom of the fencepost opposite the third tree will be found a small pasteboard box.

The messenger will place the answer in this box and return immediately to Summit.

If you attempt any treachery or fail to comply with our demands stated, you will never see your boy again.

If you pay the money as demanded, he will be returned to you safe and well within three hours. These terms are final and if you do not accede to them no further communication will be attempted.

Two Desperate Men

I addressed this letter to Dorset and put it in my pocket. As I was about to start, the kid comes up to me and says:

"Aw, Snake-eye, you said I could play the Black Scout while you was gone."

"Play it, of course," ~~says I~~. "Mr. Bill will play with you. What kind of a game is it?"

"I'm the Black Scout," ~~says Red Chief~~, "and I have to ride to the stockade to warn the settlers that the Indians are coming. I'm tired of playing Indian myself. I want to be the Black Scout."

"All right," ~~says I~~. "It sounds harmless to me. I guess Mr. Bill will help you foil the pesky savages."

"What am I to do?" ~~asks Bill, looking at the kid suspiciously.~~

"You are the hoss," ~~says Black Scout~~. "Get down on your hands and knees. How can I ride to the stockade without a hoss?"

"You better keep him interested," ~~said I,~~ "till we get the scheme going. Loosen up."

Bill gets down on his all fours, and a look comes in his eye like a rabbit's when you catch it in a trap.

"How far is it to the stockade, kid?" ~~he asks in a husky manner of voice~~.

"Ninety miles," ~~says the Black Scout~~. "And you have to hump yourself to get there on time. Whoa, now!"

The Black Scout jumps on Bill's back and digs his heels in his side.

"For Heaven's sake," ~~says Bill,~~ "hurry back, Sam, as soon as you can. I wish we hadn't made the ransom more than a thousand. Say, you quit kicking me or I'll get up and warm you good."

I walked over to Poplar Cove and sat around the post-office and store, ~~talking with the chawbacons that came in to trade~~. One whiskerando, [old man] says that he hears Summit is all upset on account of Elder Ebenezer Dorset's boy having been lost or stolen. That was all I wanted to know. ~~I bought some smoking tobacco, referred casually to the price of black-eyed peas, posted my letter surreptitiously, and came away. The postmaster said the mail carrier would come by in an hour to take the mail on to Summit.~~

When I got back to the cave, Bill and the boy were not to be found. ~~I explored the vicinity of the cave and risked a yodel or two, but there was no response.~~

~~So I lighted my pipe and sat down on a mossy bank to await developments.~~

In about half an hour I heard the bushes rustle, and Bill wabbled out into the little glade in front of the cave. Behind him was the kid, stepping softly like a scout, with a broad grin on his face. Bill stopped, took off his hat, and wiped his face with a red handkerchief. The kid stopped about eight feet behind him.

"Sam," ~~says Bill~~, "I suppose you'll think I'm a renegade, but I couldn't help it. ~~I'm a grown person with masculine proclivities and habits of self-defense, but there is a time when all systems of egotism and predominance fail.~~ The boy is gone. I have sent him home. All is off. ~~There was martyrs in old times," goes on Bill, "that suffered death rather than give up the particular graft they enjoyed. None of 'em ever was subjugated to such supernatural tortures as I have~~ been. I tried to be faithful to our articles of depredation; but there came a limit."

"What's the trouble, Bill?" ~~I asks him.~~

"I was rode," ~~says Bill~~, "the ninety miles to the stockade, not barring an inch. Then, when the settlers was rescued, I was given oats. Sand ain't a palatable substitute. ~~And then, for an hour I had to try to explain to him why there was nothin' in holes, how a road can run both ways, and what makes the grass green. I tell you, Sam, a~~

~~human can only stand so much~~. I takes him by the neck of his clothes and drags him down the mountain. ~~On the way he kicks my legs black-and-blue from the knees down; and I've got to have two or three bites on my thumb and hand cauterized~~.

"But he's gone" ~~continues Bill~~ "gone home. ~~I showed him the road to Summit and kicked him about eight feet nearer there at one kick~~. I'm sorry we lose the ransom; but it was either that or Bill Driscoll to the madhouse."

~~Bill is puffing and blowing, but there is a look of ineffable peace and growing content on his rose-pink features.~~

"Bill," ~~says I~~, "there isn't heart disease in your family, is there?"

"No," ~~says Bill~~, "nothing chronic except malaria and accidents. Why?"

"Then you might turn around," ~~says I~~, "and have a look behind you."

Bill turns and sees the boy, and loses his complexion and sits down plump on the ground and begins to pluck aimlessly at grass and little sticks. ~~For an hour~~ I was afraid for his mind. And then I told him that my scheme was to put the whole job through immediately, and that we would get the ransom and be off with it by midnight if old Dorset fell in with our proposition. ~~So Bill braced up enough to give the kid a weak sort of a smile and a promise to play the Russian in a Japanese war with him as soon as he felt a little better.~~

I had a scheme for collecting that ransom, ~~without danger of being caught by counterplots~~, that ought to commend itself to professional kidnappers. The tree under which the answer was to be left—and the money later on—was close to the road fence with big bare fields on all sides. ~~If a gang of constables should be watching for anyone to come for the note, they could see him a long way off crossing the fields or in the road. But no, sirree!~~ At half-past eight I was up in that tree as well hidden as a tree toad, waiting for the messenger to arrive.

Exactly on time a half-grown boy rides up the road on a bicycle, locates the pasteboard box at the foot of the fence posts, slips a folded piece of paper into it, and pedals away again back toward Summit.

I waited an hour and then concluded the thing was square. I slid down the tree, got the note, slipped along the fence till I struck the woods, and was back at the cave in another half an hour. I opened the note, got near the lantern, and read it to Bill. It was written with a pen in a crabbed hand, and the sum and substance of it was this:

Two Desperate Men.

Gentlemen: I received your letter today by post, in regard to the ransom you asked for the return of my son. I think you are a little high in your demands, and I hereby make you a counter-proposition, which I am inclined to believe you will accept. You bring Johnny home and pay me two hundred and fifty dollars in cash, and I agree to take him off your hands. You had better come at night, for the neighbors believe he is lost, and I couldn't be responsible for what they would do to anybody they saw bringing him back.

Very respectfully,

Ebenezer Dorset

"Great pirates of Penzance!" says I. "Of all the impudent—"

But I glanced at Bill and hesitated. He had the most appealing look in his eyes I ever saw on the face of a dumb or a talking brute.

"Sam," says he, "what's two hundred and fifty dollars after all? We've got the money. One more night of this kid will send me to a bed in Bedlam. Besides being a thorough gentlemen, I think Mr. Dorset is a spendthrift for making us such a liberal offer. You ain't going to let the chance go, are you?"

"Tell you the truth, Bill," says I, "this little ewe lamb has somewhat got on my nerves too. We'll take him home, pay the ransom, and make our get-away."

We took him home that night. We got him to go by telling him that his father had bought a silver-mounted rifle and a pair of moccasins for him and we were going to hunt bears the next day.

It was just twelve o'clock when we knocked at Ebenezer's front door. Just at the moment when I should have been abstracting the fifteen hundred dollars from the box under the tree, according to the original proposition, Bill was counting out two hundred and fifty dollars into Dorset's hand.

When the kid found out we were going to leave him at home, he started up a howl like a calliope and fastened himself as tight as a leech to Bill's leg. His father peeled him away gradually, like a porous plaster.

"How long can you hold him?" asks Bill.

"I'm not as strong as I used to be," says old Dorset, "but I think I can promise you ten minutes."

"Enough," says Bill. "In ten minutes I shall cross the Central, Southern, and Middle Western States, and be legging it trippingly for the Canadian border." And, as dark as it was, and as fat as Bill was, and as good a runner as I am, he was a good mile and a half out of Summit before I could catch up with him.

One additional problem in the reading of narrative is that there is a tendency to bring vitality and life to the dialogue sections and then a temptation to drop vitality, interest, and color in the reading of the descriptive, narrative, and expository sections. The mood the author intended to create in his story, the explanations he felt necessary for the total effect are vitally important. They are the framework around which the plot revolves and they are the setting in which the characters move. So it is a purely mechanical reading

YOUR ROLE IN ORAL INTERPRETATION

that emphasizes dialogue only and forgets the reasons for the dialogue. In addition, much of the suspense is built in the expository and narrative sections.

For example, Ernest Hemingway's *The Old Man And the Sea* has very little dialogue. Yet, the battle of the old man to catch the big fish and then to get it back to land is a vital, exciting, emotionally moving battle—the core of the book. The reader cannot go over any of these sections lightly. He must use a faster pace in the exciting sections dealing with the catch itself; he must show the relief when he lands the fish; he must indicate the panic the old man feels as the sharks attack the big fish.

One final short story is included here for your study. No cutting has been done. Read the story and decide what must be done to make it an effective and very real account of the feelings of the two officers who have the awesome task of burying a comrade on the battlefield.

THE UPTURNED FACE

STEPHEN CRANE

"What will we do now?" said the adjutant, troubled and excited.

"Bury him," said Timothy Lean.

The two officers looked down close to their toes where lay the body of their comrade. The face was chalk-blue; gleaming eyes stared at the sky. Over the two upright figures was a windy sound of bullets, and on the top of the hill Lean's prostrate company of Spitzbergen infantry was firing measured volleys.

"Don't you think it would be better . . ." began the adjutant. "We might leave him until tomorrow." "No," said Lean. "I can't hold that post an hour longer. I've got to fall back, and we've got to bury old Bill."

"Of course," said the adjutant, at once ."Your men got entrenching tools?"

Lean shouted back to his little line, and two men came slowly, one with a pick, one with a shovel. They started in the direction of the Rostina sharpshooters. Bullets cracked near their ears. "Dig here," said Lean gruffly. The men, thus caused to lower their glances to the turf, became hurried and frightened, merely because they could not look to see whence the bullets came. The dull beat of the pick striking the earth sounded amid the swift snap of close bullets. Presently the other private began to shovel.

"I suppose," said the adjutant, slowly, "we'd better search his clothes for—things."

Lean nodded. Together in curious abstraction they looked at the body. Then Lean stirred his shoulders suddenly, arousing himself.

"Yes," he said, "we'd better see what he's got." He dropped to his knees, and his hands approached the body of the dead officer. But his hands wavered over the buttons of the tunic. The first button was brick-red with drying blood, and he did not seem to dare touch it.

"Go on," said the adjutant, hoarsely.

Lean stretched his wooden hand, and his fingers fumbled with the blood-stained buttons. At last he rose with ghastly face. He had gathered a watch, a whistle, a pipe, a tobacco-pouch, a handkerchief, a little case of cards and papers. He looked at the adjutant. There was a silence. The adjutant was feeling that he had been a coward to make Lean do all the grisly business.

"Well," said Lean, "that's all, I think. You have his sword and revolver?"

"Yes," said the adjutant, his face working, and then he burst out in a sudden strange fury at the two privates. "Why don't you hurry up with that grave? What are you doing, anyhow? Hurry, do you hear? I never saw such stupid . . ." Even as he cried out in his passion the two men were laboring for their lives. Ever overhead the bullets were spitting.

The grave was finished. It was not a masterpiece—a poor little shallow thing. Lean and the adjutant again looked at each other in a curious silent communication.

Suddenly the adjutant croaked out a weird laugh. It

YOUR ROLE IN ORAL INTERPRETATION

was a terrible laugh, which had its origin in that part of the mind which is first moved by the singing of the nerves. "Well," he said humorously to Lean, "I suppose we had best tumble him in."

"Yes," said the adjutant. Then, apparently remembering that he had made Lean search the body, he stooped with great fortitude and took hold of the dead officer's clothing. Lean joined him. Both were particular that their fingers should not feel the corpse.

They tugged away; the corpse lifted, heaved, toppled, flopped into the grave, and the two officers, straightening, looked again at each other—they were always looking at each other. They sighed with relief.

The adjutant said, "I suppose we should—we should say something. Do you know the service, Tim?"

"They don't read the service until the grave is filled in," said Lean, pressing his lips to an academic expression.

"Don't they?" said the adjutant, shocked that he had made the mistake. "Oh, well," he cried, suddenly, "let us—let us say something—while he can hear us."

"All right," said Lean. "Do you know the service?"

"I can't remember a line of it," said the adjutant.

Lean was extremely dubious. "I can repeat two lines, but . . ."

"Well, do it," said the adjutant. "Go as far as you can. That's better than nothing. And the beasts have got our range exactly."

Lean looked at his two men. "Attention," he barked. The privates came to attention with a click, looking much aggrieved. The adjutant lowered his helmet to his knee. Lean, bareheaded, stood over the grave. The Rostina sharpshooters fired briskly.

"O Father, our friend has sunk in the deep waters of death, but his spirit has leaped toward Thee as the bubble arises from the lips of the drowning. Perceive, we beseech, O Father, the little flying bubble, and . . ."

Lean, although husky and ashamed, had suffered no hesitation up to this point, but he stopped with a hopeless feeling and looked at the corpse.

The adjutant moved uneasily, "And from Thy superb heights . . ." he began and then he too came to an end.

"And from Thy superb heights," said Lean.

The adjutant suddenly remembered a phrase in the back part of the Spitzbergen burial service, and he exploited it with the triumphant manner of a man who has recalled everything and can go on.

"O God, have mercy. . . ."

"O God, have mercy . . ." said Lean.

"Mercy," repeated the adjutant, in quick failure.

"Mercy," said Lean. And then he was moved by some violence of feeling, for he turned suddenly upon his two men and tigerishly said, "Throw the dirt in."

The fire of the Rostina sharpshooters was accurate and continuous.

One of the aggrieved privates came forward with his shovel. He lifted his first shovel-load of earth, and for a moment of inexplicable hesitation it was held poised above this corpse, which from its chalk-blue face looked keenly out from the grave. Then the soldier emptied his shovel on—on the feet.

Timothy Lean felt as if tons had been swiftly lifted from off his forehead. He had felt that perhaps the private might empty the shovel on—on the face. It had been emptied on the feet. There was a great point gained there—ha, ha!—the first shovelful had been emptied on the feet. How satisfactory!

The adjutant began to babble. "Well, of course—a man we've messed with all these years—impossible—you can't, you know, leave your intimate friends rotting on the field. Go on, for God's sake, and shovel, you."

The man with the shovel suddenly ducked, grabbed his left arm with his right hand, and looked at his officers for orders. Lean picked the shovel from the ground. "Go to the rear," he said to the wounded man. He also addressed the other private. "You get under cover, too; I'll finish this business."

The wounded man scrambled hard still for the top of

YOUR ROLE IN ORAL INTERPRETATION

the ridge without devoting any glances to the direction from whence the bullets came, and the other man followed at an equal pace; but he was different, in that he looked back anxiously three times.

This is merely the way—often—of the hit and unhit.

Timothy Lean filled the shovel, hesitated, and, in a movement which was like a gesture of abhorrence, he flung the dirt into the grave, and as it landed it made a sound—plop. Lean suddenly stopped and mopped his brow—a tired laborer.

"Perhaps we have been wrong," said the adjutant. His glance wavered stupidly. "It might have been better if we hadn't buried him just at this time. Of course, if we advance tomorrow the body would have been . . ."

"Damn you," said Lean, "shut your mouth." He was not the senior officer.

He again filled the shovel and flung the earth. Always the earth made that sound—plop. For a space Lean worked frantically, like a man digging himself out of danger.

Soon there was nothing to be seen but the chalk-blue face. Lean filled the shovel. "Good God," he cried to the adjutant. "Why didn't you turn him somehow when you put him in? This . . ." Then Lean began to stutter.

The adjutant understood. He was pale to the lips. "Go on, man," he cried, beseechingly, almost in a shout.

Lean swung back the shovel. It went forward in a pendulum curve. When the earth landed it made a sound —plop.

Summary

Prose is generally categorized as fiction and nonfiction. Nonfiction concerns itself primarily with explanation and persuasion. It finds its outlet through essays, editorials, diaries, histories, and letters. Fiction finds its outlet through short stories, novels, fables, and tales.

Prose may also be looked at in another way as descriptive, expository, and narrative. Descriptive prose is marked by its reliance on imagery. When cutting descriptive prose, follow the general rule to cut down but not out. Retain the most vivid elements of descriptive writing.

Expository prose is writing which concerns itself directly, by way of explanation or persuasion, with ideas or principles.

Narrative prose tells a story. It has setting, plot, and characters, and moves through one or more climaxes. It is characterized by action. It combines suspense, romance, excitement, tragedy, and comedy all at once in one selection and treats any one of them alone in another selection.

Several general rules for effective cutting of narrative prose should be considered:

1. Choose a selection that generally fits time requirements. Then cutting will be minimal.
2. Cut minor characters.
3. Where possible cut in large segments rather than in small bits.
4. Paraphrase in order not to leave large gaps in meaning.
5. Cut "he said's" wherever possible.
6. Be certain that neither the author's purpose nor his style has been distorted by your cutting.

❧ CHAPTER 11

How do I read drama?

DRAMA IS A MIRROR OF LIFE. It comments on social problems, on matters of national and international importance, on the weakness, strengths, and foibles of human nature—on life itself. It is often born of narrative prose, but it creates vivid life from the silent pages of a book.

The History of Drama

It is in the oral reading of drama that most theorists clash. The conflict between drama and oral interpretation has been dealt with in a previous chapter. Actually, drama and oral interpretation are closely allied in their respective histories. Drama was the original form. It is older than religion. Theatre began with the first man who thought that by imitating animals around the camp fire he could increase the game and insure good hunting. As man moved past the imitative stage and began to express himself in dance and in rituals, drama and theatre as such moved with him.

Such was drama until the classical period in Greece when theatre took on its first genuine form. Greek theatre concentrated on three types of plays: tragedies, based on noble themes and heroic legends of the gods; satyrs, burlesques of such legends; and comedies, dealing with the farcical aspects of human life. Drama, in Greece, grew out of the dithyramb, a choral hymn of praise to Dionysus, the god of wine and fertility. Later, the first actor was born when Thespis moved out of the chorus and took on the role of narrator and later became a specific character. From this time on drama became a vital part of the cultural life of the Greeks. Plays were given in open-air amphitheatres, and, for the most part, the themes were noble and tragic, although such writers as Aristophanes chose to satirize life.

Greece produced such playwrights as Sophocles, Asechylus, Euripides, and Aristophanes. Interestingly enough, masks were used in many of the plays for character differentiation. Many interpretative students would probably prefer using masks today rather than be faced with the need to create character differences through vocal and bodily interpretation.

As was the case with oral interpretation, when the cultural life of Greece died, the theatre largely died with it, not to return until the Middle Ages when it was reborn within the church. It had been the church's resentment of prior secular activities that had helped to bring about the demise of the theatre. In Rome, for instance, theatre was very undistinguished, with emphasis on games and dances in celebration of sports and on the bawdy and the immoral.

When drama did return, it was part of the High Mass; words or chants were offered in the service. Soon, however, when both rituals and priests began to be satirized and bawdy references to sex and immorality took over, the church banned such plays. The companies, made up of members of craft guilds—labor unions of the time—then moved out of doors. They went from town to town on wagons, displaying their theatrical wares. The themes most in favor were dramatizations of the Old and New Testaments—and the ever present bawdy satirical interpretations of the theological doctrines.

By the time of the Renaissance, there was renewed interest in drama, as there had been in oral reading. But the period was marked by a lack of actual plays. One of the most popular forms of entertainment in Italy was the commedia dell'arte where a "situation" was improvised and jokes were interjected into what little plot there was. The characters again wore masks and highly colored costumes, and uninhibited actions and comedy were primary features.

It was in Spain that playwriting as an art began to emerge, principally in the persons of Lope de Rueda, Lope de Vega, Cervantes, and Calderon.

England was also seeing a rebirth of drama. Plays were acted for both the courts and the public, and gruesome, rather bloody stories were popular. This paralleled the writings of Seneca in the oral reading field. Then, in the last half of the reign of Queen

Elizabeth, theatre was suddenly shot into orbit with the writings of such playwrights as Christopher Marlowe, Thomas Kyd, Ben Jonson, and, of course, William Shakespeare.

In France there was a good deal of activity; mystery plays, those with basically religious themes, were given in open fields, public squares, palaces, and even cemeteries. Corneille, Racine, and Molière were the classic contributors to the drama, although Alexandre Hardy was the first professional playwright of France. It was Molière, however, who with his brilliantly satirical comedies brought lustre to French drama. Many of his plays are performed today, such as *Tartuffe, Le Malade Imaginaire, The School for Wives, Le Bourgeois Gentilhomme,* and *The Doctor in Spite of Himself.* Any of these plays today provide excellent material for the oral interpreter.

In England, with the advent of Cromwell and the upsurge of the Puritan theology, the theatre died down, but it was later given new life, a new spice, with the Restoration period. A favorite theme was heartless seduction and sophisticated evil, and Sir George Etherege, William Congreve, and William Wycherley were three of the most noted playwrights. Wycherley's *Country Wife* is performed even today. The period also saw the emergence of the first actress on stage—up to this time young boys had played the women's roles—and the appearance of David Garrick, England's greatest actor.

The eighteenth century was also distinguished by the fine comedies of Oliver Goldsmith and Richard Brinsley Sheridan. Goldsmith's *She Stoops to Conquer* and Sheridan's *The Rivals* and *School for Scandal* are popular comedies and offer good scenes for interpretative reading. John Gay was another who achieved fame with his *The Beggar's Opera,* from which *The Threepenny Opera* was taken.

Drama was also moving ahead in Germany with the works of Johann Friedrich Schiller and Goethe. The latter's *Faust* is one of the world's best known dramas.

In the nineteenth century, all over Europe, romanticism and melodrama were popular, but the theatre began to emerge as a medium for social protest. Henrik Ibsen became one of the most vocal figures with such plays as *Hedda Gabler, Ghosts, The Master Builder,* and others. And in France, Emile Zola and André Antoine spearheaded, through the Theatre Libre, the movement called "naturalism." It was a move to bring to drama the utter reality and naturalness of life, to escape from some of the artifices and excesses that had invaded the theatre in some areas. In a way it paralleled the naturalist vs. mechanical conflict of the elocution period.

In Russia at the time there emerged a man who exerted one of the greatest influences on drama and on acting—Constantine Stanislavsky. His work with the Moscow Art Theatre remains even today an integral part of the growth of drama. His was a protest against all the old ideas of acting, the falseness, the artifices; it was an attempt to bring in a more realistic approach to the art of acting. Some of his theories of characterization could be studied advantageously by interpreters without, of course, the emphasis on such total involvement.

And so we enter the twentieth century with the works of such playwrights as Eugene O'Neill, who, in his way, adapted techniques from the past. He borrowed the use of masks from the Greeks in *Great God Brown* and based *Mourning Becomes Electra* on the Greek trilogy. His *Long Day's Journey Into Night* is an expression of nineteenth-century naturalism, and he has also dealt in noble terms with the problems of today.

Arthur Miller has been an extension of O'Neill's tragic themes with such plays as *Death of a Salesman, After the Fall,* and *Incident at Vichy;* Tennessee Williams has provided further probing into the weaknesses of mankind with such works as *Streetcar Named Desire, Suddenly Last Summer,* and *Glass Menagerie.*

It was in the latter part of the nineteenth century and the first part of the twentieth century that one of the greatest satirists and social protesters arose—George Bernard Shaw. His *Mrs. Warren's Profession* is a biting social commentary; *Major Barbara* deals with religion; and his *Pygmalion* has achieved world-wide fame in both the play form, and as a Broadway musical and a movie known as *My Fair Lady.* Among his other works are *Arms and the Man, Caesar and Cleopatra,* and *St. Joan.*

The modern day drama has also seen the emergence of a form of playwriting known as avant-garde—an outgrowth of surrealism and existentialism which unites often obscure philosophy and drama. It has also been called the "theatre of the absurd" and projects reality beyond logic and literal observation. Some of the more notable examples are Eugene Ionesco's *The Chairs* and *The Bald Soprano,* Jean-Paul Sartre's *No Exit,* Jean Genet's *The Balcony,* and Samuel Beckett's *Waiting for Godot.*

Thus drama continues to move and to change both in theory and style, just as oral interpretation does. The two have a very similar history.

YOUR ROLE IN ORAL INTERPRETATION

Structure of the Play

A play is a story—or at times an idea—told in dialogue form. Usually it contains three acts, although in the beginning there was no specific act separation. Plays went to five acts during Shakespeare's time, then to four and finally three. There are, of course, exceptions. Structurally, the form can vary. John Osborne's *Inadmissible Evidence* has two acts; Peter Weiss' *The Investigation* is not divided into acts. Eugene O'Neill's *Long Day's Journey Into Night* has four acts but his *Mourning Becomes Electra* is comprised of three plays, the first having four acts, the second five, and third four. O'Neill also separated his *Strange Interlude* into two parts with the first having five acts and the second four. He has been noted for the marathon length of his works—as well as for his brilliant use of dialogue and characterization. It was not unusual, in such plays as *Electra* and *Strange Interlude,* for the play to begin at 7:30 P.M. and end at midnight.

Some have considered that a play must have a theme, thesis, root idea, central idea, goal, aim, driving force, subject, purpose, plan, plot. But, according to Lajos Egri in his noted book on playwriting, *The Art of Dramatic Writing*, ". . . we choose the word 'premise' because it contains all the elements the other words try to express and because it is less subject to misinterpretation."[1] It is his feeling that no idea or situation was strong enough to provide a basis for a play. It must have a premise. It must head down a certain road. It must be about something.

Whatever theory is used, there is one common requirement—plays must have conflict. Certainly Mr. Egri's theory provides that essential. And certainly the reader must know the premise if he is to interpret the play meaningfully.

Stylistically speaking, plays have employed all forms or writing techniques. They have gone from the poetic form of the Greek drama to the blank verse of Shakespeare, a form also used by such modern playwrights as Maxwell Anderson in his *Winterset, Elizabeth the Queen,* and *Mary of Scotland.* Plays have also been written in almost a newspaper documentary style, as in the days of German expressionism and the "Living Newspaper" during the Depression

---

[1] Lajos Egri, The *Art of Dramatic Writing*, (New York, 1960) p. 2.

in America. A similar technique was recently used in *The Investigation*. O'Neill used a different style in *Strange Interlude*, adopting
the form of spoken thoughts similar to the "asides" in earlier melo-
dramas, although his was a far more extensive use of the device
whereby an actor speaks to the audience about what is happening
on stage—with the other actors on stage supposedly not able to hear
the comments. Generally speaking, though, the dialogue and style
of most plays are in realistic conversational form, and the three act
division is by far the most often used.

The general structure of a play is as follows: The playwright
introduces the primary problem, the conflict, and the characters of
importance usually in the first act. In the second act the conflict is
extended, new characters may be introduced, but definite steps are
taken towards the resolution of the conflict. However, as is most
often the case, the crisis, the height of the conflict, the moment of
decision where the characters turn one way or the other occurs at
the end of the second act. The third act provides the resolution of
the problem—or the submission to it—and completes the roles the
characters play in the conflict.

Let us take for an example Eugene O'Neill's autobiographical
play, *Long Day's Journey Into Night*. In the first act we meet
Tyrone, his sons Jamie and Edmund, and his wife, Mary. We learn
of the family's concern over Mary's addiction to dope and we also
learn what brought it about. We see their hope that she may be able
to defeat the addiction, but by the end of the first act we know she
is not going to win her battle. We also learn of Edmund's illness and
Jamie's furtive enjoyment of his "wild" life and his hatred for his
father. In Act Two we discover that Mary is back on dope and we
feel the deep disappointment her sons experience because of her
weakness. They confront her with their awareness of her relapse, as
does Tyrone, but she refuses to admit she has taken dope. The
separation of the members of the family increases. In the third act
Mary is even further under the influence. Her mind wanders continually back to the past and the life she once had. We learn more
of what makes Mary what she is. She completely rejects Tyrone's
condemnation for taking the dope. In the fourth act the family has
given up hope. Edmund resents his father for the penny-pinching
actions that have led Mary to drugs and have resulted in his,
Edmund's, being sent to a state hospital to be treated for consump-
tion. Jamie has left the house in anger to spend the night in town
drinking and whoring. Tyrone tries to explain why he has been so
careful with money by telling Edmund of his own unhappy, poverty-

YOUR ROLE IN ORAL INTERPRETATION

ridden childhood. Then Edmund tells his father what matters to him in life. Jamie returns after Tyrone has left and gives Edmund an account of his night—and then in a drunken and bitter moment of revelation he tells of his jealousy and hatred for Edmund because the latter has been given most of his parents' attention. Jamie brokenly confesses at the same time his love for his brother but lets us feel the depth of his aloneness. Tyrone joins his sons, condemns Jamie again for a wasted life, and at this moment Mary enters the room, now totally under the influence of dope—totally unaware of her family in the room. The final tragedy is complete. Hope has been utterly destroyed. There is no illusion.

The play extends, time-wise, from dawn to late night, and in that brief period we see the cross-currents, the complexities, the tragedies of the lives of four people.

Division into acts can also call for further division. Many times an act will be divided into scenes. Such a form is often necessary for a change in scenery within the act or for purposes of climactic structure. Each scene has its own minor climax building to the major climax and final resolution.

In spite of such division, however, the play must move smoothly from one new development to another without any abrupt change in continuity. This is not, of course, true of the structure of such plays as *The Chairs* or *Mother Courage* by Brecht or *Endgame* by Beckett as these purposely employ sudden and jarring changes of thought and idea because they were written as an existentialist revolt against the rigid structuring of writing. But the average play moves with smooth transitions.

Richard Brinsley Sheridan's *The School for Scandal* is carefully plotted. Each scene moves into another one smoothly, but the scenes are complete within themselves. An excellent example is the famous closet scene.

Excerpt from THE SCHOOL FOR SCANDAL

RICHARD BRINSLEY SHERIDAN

(*A Library in Joseph Surface's House. Joseph Surface and Servant.*)

JOSEPH SURFACE.   No letter from Lady Teazle?

SERVANT.   No, sir.

JOSEPH SURFACE (*aside*).   I am surprised she has not sent, if she is prevented from coming. Sir Peter certainly does not suspect me. Yet I wish I may not lose the heiress through the scrape I have drawn myself into with the wife. However, Charles's imprudence and bad character are great points in my favor.

(*Knocking*)

SERVANT. Sir, I believe that must be Lady Teazle.

JOSEPH SURFACE. Hold! See whether it is or not before you go to the door. I have a particular message for you if it should be my brother.

SERVANT. 'Tis her ladyship, sir; she always leaves the chair at the milliner's in the next street.

JOSEPH SURFACE. Stay, stay! Draw that screen before the window—that will do. My opposite neighbor is a maiden lady of so curious a temper.

(*Servant draws the screen, and exits*)

I have a difficult hand to play in this affair. Lady Teazle has lately suspected my views on Maria; but she must by no means be let into that secret—at least, till I have her more in my power.

(*Enter Lady Teazle*)

LADY TEAZLE. What, sentiment in soliloquy now? Have you been very impatient? O lud! don't pretend to look grave. I vow I couldn't come before.

JOSEPH SURFACE. O madam, punctuality is a species of constancy very unfashionable in a lady of quality.

LADY TEAZLE. Upon my word, you ought to pity me. Do you know Sir Peter is grown so ill-natured to me of late, and so jealous of Charles too—that's the best of the story, isn't it?

JOSEPH SURFACE (*aside*). I am glad my scandalous friends keep that up.

LADY TEAZLE. I am sure I wish he would let Maria marry him, and then perhaps he would be convinced; don't you, Mr. Surface?

JOSEPH SURFACE (*aside*). Indeed I do not—(*aloud*) Oh, certainly I do! for then my dear Lady Teazle would also be convinced how wrong her suspicions were of my having any design on the silly girl.

YOUR ROLE IN ORAL INTERPRETATION

LADY TEAZLE. Well, well, I'm inclined to believe you. But isn't it provoking to have the most ill-natured things said of one? And there's my friend Lady Sneerwell has circulated I don't know how many scandalous tales of me, and all without any foundation, too; that's what vexes me.

JOSEPH SURFACE. Ay, madam, to be sure, that is the provoking circumstance—without foundation. Yes, yes, there's the mortification, indeed; for, when a scandalous story is believed against one, there certainly is no comfort like the consciousness of having deserved it.

LADY TEAZLE. No, to be sure, then I'd forgive their malice; but to attack me, who am really so innocent, and who never say an ill-natured thing of anybody—that is, of any friend; and then Sir Peter, too, to have him so peevish, and so suspicious, when I know the integrity of my own heart—indeed 'tis monstrous!

JOSEPH SURFACE. But, my dear Lady Teazle, 'tis your own fault if you suffer it. When a husband entertains a groundless suspicion of his wife, and withdraws his confidence from her, the original compact is broken, and she owes it to the honor of her sex to endeavor to outwit him.

LADY TEAZLE. Indeed! So that, if he suspects me without cause, it follows, that the best way of curing his jealousy is to give reason for't?

JOSEPH SURFACE. Undoubtedly—for your husband should never be deceived in you: and in that case it becomes you to be frail in compliment to his discernment.

LADY TEAZLE. To be sure, what you say is very reasonable, and when the consciousness of my innocence—

JOSEPH SURFACE. Ah, my dear madam, there is the great mistake; 'tis this very conscious innocence that is of the greatest prejudice to you. What is it makes you negligent of forms and careless of the world's opinion? why, the consciousness of your own innocence. What makes you thoughtless in your conduct and apt to run into a thousand little imprudences? why, the consciousness of your own innocence. What makes you impatient of Sir Peter's tem-

per, and outrageous at his suspicions? why, the consciousness of your innocence.

LADY TEAZLE. 'Tis very true!

JOSEPH SURFACE. Now, my dear Lady Teazle, if you
would but once make a trifling faux pas, you can't conceive how cautious you would grow, and how ready to
humor and agree with your husband.

LADY TEAZLE. Do you think so?

JOSEPH SURFACE. Oh, I'm sure on't! and then you would
find all scandal would cease at once, for—in short, your
character at present is like a person in a plethora, absolutely dying from too much health.

LADY TEAZLE. So, so; then I perceive your prescription is
that I must sin in my own defence, and part with my
virtue to preserve my reputation?

JOSEPH SURFACE. Exactly so, upon my credit, ma'am.

LADY TEAZLE. Well, certainly this is the oddest doctrine,
and the newest receipt for avoiding calumny.

JOSEPH SURFACE. An infallible one, believe me. Prudence, like experience, must be paid for.

LADY TEAZLE. Why, if my understanding were once
convinced—

JOSEPH SURFACE. Oh, certainly, madam, your understanding should be convinced. Yes, yes—Heaven forbid I
should persuade you to do anything you thought wrong.
No, no, I have too much honor to desire it.

LADY TEAZLE. Don't you think we may as well leave
honor out of the argument? (*rises*)

JOSEPH SURFACE. Ah, the ill effects of your country education, I see, still remain with you.

LADY TEAZLE. I doubt they do, indeed; and I will fairly
own to you, that if I could be persuaded to do wrong, it
would be by Sir Peter's ill usage sooner than your honorable logic, after all.

JOSEPH SURFACE. Then, by this hand, which he is un-
worthy of— (*taking her hand*)

(*Enter Servant*)

'Sdeath, you blockhead—what do you want?

YOUR ROLE IN ORAL INTERPRETATION

SERVANT. I beg your pardon, sir, but I thought you would not choose Sir Peter to come up without announcing him.

JOSEPH SURFACE. Sir Peter!—Oons—the devil!

LADY TEAZLE. Sir Peter! O lud! I'm ruined! I'm ruined!

SERVANT. Sir, 'twasn't I let him in.

LADY TEAZLE. Oh! I'm quite undone! What will become of me now, Mr. Logic?—Oh! mercy, he's on the stairs— I'll get behind here—and if ever I'm so imprudent again— (*Goes behind the screen*)

(*At this point, Sir Peter Teazle arrives and tells Sir Joseph he fears his wife, Lady Teazle, is being untrue to him. The man in question he believes to be Joseph's brother, Charles. Sir Peter also says he has left the bulk of his fortune to his wife, a fact that does not escape Lady Teazle as she hides behind the screen. Sir Peter then discusses his views about Joseph's alleged attention to a milliner. Their conversation is interrupted with the announcement that Charles demands admittance. Sir Peter is about to hide when he spies a skirt behind the screen, but Sir Joseph assures him it is only the milliner who has been plaguing him. Sir Peter goes into a closet. Charles enters and he and Joseph discuss Sir Peter's feelings about Charles's attentions to Lady Teazle, and Charles says he always thought it was Joseph who was being attentive to her and receiving the attentions. Joseph, not wishing Sir Peter to hear more, says Sir Peter is hiding in the closet, so Charles says he is only playing a joke on Joseph. Then Sir Peter comes out and says he knew of Joseph's interest in the milliner and she was hiding behind the screen. Charles pulls down the screen. Now continue the scene.*)

(*Joseph Surface enters just as Charles throws down the screen*)

CHARLES SURFACE. Lady Teazle, by all that's wonderful!

SIR PETER. Lady Teazle, by all that's damnable!

CHARLES SURFACE. Sir Peter, this is one of the smartest French milliners I ever saw. Egad, you seem all to have been diverting yourselves here at hide and seek, and I don't see who is out of the secret. Shall I beg your ladyship to inform me? Now a word!—Brother, will you be pleased to explain this matter? What! is Morality dumb too?—Sir Peter, though I found you in the dark, perhaps you are not so now! All mute! Well—though I can make nothing of the affair, I suppose you perfectly understand one another; so I'll leave you to yourselves. (*going*) Brother, I'm sorry to find you have given that worthy man grounds for so much uneasiness—Sir Peter! there's nothing in the world so noble as a man of sentiment!

(*Exit Charles Surface. They stand for some time looking at each other.*)

JOSEPH SURFACE. Sir Peter—notwithstanding—I confess —that appearances are against me—if you will afford me your patience—I make no doubt—but I shall explain everything to your satisfaction.

SIR PETER. If you please, sir.

JOSEPH SURFACE. The fact is, sir, that Lady Teazle, knowing my pretensions to your ward Maria—I say, sir, Lady Teazle, being apprehensive of the jealousy of your temper—and knowing my friendship to the family—she, sir, I say—called here—in order that—I might explain these pretensions—but on your coming—being apprehensive—as I said—of your jealousy—she withdrew—and this, you may depend on it, is the whole truth of the matter.

SIR PETER. A very clear account, upon my word; and I dare swear the lady will vouch for every article of it.

LADY TEAZLE. For not one word of it, Sir Peter!

SIR PETER. How! don't you think it worth while to agree in the lie?

LADY TEAZLE. There is not one syllable of truth in what that gentleman has told you.

SIR PETER. I believe you, upon my soul, ma'am!

JOSEPH SURFACE (*aside to Lady Teazle*). 'Sdeath, madam, will you betray me?

LADY TEAZLE. Good Mr. Hypocrite, by your leave, I'll speak for myself.

SIR PETER. Ay, let her alone, sir: you'll find she'll make a better story than you, without prompting.

LADY TEAZLE. Hear me, Sir Peter! I came here on no matter relating to your ward, and even ignorant of this

YOUR ROLE IN ORAL INTERPRETATION

gentleman's pretensions to her. But I came, seduced by his insidious arguments, at least to listen to his pretended passion, if not to sacrifice your honor to his baseness.

SIR PETER. Now, I believe, the truth is coming, indeed!

JOSEPH SURFACE. The woman's mad!

LADY TEAZLE. No, sir; she has recovered her senses, and your own arts have furnished her with the means. Sir Peter, I do not expect you to credit me—but the tenderness you express for me, when I am sure you could not think I was a witness to it, has penetrated so to my heart, that had I left the place without the shame of this discovery, my future life should have spoken the sincerity of my gratitude. As for that smooth-tongued hypocrite, who would have seduced the wife of his too credulous friend, while he affected honorable addresses to his ward—I behold him now in a light so truly despicable that I shall never again respect myself for having listened to him.

(*Exit Lady Teazle*)

JOSEPH SURFACE. Notwithstanding all this, Sir Peter, Heaven knows—

SIR PETER. That you are a villain! and so I leave you to your conscience.

JOSEPH SURFACE. You are too rash, Sir Peter; you shall hear me. The man who shuts out conviction by refusing to—

(*Exeunt, Joseph Surface talking*)

Physical Description

The playwright, in addition to structuring his work so that it clearly presents the story, must describe in detail what is in the set—where the doors are, what furniture is present, what kind of light is in the room. Also he must describe the characters. O'Neill goes into great detail in the description of the main characters while others deal quite superficially with character description. In *Long Day's Journey Into Night*, O'Neill lets the reader know all about the house, the people, the atmosphere.

UNDERSTANDING LITERATURE

From LONG DAY'S JOURNEY INTO NIGHT

EUGENE O'NEILL

Scene: Living room of James Tyrone's summer home on a morning in August, 1912.

At rear are two double doorways with portieres. The one at right leads into a front parlor with the formally arranged, set appearance of a room rarely occupied. The other opens on a dark, windowless back parlor, never used except as a passage from living room to dining room. Against the wall between the doorways is a small bookcase, with a picture of Shakespeare above it, containing novels by Balzac, Zola, Stendhal, philosophical and sociological works by Schopenhauer, Nietzsche, Marx, Engels, Kropotkin, Max Sterner, plays by Ibsen, Shaw, Strindberg, poetry by Swinburne, Rossetti, Wilde, Ernest Dowson, Kipling, etc. In the right wall, rear, is a screen door leading out on the porch which extends halfway around the house. Farther forward, a series of three windows looks over the front lawn to the harbor and the avenue that runs along the water front. A small wicker table and an ordinary oak desk are against the wall, flanking the windows. In the left wall, a similar series of windows looks out on the grounds in back of the house. Beneath them is a wicker couch with cushions, its head toward rear. Farther back is a large, glassed-in bookcase with sets of Dumas, Victor Hugo, Charles Lever, three sets of Shakespeare, the *World's Best Literature* in fifty large volumes, Hume's *History of England,* Thiers' *History of the Consulate and Empire,* Smollett's *History of England,* Gibbon's *Roman Empire* and miscellaneous volumes of old plays, poetry, and several histories of Ireland. The astonishing thing about these sets is that all the volumes have the look of having been read and reread.

The hardwood floor is nearly covered by a rug, inoffensive in design and color. At center is a round table with a green shaded reading lamp, the cord plugged in one of the four sockets in the chandelier above. Around the table within reading-light range are four chairs, three of them wicker armchairs, the fourth (at right front of table) a varnished oak rocker with leather bottom. It is around 8:30. Sunshine comes through the windows at right. And as the curtain rises, the family have just finished breakfast. Mary Tyrone and her husband enter together from the back parlor, coming from the dining room.

Mary is fifty-four, about medium height. She still has a young, graceful figure, a trifle plump, but showing little evidence of middle-aged waist and hips, although she is not tightly corseted. Her face is distinctly Irish in type. It must once have been extremely pretty, and is still striking. It does not match her healthy figure but is thin and pale with the bone structure prominent. Her nose is long and straight, her mouth wide with full, sensitive lips. She uses no rouge or any sort of makeup. Her high forehead is framed by thick, pure white hair. Accentuated by her pallor and white hair, her dark brown eyes appear black. They are unusually large and beautiful, with black brows and long curling lashes.

What strikes one immediately is her extreme nervousness. Her hands are never still. They were once beautiful hands, with long, tapering fingers, but rheumatism has knotted the joints and warped the fingers, so that now they have an ugly crippled look. One avoids looking at them, the more so because one is conscious she is sensitive about their appearance and humiliated by her inability to control the nervousness which draws attention to them. She is dressed simply but with a sure sense of what becomes her. Her hair is arranged with fastidious care. Her voice is soft and attractive. When she is merry, there is a touch of Irish lilt in it.

Her most appealing quality is the simple, unaffected charm of a shy convent-girl youthfulness she has never lost—an innate unworldly innocence.

While O'Neill describes setting and characters in detail, no such care is exercised by such classical playwrights as Shakespeare. He merely names the locale of the scene and devotes no space at all to a description of the characters. Such detail he leaves to the actor. And, as such, he provides the actor—or the reader—with a very real challenge.

Climax in Drama

The playwright must be concerned with structural climaxes to a scene. He must think, too, of the effect of such technical devices as a curtain's falling on a peak moment, of lights being used to heighten a scene. For instance, in Arthur Miller's *All My Sons,* the confrontation scene between the father and the son at the end of the second act is carefully motivated. The climax is the high point of the play. It is the moment toward which all events previously have been building, and it is the moment calling for the final resolution in the third act. The effect of the falling curtain and the dimming lights add greatly to the emotional impact of the scene.

The playwright, however, is often at the mercy of other people involved in the production. A director may interpret the play in a different manner from that intended by the author. And the director can further add to this conception by directing the actors to play their roles in a manner consistent with his interpretation. In some cases, it is true that the playwright demands and is given a voice in the direction of his play. Then he can insist his intentions and premises be retained. But, often, particularly if he is not a playwright of recognized stature, he is powerless to prevent misinterpretations of his work.

Sometimes, however, such misinterpretations can work to the benefit of the playwright. When *Arsenic and Old Lace* was presented for production, the author saw it as a serious play. The director decided it would be great comedy and staged it as a comedy. The play became a smash hit.

The Reading of Drama

Perhaps in no other literature is involvement with characters more important than in drama because in the reading of drama you must present in a realistic manner the stories of people, their conflicts,

YOUR ROLE IN ORAL INTERPRETATION

their dreams, their hopes. And you breathe life into them only through their dialogue. Consequently, it is imperative in choosing a play that you read it in its entirety. Do not make the mistake of reading only a scene because that scene can very often not present the clear picture of either the plot or the people involved, and meaning will be distorted.

CHARACTERIZATION

The principal concern in the reading of a play is to know the characters you read. And you must know *all* about them—and then identify their differences through vocal and physical details.

If you are reading a scene with two or three people—it is never wise to try to do more than three—their differences should be brought about through your characterization. In *Becket*, the King is inclined to be temperamental, impulsive, excitable, and very sensitive. These characteristics would guide you in your reading of the part. Becket, on the other hand, particularly in the last half of the play, has a quiet inner strength, a confidence, a peace. There *is* a difference between these two men as there is between any two people. The King would probably speak in a higher voice, at a somewhat faster rate (at least in some scenes where a faster pace would be required). Becket would be read with a calmer, slower pace, with a lower tone, though earlier in the play, when they are friends living the full life, Becket is more outwardly vigorous, more expansive, less reserved. An equally dramatic contrast exists in the fourth act of *Long Day's Journey Into Night*, where Tyrone and Edmund are both drunk. But—Tyrone is the father, an older person with more maturity and strength. Edmund, on the other hand, is not well. He is frail, younger, highly sensitive, a dreamer.

A reader, in his introduction, must always inform his audience of the events that have taken place prior to the beginning of the scene to be read. It need not be a long, detailed summary. Only the most essential facts should be given so that the audience may have a clear concept of the people and the situation. The reader is not obligated to tell what happens after the scene is over.

To help the reader in presenting clear-cut and firm characterizations in the reading of drama, the playwright often provides excellent clues as to the type of emotion demanded in a scene. After the name of the character, the author will insert in parenthesis such words as "angrily," "slowly," "spirited," and so forth. And at other times, he may interrupt the dialogue in a scene to indicate the pause for a character's reflection or a sudden change in attitude or mood, such as, "he pauses, glares at Mary, and then slowly and with anger, he turns on her."

All such clues add to the reader's understanding of the people in the play, but they should not be read aloud by the interpreter. They are his clues to interpretation.

The playwright reveals much of the characters' feelings in their dialogue, also. For example, note how Hamlet tells his innermost thoughts and emotions in such soliloquies as "To be or not to be" and "Oh, that this too too solid flesh would melt." Both of these speeches give the reader clues as to the type of person Hamlet is. In addition, other characters in the play tell much about other personalities, all of which are significant clues to the interpreter. In Jean Anouilh's *Becket,* the King in the opening scene not only tells the kind of person Becket was, but he also reveals much of their past association.

BECKET

JEAN ANOUILH

Act One

The King enters from the back. He is wearing his crown, and is naked under a big cloak. The King hesitates a moment before the tomb; then removes his cloak with a swift movement and the Page takes it away. He falls to his knees on the stone floor and prays, alone, naked, in the middle of the stage. Behind the pillars, in the shadows, one senses the disquieting presence of unseen lookers-on.
KING. Well, Thomas Becket, are you satisfied? I am naked at your tomb and your monks are coming to flog me. What an end to our story! You, rotting in this tomb, larded with my barons' dagger thrusts, and I, naked, shivering in the draughts, and waiting like an idiot for those brutes to come and thrash me. Don't you think we'd have done better to understand each other?

YOUR ROLE IN ORAL INTERPRETATION

Becket in his Archbishop's robes, just as he was on the day of his death, has appeared on the side of the stage, from behind a pillar. He says softly:

BECKET. Understand each other? It wasn't possible.

KING. I said, "In all save the honor of the realm." It was you who taught me that slogan, after all.

BECKET. I answered you. "In all save the honor of God." We were like two deaf men talking.

KING. How cold it was on that bare plain at La Ferté-Bernard, the last time we two met! It's funny, it's always been cold, in our story. Save at the beginning, when we were friends. We had a few fine summer evenings together, with the girls. . . .

He says suddenly:

Did you love Gwendolen, Archbishop? Did you hate me, that night when I said, "I am the King," and took her from you? Perhaps that's what you never could forgive me for?

BECKET (*Quietly*). I've forgotten.

KING. Yet we were like two brothers, weren't we—you and I? That night it was a childish prank—a lusty lad shouting "I am the King!" . . . I was so young. . . . And every thought in my head came from you, you know that.

BECKET (*Gently, as if to a little boy*). Pray, Henry, and don't talk so much.

KING. (*Irritably*). If you think I'm in the mood for praying at the moment . . .

Becket quietly withdraws into the darkness and disappears during the King's next speech.

I can see them through my fingers, spying on me from the aisles. Say what you like, they're an oafish lot, those Saxons of yours! To give oneself over naked to those ruffians! With my delicate skin. . . . Even you'd be afraid. Besides, I'm ashamed. Ashamed of this whole masquerade. I need them though, that's the trouble. I have to rally them to my cause, against my son, who'll gobble up my kingdom if I let him. So I've come to make my peace with their saint. You must admit it's funny. You've become a saint and here am I, the King, desper-

ately in need of that great amorphous mass which could do nothing, up till now, save lie inert beneath its own enormous weight, cowering under blows, and which is all-powerful now. What use are conquests, when you stop to think? They are England now, because of their vast numbers, and the rate at which they breed—like rabbits, to make good the massacres. But one must always pay the price—that's another thing you taught me, Thomas Becket, when you were still advising me. . . . You taught me everything. . . . (*Dreamily*) Ah, those were happy times. . . . At the peep of dawn—well, our dawn that is, around noon, because we always went to bed very late—you'd come into my room, as I was emerging from the bathhouse, rested, smiling, debonair, as fresh as if we'd never spent the entire night drinking and whoring through the town.
He says a little sourly:
That's another thing you were better at than me. . . .

Becket also shows the change within himself in his confession scene.

Act Three

BECKET. Yet it would be simple enough. Too simple perhaps. Saintliness is a temptation too. Oh, how difficult it is to get an answer from You, Lord! I was slow in praying to You, but I cannot believe that others, worthier than I, who have spent years asking You questions, have been better than myself at deciphering Your real intentions. I am only a beginner and I must make mistake after mistake, as I did in my Latin translations as a boy, when my riotous imagination made the old priest roar with laughter. But I cannot believe that one learns Your language as one learns any human tongue, by hard studying, with a dictionary, a grammar and a set of idioms. I am sure that to the hardened sinner, who drops to his knees for the first time and murmurs Your name, marveling, You tell him all Your secrets, straightaway, and that he understands. I have served You like a dilettante, surprised that I

could still find my pleasure in Your service. And for a long time I was on my guard bcause of it. I could not believe this pleasure would bring me one step nearer You. I could not believe that the road could be a happy one. Their hair shirts, their fasting, their bells in the small hours summoning one to meet You, on the icy paving stones, in the sick misery of the poor ill-treated human animal—I cannot believe that all these are anything but safeguards for the weak. In power and in luxury, and even in the pleasures of the flesh, I shall not cease to speak to You, I feel this now. You are the God of the rich man and the happy man too, Lord, and therein lies Your profound justice. You do not turn away Your eyes from the man who was given everything from birth. You have not abandoned him, alone in his ensnaring facility. And he may be Your true lost sheep. For Your scheme of things, which we mistakenly call Justice, is secret and profound and You plumb the hidden depths of poor men's puny frames as carefully as those of kings. And beneath those outward differences, which blind us, but which to You are barely noticeable; beneath the diadem or the grime, You discern the same pride, the same vanity, the same petty, complacent preoccupation with oneself. Lord, I am certain now that You meant to tempt me with this hair shirt, object of so much vapid self-congratulation! this bare cell, this solitude, this absurdly endured winter cold—and the conveniences of prayer. It would be too easy to buy You like this, at so low a price. I shall leave this convent, where so many precautions hem You round. I shall take up the miter and the golden cope again, and the great silver cross, and I shall go back and fight in the place and with the weapons it has pleased You to give me. It has pleased You to make me Archbishop and to set me, like a solitary pawn, face to face with the King, upon the chessboard. I shall go back to my place, humbly, and let the world accuse me of pride, so that I may do what I believe is my life's work. For the rest, Your will be done.
He crosses himself.

The mechanical idea of placing one character to your left, another to your right, and one in the middle for differentiation and location, has been suggested by a number of authorities, but we have found that great care must be used with this method, for there is often the danger of confusing character location, and a mix-up in placement often causes confusion and a loss of attention on the part of the audience. Such a service can also lead to the kind of reading which is comparable to watching a tennis match. The mechanics of locating characters can get in the way of the material.

Others have suggested a higher voice for one part and a lower voice for the other. The mere matter of raising or lowering a voice does not, however, assure a meaningful characterization.

A man's reading of a woman's part might be handled with a higher tone but it should not be so high that it sounds more like a squeak. In the same way, a girl trying to lower her voice just to portray a man can often distort the character of the man completely and make her look understandably ridiculous. If you get the characters in mind clearly, if you know what kinds of people they are, how they feel and react in a scene, how these emotions and feelings change with the progress of the scene, and how they relate to other characters, you will make the distinctions without any artifices.

To help the reader in another way to interpret characters, other clues are provided in the dialogue. A person who speaks in a coarse, ungrammatical manner is generally an uneducated person, or he is perhaps speaking in a style peculiar to a certain locale. For instance, those from the deep South have their own style of speaking, and playwrights usually convey that style in their manner of writing. On the other hand, a person using a wide vocabulary and speaking with an understanding of the niceties of language is ordinarily educated, refined, from a higher level of society. Such dialogue is in itself a valuable clue to the interpreter. An excellent example is a comparison of the dialogue of Professor Higgins with that of Liza in the earlier scenes of the play *Pygmalion*.

In the reading of dialogue, it is necessary to remember that you cannot build a scene towards a climax by pausing after each character's speech. To do so completely stops movement, and in drama a scene must move. If you find yourself reading a scene with two people who talk in very short segments of dialogue, your problems will be evident. If the scene calls for a glib, conversational quality, such as is found in Noel Coward's *Private Lives* or

Blithe Spirit, pauses between speeches would utterly destroy Coward's intent. Learn to change from one character to another quickly and with consistency. However, when pauses are called for (and often the author indicates these pauses), you should take advantage of them, for they heighten a change in emotion or idea. They are there for a purpose. It is not always wise to read a scene where the dialogue is too curt because changing character rapidly imposes too much of a problem for the reader.

One of the crucial lessons in the reading of drama is to learn when the characters' ideas or moods change. These must be clearly brought out to elicit the full meaning of the scene or the dialogue. If the reader does not know the emotion inherent in a scene and how and why that emotion changes, he is unable to read with full meaning.

In *Becket,* one of the most dramatic moments comes in the scene on the beach where Becket and the King meet after having been separated. Here are two proud men, yet both want, deep within themselves, to reach out to the other, to tear down the reserves, to recapture the closeness they once felt. They are unable to do so because of conflicting ideals. The King cannot let himself give in to Becket, and Becket cannot go back on his faith to accede to the King's wishes. The reader must show this conflict, the invisible wall that separates the men, and he must reveal the inner conflicts as the scene progresses.

The moods change in this manner. On the first meeting there is a quietness, an uneasiness, an appraisal of each other, an indulgence in idle remarks to keep from facing the central conflict. The emotion suddenly changes when Becket makes his first reference to God and the King says, "If we start straightway, we're sure to quarrel! Let's talk about trivial things." There has been a momentary flare-up and then a mechanical return to matters of insignificance. The King is petulant, bored, fighting within himself as he talks about horses, hawks, his son. Then the mood changes, particularly with the King, to one of pleasurable reminiscence as he speaks of the old days. Yet, mingled with this reminiscence is evidence of the King's annoyance at Becket's dedication to the faith. Finally, unable to contain his feelings he bursts out with "Becket, I'm bored!" And immediately he cries out for Becket's help.

Shortly after, both Becket and the King make clear what their obligations are. The King asks Becket if he will make a concession but Becket refuses to change his principles, and the King then offers

UNDERSTANDING LITERATURE

him a chance to return to England. Suddenly, they both express the physical coldness they feel—but it is the coldness of two men who cannot return to what they once were.

Unable to keep inside any longer his vital concern over the loss of friendship, the King blurts out, "You never loved me, did you, Becket?" Becket reaffirms his love for the King but more for his God. Then the King, in another switch of emotion, cries, "I never should have seen you again. It hurts too much." We are now at the point where the King expresses what he really feels. When Becket tries to comfort him, the King's pride again returns and he insists he wants no pity. And so the two men part—never to see one another again.

In Elmer Rice's *The Adding Machine*, both Mrs. Zero and Mr. Zero have long soliloquies. Mrs. Zero is a gossip in one part of the dialogue, a nagging wife in another, a jealous woman in still another, while Mr. Zero goes from man's pride in being reliable at his work to sensual interest in another woman, to self-defense and rationalization about killing a man, to his prejudices about Negroes and Jews. His lack of culture and background is evident in the type of dialogue and in the principles and bias expressed.

The reader must remember that no character remains the same within a given framework of time. He moves from one mood to another, often with startling rapidity. The Old Man in Ionesco's *The Chairs* moves back and forth from one mood to another abruptly and sharply. In one scene in the beginning of the play, he is reminiscent about the days now gone. He is dreamy, very old. Then suddenly he changes into a spasm of crying for his dead mother. He goes back to his earlier days as he weeps convulsively. From that mood he as quickly turns to the "reality" (if it can be called that) of the present moment.

To fully realize such changes, pacing is very important. In the beginning of *The Chairs*, the pace is slow, dreamy; there is a sense of pervading unreality. Then there is a change to a faster pace as the Old Man becomes annoyed with the Old Woman. The little argument ends almost as soon as it begins, and then to please the Old Woman, the Old Man starts to tell the age-old story. The pace is slow at first as they speak of the city they once knew; then it quickens as they start the hysterical laughter. Gradually exhausted by the laughing, they return to the slow, languid pace for just a moment, and then a faster, more explosive kind of pacing follows as the Old Man begins his crying again for his mother. And so the play switches from one pacing to another, from the hectic rapidity of the arrival of the guests, to the reminiscence with guests about the past and a quieter, slower pace. And so on.

The reader, as can be seen, has a tremendous task in the reading of drama. That is one reason why his involvement must be deep enough to handle such demands. Drama requires more subjectivity than objectivity if it is to reflect life. It requires facility in the handling of emotion and in perception of changes in the structure. Students may fear this assignment more than others in the beginning, but perhaps because drama enables them to break down their reserve in many cases, the assignment usually becomes most enjoyable.

Choosing the Scene

The reader faced with the task of selecting a scene has a most difficult job. As a beginning point the entire play, or at least a good condensation of the play, must be read. You cannot summarily select a scene without knowing how it relates to the rest of the play. For example, if you read the second scene between the Public and the Private Gar in *Philadelphia, Here I Come*, you would have no understanding of the relationship between the two. You might assume they were two separate people instead of one being the other's alter ego. Or if you were to choose only the beach scene from *Becket* you would have no awareness of the basis for that scene.

It is also important to select a scene that fits your sex and maturity. For instance, it would not be advisable for a girl to attempt the scene between the Captain and Mr. Roberts in *Mister Roberts*. She would not be able to give a very true or honest interpretation of these two men. She simply would not have the physical voice or force needed. As far as maturity is concerned, any one who has not experienced life in its more complex aspects, who has never known a marriage that has degenerated, for example, would not be able to give any depth to the reading of a play like *Who's Afraid of Virginia Woolf*.

Another consideration in the selection of a scene is that it must be able to stand alone. The reader might decide to do the scene in the first act of C. S. Forrester's *Payment Deferred* where Marble meets his nephew for the first time and plots his murder. Or he might do the scene where father and son face each other realistically in *The Subject Was Roses*.

A scene should be chosen that begins at a definite point and builds to a climax. The following scene from *Taming of the Shrew* is an excellent example of such a scene.

TAMING OF THE SHREW

WILLIAM SHAKESPEARE

Characters: PETRUCHIO   KATHARINA

(*Petruchio, a man of the world, has decided to wed Katharina the shrew, a woman whom no man has been able to tame. Petruchio is as much enamoured of her dowry as he is of Katharina. He begins his unusual courting in this scene.*)

PETRUCHIO.   Good morrow, Kate; for that's your name, I
    hear.
KATHARINA.   Well have you heard, but something hard of
    hearing:
They call me Katharine that do talk of me.
PETRUCHIO.   You lie, in faith, for you are called plain Kate.
And bonny Kate, and sometimes Kate the Curst;
But Kate, the prettiest Kate in Christendom,
Kate of Kate-Hall, my superdainty Kate,
For dainties are all Kates—and therefore, Kate,
Take this of me, Kate of my consolation:
Hearing thy mildness praised in every town,
Thy virtues spoke of, and thy beauty sounded,
Yet not so deeply as to thee belongs,
Myself am moved to woo thee for my wife.
KATHARINA.   Moved! in good time. Let him that moved
    you hither
Remove you hence. I knew you at the first
You were a movable.
PETRUCHIO.   Why, what's a movable?
KATHARINA.   A joined stool.
PETRUCHIO.   Thou hast hit it. Come, sit on me.

KATHARINA. Asses are made to bear, and so are you.

PETRUCHIO. Women are made to bear, and so are you.

KATHARINA. No such jade as you, if me you mean.

PETRUCHIO. Alas, good Kate, I will not burden thee!
For knowing thee to be but young and light—

KATHARINA. Too light for such a swain as you to catch,
And yet as heavy as my weight should be.

PETRUCHIO. Should be! should—buzz!

KATHARINA. Well ta'en, and like a buzzard.

PETRUCHIO. O slow-winged turtle! shall a buzzard take
thee?

KATHARINA. Ay, for a turtle, as he takes a buzzard.

PETRUCHIO. Come, come, you wasp. I' faith, you are too
angry.

KATHARINA. If I be waspish, best beware my sting.

PETRUCHIO. My remedy is then to pluck it out.

KATHARINA. Aye, if the fool could find it where it lies.

PETRUCHIO. Who knows not where a wasp does wear his
sting?
In his tail.

KATHARINA. In his tongue.

PETRUCHIO. Whose tongue?

KATHARINA. Yours, if you talk of tails; and so farewell.

PETRUCHIO. What, with my tongue in your tail? nay, come
again,
Good Kate, I am a gentleman.

KATHARINA. That I'll try.

(*She strikes him*)

PETRUCHIO. I swear I'll cuff you if you strike again.

KATHARINA. So may you lose your arms.
If you strike me, you are no gentleman,
And if no gentleman, why then no arms.

PETRUCHIO. A herald, Kate? O, put me in thy books!

KATHARINA. What is your crest? a coxcomb?

PETRUCHIO. A combless cock, so Kate will be my hen.

KATHARINA. No cock of mine. You crow too like a craven.

PETRUCHIO. Nay, come, Kate, come. You must not look
so sour.

KATHARINA. It is my fashion when I see a crab.

PETRUCHIO. Why, here's no crab, and therefore look not
sour.

KATHARINA. There is, there is.

PETRUCHIO. Then show it me.

KATHARINA. Had I a glass, I would.

PETRUCHIO. What, you mean my face?

KATHARINA. Well aimed of such a young one.

PETRUCHIO. Now, by Saint George, I am too young for
you.

KATHARINA. Yet you are withered.

PETRUCHIO. 'Tis with cares.

KATHARINA. I care not.

PETRUCHIO. Nay, hear you, Kate. In sooth you scape
not so.

KATHARINA. I chafe you, if I tarry. Let me go.

PETRUCHIO. No, not a whit. I find you passing gentle.
'Twas told me you were rough and coy and sullen,
And now I find report a very liar;
For thou are pleasant, gamesome, passing courteous,
But slow in speech, yet sweet as springtime flowers.
Thou canst not frown, thou canst not look askance,
Nor bite the lip, as angry wenches will,
Nor hast thou pleasure to be cross in talk,
But thou with mildness entertain'st thy wooers,
With gentle conference, soft and affable.
Why does the world report that Kate doth limp?
O slanderous world! Kate like the hazel twig
Is straight and slender, and as brown in hue
As hazel nuts, and sweeter than the kernels.
O, let me see thee walk. Thou dost not halt.

KATHARINA. Go, fool, and whom thou keep'st command.

PETRUCHIO. Did ever Dian so become a grove
As Kate this chamber with her princely gait?
O, be thou Dian, and let her be Kate
And then let Kate be chaste and Dian sportful!

KATHARINA. Where did you study all this goodly speech?

PETRUCHIO. It is extempore, from my mother wit.

KATHARINA. A witty mother! Witless else her son.

YOUR ROLE IN ORAL INTERPRETATION

PETRUCHIO. Am I not wise?

KATHARINA. Yes. Keep you warm.

PETRUCHIO. Marry, so I mean, sweet Katharine, in thy
   bed.
And therefore, setting all this chat aside,
Thus in plain terms: Your father hath consented
That you shall be my wife, your dowry 'greed on,
And, will you, nill you, I will marry you.
Now Kate, I am a husband for your turn.
For, by this light whereby I see thy beauty.
Thy beauty, that doth make me like thee well,
Thou must be married to no man but me;
For I am he am born to tame you Kate,
And bring you from a wild Kate to a Kate
Conformable as other household Kates.
Here comes your father. Never make denial.
I must and will have Katharine to my wife.

It is unwise to select any scene which relies heavily on props
and which demands a great deal of action. It is equally bad to
choose one that has too many characters. Because props are unnecessary for the clarity of the scenes and because the plot involves
only two characters, William Gibson's *Two for the Seesaw* is a
good choice. The confrontation scene between Pizarro and Ata-
hualpa in the last act of *Royal Hunt of the Sun* would be another
wise choice since it does not depend on any technical effects for its
impact. Likewise, the first scene in Oliver Goldsmith's *She Stoops
to Conquer* between Mr. and Mrs. Hardcastle would make an
effective reading. The King's great speech about love in the end of
the first act of *Camelot* would be excellent too; it deals only with the
King and is complete within itself.

It is also wise not to choose a scene that has several character
entrances and exits as these are difficult to convey with ease.
Wherever possible, such exits and entrances should be cut, but if
this is not possible, the reader should insert a line or a word to
indicate the person has exited. If a character enters, the reader
could turn his head to the left or to the right, give a sign of recognition, and perhaps mention the person's name. Often, of course, the
person leaving has a line such as "I have to go now" or "see you

later" which makes it clear he is exiting. No added information is then needed, and the reader does not say "he exits" or "he enters." Nor does he read such stage directions as "he moved about the room restlessly, then sat down on the sofa, and put his head in his hands . . ." And obviously the reader doesn't read any directions about the mood the character is experiencing, such as "angrily." It is up to the voice, the characterization, to convey this mood.

Is it possible to do more than one scene from a play? This is a question often asked by students. Yes, if proper narrative comment is provided to give a bridge between scenes. While the authors prefer to avoid the need for narrative abridgement, at times it can be used effectively. For example, one could do a reading of *Becket* with narrative continuity. The sequence would be this: the King's speech in the beginning at Becket's tomb; the King's appointment of Becket as Archbishop; Becket's confession in the church; the first conflict between the King and Becket; and finally, the scene at the beach.

However, it is better to select a complete scene or a long speech for oral reading. The narrative technique is more often used for a professional reading of an entire play with necessary cuts.

The Cutting of a Play

There are not too many general rules about cutting a play. The more specific considerations will be dealt with here.

It is always wise to cut minor characters that do not contribute materially or meaningfully to the scene. But make sure these characters do not, in total aspect, play significant parts in the scene. Omit repetition of thought or idea in scenes. If one character makes the point with his dialogue, there is no need for another to repeat the same thought. Select a scene that does not have too many exits and entrances. Cut out exits and entrances whenever possible. At times, one scene can be telescoped into another for a more cohesive whole and for complete development of some conflict. Cut out intervening dialogue that does not advance the progress of the scene.

Elements of the scene which are designed more for playing on the stage and not for clear interpretation by a reader should be cut. In short, some scenes depend largely on lighting and sound effects for a complete response. Such scenes should be omitted. Remember, you are obligated to read the scene and make it meaningful, to give the desired response; the only equipment you have is your voice and your body through your emotional response to the material.

If a scene is interrupted by comments from other characters, outside of the central figures you are dealing with, omit these characters. For instance, in the play within the play scene in *A Midsummer Night's Dream,* your concentration is on Bottom, Quince, and other townsfolk. As a result the comments of Theseus, Demetrius, and the others are not essential.

Naturally, you should omit all stage directions. These are not to be read—except on rare occasions when some comment or direction is necessary for clarity. To drop into the role of narrator or expositor would cause you to lose too much contact with the essential part of your material—the dialogue.

These are a few points to consider. To explain further, let us look at this scene from *A Midsummer Night's Dream* and note the cuts.

A MIDSUMMER NIGHT'S DREAM
WILLIAM SHAKESPEARE

Re-enter Philostrate.

PHILOSTRATE. So please your grace, the Prologue is address'd.

THESEUS. Let him approach. (*Flourish of trumpets*)

Enter Quince for the Prologue.

PROLOGUE. If we offend, it is without good will.
That you should think we come not to offend,
But with good will. To show our simple skill,
That is the true beginning of our end.
Consider then, we come but in despite.
We do not come, as minding to content you,
Our true intent is. All for your delight,
We are not here. That you should here repent you,
The actors are at hand; and, by their show,
You shall know all, that you are like to know.

THESEUS. This fellow doth not stand upon points.

LYSANDER. He hath rid his prologue like a rough colt; he knows not the stop. A good moral, my lord: it is not enough to speak, but to speak true.

HIPPOLYTA. Indeed he hath played on his prologue like a child on a recorder; a sound, but not in government.

UNDERSTANDING LITERATURE

THESEUS. ~~His speech was like a tangled chain; nothing impaired, but all disordered. Who is next?~~

Enter Pyramus and Thisby, Wall, Moonshine, and Lion.

PROLOGUE.   Gentles, perchance you wonder at this show;
But wonder on, till truth makes all things plain.
This man is Pyramus, if you would know;
This beauteous lady Thisby is certain.
This man, with lime and rough-cast, doth present
Wall, that vile Wall which did these lovers sunder;
And through Wall's chink, poor souls, they are content
To whisper. At the which let no man wonder.
This man, with lanthorn, dog, and bush of thorn,
Presenteth Moonshine; for, if you will know,
By moonshine did these lovers think no scorn
To meet at Ninus' tomb, there, there to woo.
This grisly beast, which Lion hight by name,
The trusty Thisby, coming first by night,
Did scare away, or rather did affright;
And, as she fled, her mantle she did fall,
Which Lion vile with bloody mouth did stain.
Anon comes Pyramus, sweet youth and tall,
And finds his trusty Thisby's mantle slain:
Whereat, with blade, with bloody blameful blade,
He bravely broach'd his boiling bloody breast:
And Thisby, tarrying in mulberry shade,
His dagger drew, and died. For all the rest,
Let Lion, Moonshine, Wall and lovers twain
At large discourse, while here they do remain.

Exeunt Prologue, Pyramus, Thisby, Lion, and Moonshine.

THESEUS.   I wonder if the lion be to speak.

DEMETRIUS.   No wonder, my lord: one lion may, when many
asses do.

WALL.   In this same interlude it doth befall
That I, one Snout by name, present a wall;
And such a wall, as I would have you think,
That had in it a crannied hole or chink,
Through which the lovers, Pyramus and Thisby,
Did whisper often very secretly.

YOUR ROLE IN ORAL INTERPRETATION

This loam, this rough-case, and this stone, doth show
That I am the same wall; the truth is so:
And this the cranny is, right and sinister,
Through which the fearful lovers are to whisper.

THESEUS. ~~Would you desire lime and hair to speak better?~~
DEMETRIUS. ~~It is the wittiest partition that ever I heard~~
~~discourse, my lord.~~
THESEUS. Pyramus draws near the wall: silence!

Re-enter Pyramus.

PYRAMUS. O grim-look'd night! O night with hue so
black!
O night, which ever art when day is not!
O night, O night! alack, alack, alack,
I fear my Thisby's promise is forgot!
And thou, O wall, O sweet, O lovely wall,
That stand'st between her father's ground and mine!
Show me thy chink, to blink through with mine eyne!
(*Wall holds up his fingers*)
Thanks, courteous wall; Jove shield thee well for this!
But what see I? No Thisby do I see.
O wicked wall, through whom I see no bliss!
Cursed be thy stones for thus deceiving me!

THESEUS. The wall, me thinks, being sensible, should curse
again.
PYRAMUS. No, in truth, sir, he should not. "Deceiving me"
is Thisby's cue: she is to enter now, and I am to spy
her through the wall. You shall see, it will fall pat as I
told you. Yonder she comes.

Re-enter Thisby.

THISBY. O wall, full often hast thou heard my moans,
For parting my fair Pyramus and me!
My cherry lips have often kiss'd thy stones,
Thy stones with lime and hair knit up in thee.
PYRAMUS. I see a voice: now will I to the chink,
To spy an I can hear my Thisby's face.
Thisby!
THISBY. My love thou art, my love I think.

PYRAMUS.   Think what thou wilt, I am thy lover's grace;
And, like Limander, am I trusty still.
THISBY.   And I like Helen, till the Fates me kill.
PYRAMUS.   Not Shafalus to Procrus was so true.
THISBY.   As Shafalus to Procrus, I to you.
PYRAMUS.   Will thou at Ninny's tomb meet me straight-
way?
THISBY.   'Tide life, 'tide death, I come without delay.
Exeunt Pyramus and Thisby.
WALL.   Thus have I, wall, my part discharged so;
And being done, thus wall away doth go.
THESEUS.   Now is the mural down between the two neigh-
bors.
DEMETRIUS.   No remedy, my lord, when walls are so willful
to hear without warning.
HIPPOLYTA.   This is the silliest stuff that ever I heard.
THESEUS.   The best in this kind are but shadows; and the
worst are no worse, if imagination amend them.
HIPPOLYTA.   It must be your imagination then, and not
theirs.
THESEUS.   If we imagine no worse of them than they of
themselves, they may pass for excellent men. Here
come two noble beasts in, a man and a lion.
Re-enter Lion and Moonshine.
LION.   You, ladies, you, whose gentle hearts do fear
The smallest monstrous mouse that creeps on floor,
May now perchance both quake and tremble here,
When lion rough in wildest rage doth roar,
Then know that I, one Snug the joiner, am
A lion-fell, nor else no lion's dam;
For, if I should as lion come in strife
Into this place, 'twere pity on my life.
THESEUS.   A very gentle beast, and of good conscience.
DEMETRIUS.   The very best at a beast, my lord, that e'er
I saw.
LYSANDER.   This lion is a very fox for his valor.
THESEUS.   True; and a goose for his discretion.

YOUR ROLE IN ORAL INTERPRETATION

DEMETRIUS. Not so, my lord; for his valor cannot carry his discretion; and the fox carries the goose.

THESEUS. His discretion, I am sure, cannot carry his valor; for the goose carries not the fox. It is well; leave it to his discretion, and let us listen to the moon.

MOONSHINE. This lanthorn doth the horned moon present—

DEMETRIUS. He should have worn the horns on his head.

THESEUS. He is no crescent, and his horns are invisible within the circumference.

MOONSHINE. This lanthorn doth the horned moon present;
Myself, the man-i'-th'-moon do seem to be.

THESEUS. This is the greatest error of all the rest; the man should be put into the lantern. How is it else the man-i'-th'-moon?

DEMETRIUS. He dares not come there for the candle; for, you see, it is already in snuff.

HIPPOLYTA. I am aweary of this moon: would he would change!

THESEUS. It appears, by his small light of discretion, that he is in the wane; but yet, in courtesy, in all reason, we must stay the time.

LYSANDER. Proceed, Moon.

MOONSHINE. All that I have to say, is, to tell you that the lanthorn is the moon; I, the man-i'-th'-moon; this thorn-bush, my thorn-bush; and this dog, my dog.

DEMETRIUS. Why, all these should be in the lantern; for all these are in the moon. But, silence! here comes Thisby.

(*Re-enter Thisby*)

THISBY. This is old Ninny's tomb. Where is my love?

LION (*Roaring*) Oh——

DEMETRIUS. Well roared, Lion.

THESEUS. Well run, Thisby.

HIPPOLYTA. Well shone, Moon. Truly, the moon shines with good grace.

(*The Lion shakes Thisby's mantle, and exits*)

THESEUS. ~~Well moused, Lion.~~

DEMETRIUS. ~~And then came Pyramus.~~

LYSANDER. ~~And so the lion vanished.~~

(*Re-enter Pyramus*)

PYRAMUS.   Sweet Moon, I thank thee for thy sunny beams;
I thank thee, Moon, for shining now so bright;
For, by thy gracious, golden, glittering gleams,
I trust to take of truest Thisby sight.
But stay, O spite!
But mark, poor knight,
What dreadful dole is here!
Eyes, do you see?
How can it be?
O dainty duck! O dear!
Thy mantle good,
What, stain'd with blood!
Approach, ye Furies fell!
O Fates, come, come,
Cut thread and thrum;
Quail, crush, conclude, and quell!

THESEUS.   This passion, and the death of a dear friend,
    would go near to make a man look sad.

HIPPOLYTA. ~~Beshrew my heart, but I pity the man.~~

PYRAMUS.   O wherefore, Nature, didst thou lions frame?
Since Lion vile hath here deflower'd my dear;
Which is—no, no—which was the fairest dame
That lives, that loved, that liked, that look'd with cheer.
Come, tears, confound;
Out, sword, and wound
The pap of Pyramus;
Ay, that left pap,
Where heart doth hop: (*Stabs himself*)
Thus die I, thus, thus, thus.
Now I am dead,
Now am I fled;
My soul is in the sky:
Tongue, lose thy light;
Moon, take thy flight: (*Exit Moonshine*)
Now die, die, die, die, die. (*Dies*)

YOUR ROLE IN ORAL INTERPRETATION

The Readers' Theatre

In recent years there has been a most interesting new development in the interpretative field—the group reading of a play or some other kind of dramatic work. Known as Readers' Theatre, it is an adroit combination of the techniques of acting and interpretation.

In this form of dramatic literature, a certain number of readers join together for the reading. Each reads one part—just as an actor plays only one role. Each is responsible for the interpretation of that part, and yet he must relate himself and his part clearly to that of the other readers—and to the author's primary intent.

The technique of the actor comes into real focus here. While the readers do not memorize the lines, as actors do, and while they are not in costume or surrounded by props and a full array of lights, they must work together in a cohesive unit to build the reading to the necessary climax, to provide utter believability in the roles they are playing. There must be the same mutual "playing together" as there is in acting.

Such a field has found both cultural and commercial favor in recent years. Notable examples have been *Don Juan in Hell, John Brown's Body,* and *Spoon River Anthology.* Agnes Moorehead, Charles Boyer, Sir Cedric Hardwicke, and Charles Laughton made the first big impression with their reading of *Don Juan in Hell* by Shaw. Dressed in evening clothes, they managed to convey the full intent and scope of the play. While they remained interpreters, they also could not disguise the fact that much of their ability as actors was in evidence. Tyrone Power, Judith Anderson, and Raymond Massey appeared in the cast of *John Brown's Body. Spoon River Anthology* featured Betty Garrett, Robert Elston, and others.

The Readers' Theatre idea has also found favor in such universities as UCLA where, under the direction of Dr. George Savage, readings have been held of new, unpublished plays. Students in theatre read the various roles, but not in costume. They occasionally will indulge in some stage movement, but as a rule they stand at rostrums or without stands and read the play. In the readings, however, the same emphasis is put on building to climaxes, characterization, and proper pacing as would be found in the theatre.

There are varying ideas on how much Readers' Theatre should adopt the characteristics of the stage play. Some decry any attempt by the readers to play scenes facing each other as would be the case on the stage. These theorists believe that at all times the dialogue should be directed to the audience. Others feel such an "out front" attack is artificial and phony and destroys the illusion. They contend that it makes no vital difference whether the readers face the audience or their fellow players as long as the purpose of the play is achieved.

Your authors have seen readings done in both manners and we are inclined to go along with the idea that the direction of the reader's contact is not at all as vital as is the interpretation. It seems far more natural for readers to be actively interplaying with each other than to try to place an artificial barrier between themselves just to make certain that no semblance of acting technique is involved. This seems like drawing a fine line. In scenes where a reader can logically direct his lines to the audience, he should do so, but when the dialogue compels him to give his attention to another reader, it seems artificial to look at the audience instead. This technique serves to draw attention away from the material and toward the style of delivery.

There are also various ideas as to the manner of "staging" such group readings. Some believe that when a character exits, the reader should turn his back to the audience or step back a few paces. An entrance should be made, according to this theory, by facing the audience again and advancing to the stand. Others find a simpler way of designating exits and entrances. When an interpreter has finished his scene, he merely sits down. When he makes an entrance again, he rises and resumes his place at the stand. There is no rigid rule for the mechanical handling of such movements.

Usually, it is advisable to employ the services of a narrator to set the scene, to comment on actions that the readers cannot convey, and to indicate such matters as change of time. However, his role should be kept to a minimum since the focus should be on the readers and the play.

The Readers' Theatre is a most important advancement in that it provides a chance to bring dramatic literature to people who might never have the chance of seeing it. Often the costs of producing a play are too prohibitive for some organizations, and yet there is the desire to bring such literature to their community. Consequently, the reading of a play, which involves no building of sets, no expensive array of lights, no costumes, permits them to bring to life the literature of drama. It has also been found to be an excellent way of testing the works of new and undiscovered playwrights. Many have discovered that the readings of their plays reveal merits and faults that can be developed and corrected before submitting the work to an actual producer for a full scale production.

Nevertheless, Readers' Theatre is a very real merging of the two allied arts—interpretation and acting. It borrows a little from each and yet intrudes upon neither.

Recordings of Plays

Of particular interest and value to readers of drama are the many recordings of dramatic interpretations by noted actors. While it is true that most of these recordings have a cast of players rather than a single performer, and though these cast albums are more Readers' Theatre than individual interpretation, the mere fact that recording companies have gone to the expense of creating such records indicates a wide enough public interest in the art to warrant the expenditure.

Certainly any serious student of oral interpretation should acquaint himself with these recordings, for he can learn much about the art by listening to the "experts." It is not that the student should set out to imitate the readings—his interpretation must be part of him—but he can gain valuable aids in content analysis, in the use of pauses and pacing, and in characterization. Two records of note are Jason Robards' *Readings from the Works of Eugene O'Neill* on Columbia and Ingrid Bergman's *The Human Voice*, a one-woman drama. Robards' album contains scenes from *Long Day's Journey Into Night, A Moon for the Misbegotten, The Hairy Ape,* and *The Iceman Cometh.* The actor is noted for his interpretations of O'Neill. He also is featured on a recording of *Hughie,* with Jack Dodson, also by O'Neill.

Miss Bergman's *The Human Voice* for Caedmon is a drama by Jean Cocteau, told entirely by a woman on the telephone. While it may be considered by some as more acting than interpretation, it must be remembered that Miss Bergman creates the illusion solely by the use of her voice with no technical help of any kind, so it would seem to be an expert example of interpretation.

There are, of course, countless other recordings. Columbia has recorded Shaw's *Don Juan in Hell,* with Charles Boyer, Sir Cedric Hardwicke, Charles Laughton, and Agnes Moorehead, as well as

John Brown's Body by Stephen Vincent Benét with Tyrone Power, Judith Anderson, and Raymond Massey. It has also given us the remarkable recording of Sir John Gielgud's production, *Ages of Man,* featuring excerpts from Shakespeare. The company's other Shakespearean albums include *Homage to Shakespeare* with Dame Edith Evans, Sir John Gielgud, and Margaret Leighton and *Soul of An Age* with Sir Michael Redgrave and Sir Ralph Richardson.

In addition, full versions of such Shakespearean plays as *Othello, Hamlet, Macbeth, King Lear,* and *Julius Caesar* have been recorded.

One of the more popular ventures has been the recording of complete plays with original casts. These are actors playing definite roles. But again you must keep in mind that the medium is the record—not the stage—and that, therefore, the performer must be more the interpreter than the actor. He uses the voice alone—and the emotional response to the material. A select list of recordings is given on the following pages:

Brecht on Brecht—featuring Dane Clark, Anne Jackson, Lotte Lenya in excerpts from the writings of Bertolt Brecht.
Dylan—by Sidney Michaels. The dramatic version of the life of Dylan Thomas, with Alec Guinness.
Everyman—the old morality play with Burgess Meredith.
Moss Hart—reading some of his own works, including *Lady in the Dark* and *Man Who Came to Dinner,* as well as excerpts from his autobiography *Act One.*
Hostage—by Brendan Behan with Geoff Garland, Julie Harris, Diane Webster, Moultrie Patten.
Krapp's Last Tape—by Samuel Beckett with Donald Davis.
Luv—by Murray Schisgall with Alan Arkin, Eli Wallach, Anne Jackson.
A Man's A Man—by Bertolt Brecht.
Arthur Miller—reading from his plays *The Crucible* and *Death of a Salesman.*
Sir Michael Redgrave—reading from Chekhov.
John Millington Synge—*Riders to the Sea.*
Strange Interlude—Eugene O'Neill's marathon play with Betty Field, Jane Fonda.
The Subject Was Roses—Pulitzer Prize play by Frank Gilroy, with Jack Albertson, Irene Dailey, Martin Sheen.
Under Milkwood—another example of Readers' Theatre. A reading of the work by Dylan Thomas.
Waiting for Godot—by Samuel Beckett with Bert Lahr, E. G. Marshall, Kurt Kasznar.

YOUR ROLE IN ORAL INTERPRETATION

Who's Afraid of Virginia Woolf—Edward Albee's play with the original
Broadway cast: Arthur Hill, Uta Hagen, George Grizzard, and
Melinda Dillon.
The Zoo Story—by Edward Albee with Mark Richardson and William
Daniels.

Caedmon Records offers many selections, including the following:
The Balcony—by Jean Genet.
The Glass Menagerie—by Tennessee Williams with Montgomery Clift,
Julie Harris, Jessica Tandy, and David Wayne.
St. Joan—by George Bernard Shaw, with Siobhan McKenna.
Marat/Sade—by Peter Weiss with the original London and New York cast.
Uncle Vanya—by Anton Chekhov with Sir Laurence Olivier.

The Shakespeare Recording Society, in association with Caedmon,
offers the following records of Shakespearean works:
Measure for Measure with John Gielgud and Margaret Leighton.
The Taming of the Shrew with Trevor Howard and Margaret Leighton.
Twelfth Night with Siobhan McKenna.
The Winter's Tale with Sir John Gielgud.
Richard II with Sir John Gielgud.
Romeo and Juliet with Claire Bloom and Albert Finney.
Macbeth with Anthony Quayle, Ffrangcan Davies.
As You Like It with Vanessa Redgrave.
Coriolanus with Richard Burton and Jessica Tandy.
Cymbeline with Claire Bloom and Pamela Brown.

RCA Victor also produces some Shakespearean records, including
scenes from the sound track of the film of *Taming of the Shrew* with
Elizabeth Taylor and Richard Burton; Sir Laurence Olivier's *Othello* and
his *Henry V*. The company has also recorded an album from the sound
track of *Man For All Seasons* by Robert Bolt.

The Theatre Recording Society has made available many theatrical
productions:
Cyrano de Bergerac with Sir Ralph Richardson and Anna Massey.
Death of a Salesman with Lee J. Cobb and Mildred Dunnock.
Lysistrata with Hermione Gingold and Stanley Holloway.
Five One-Act Plays by William Butler Yeats with Siobhan McKenna,
Patrick Magee, Cyril Cusack and Joyce Redman.
The Master Builder by Henrik Ibsen with Sir Michael Redgrave.
The Family Reunion by T. S. Eliot with Flora Robson, Paul Scofield, and
Sybil Thorndike.
She Stoops to Conquer by Oliver Goldsmith with Alastair Sim and Claire
Bloom.

The School for Scandal by Richard Brinsley Sheridan with Sir Ralph Richardson, Sir John Gielgud.

And, of course, there are many, many others.

Summary

Drama is a mirror of life, a commentary on the people who live it. As such, its history dates back to the first man who imitated animals and who indulged in rituals as a form of expression. Drama, however, began to achieve a basic form in Greece where it first saw expression in festivals to Dionysus. Greek plays as such, were of three types: tragedies, satyrs, and burlesques.

Among the more noted playwrights in Greece were Sophocles, Aeschylus, Euripides, and Aristophanes.

A highlight of the rebirth of drama occurred in England with the advent of such noted playwrights as Ben Jonson, Marlowe, Kyd, and, of course, Shakespeare.

The Restoration period in England was a glorious time for drama. With sophisticated plays of seduction and evil, and with the works of such playwrights as Richard Brinsley Sheridan and Oliver Goldsmith, theatre was indeed lively.

The nineteenth century saw drama moving into the realm of naturalism and at times voicing social protest. The twentieth century continued this trend with the works of Eugene O'Neill and Arthur Miller.

A new development of the twentieth century was the emergence of the avant-garde theatre, the "theatre of the absurd," an expression of the existentialists who revolted against the rigid principles of play construction.

A play is usually divided into three acts, often with scenes within the acts, but the structural form can vary from one act to two and three acts. Shakespeare used a five-act structure, and O'Neill employed a four-act division in some cases. He also used the trilogy as a form.

In most cases, the divisions are made as follows: The first act introduces the main characters, sets the scene, and reveals the primary conflicts. The second act develops the characters and builds to the moment of decision—the dénouement, the crisis. The third act brings about the resolution. This technique, can, of course, change according to playwrights' own theories. Avant-garde theatre observes no structural devices.

YOUR ROLE IN ORAL INTERPRETATION

The playwright often has little to say about how his work is interpreted in the theatre. The director or producer may have a different concept of the play than does the author, and the cast may be guided along the roads of that interpretation. At times, the playwright can have a voice in the direction his play is to take, but this usually occurs after he has become a success.

Readers' Theatre is a new development of oral interpretation. This consists of group readings of a play or some other form of dramatic literature. Recent examples have been *Don Juan in Hell*, *John Brown's Body*, and *Spoon River Anthology*.

This new field embraces both the techniques of acting and oral interpretation, but in that the readers read the parts, are not in costume, and have no props or array of lights, they are more closely aligned to interpretation. Yet, they must play together cohesively, respond emotionally to each other's roles, and play only one part themselves; as such they are in the realm of acting.

The techniques of staging Readers' Theatre are varied and depend usually on the attitude of the person directing the production. It is at least a new and challenging development in this long and vivid art.

How do I read poetry?

How or when poetry began as a form of expression no literary historian would venture to guess. However, it can be said that poetic expression was used together with music, dance, pagan rituals, and other rhythmic forms in early tribal ceremonials. Poetry is inherently emotional and primitive man, as well as modern, must have waxed poetic when he was under emotional stress. In any case poetry, while not the largest body of literature, has certainly been used by man to express his views about virtually every emotion and every experience his kind has had.

It is difficult to define poetry because it is such a dynamic form of expression. As quickly as someone tries to define it and thereby confine it to particular boundaries of content and structure, it shows up in a fresh new form and the definition must be revised. Therefore, no attempt to define poetry has been successful in controlling its growth or containing its shape. Even so, a look at some "definitions" by a few great poets and thinkers is in order.

William Wordsworth referred to poetry as "the imaginative expression of strong feeling, usually rhythmical . . ."

Samuel Taylor Coleridge distinguished between prose and poetry when he wrote, "Prose: words in their best order; poetry: the best words in the best order."

Archibald MacLeish said, "A poem should not *mean* but *be*."

Thomas Macaulay wrote: "By poetry we mean the art of employing words in such a manner as to produce an illusion of the imagination, the art of doing by means of words what the painter does by means of colors."

All of these definitions are as imaginative as poetry itself. Perhaps the one by Macaulay is most beneficial for you as a beginning reader, however, because you can remember all the different paintings you have seen and realize that poetry exists in an equal number of varieties and shapes. In fact, variety and shape are effective terms to use in discussing poetry.

Archibald MacLeish suggests that poetry should be an experience, not tell of one. So poetry depends a great deal on emotion and imagination in presenting its meaning. There are no bounds on the kinds of ideas on which poetry has been written. Man, nature, the joys and problems of living, and dying—all these have been given full treatment by the world's poets. Where we came from, why we are here, what happens to us at death—all these have been explored through centuries of poetry. Poetry has been written to record events, to preserve ideas and moods, to protest "wrongs" and herald "rights." It has been written in deepest sorrow and in lightest humor. No experience of man has escaped the poet's palette. And we can be glad that it hasn't. But let's take a closer look at the contents of poetry.

The Contents of Poetry

What do we mean when we say poetry is emotional and imaginative? The definition by Coleridge is the first clue. "The best words in the best order," he said. His idea of the "best words" leads us into a discussion of poetic imagery. The poet relies heavily on imagery to put across his meaning. Read the following lines of poetry by John Donne and you'll quickly see the imaginative use of words. The lines are taken from his poem "The Indifferent."

I can love both fair and brown:
Her whom abundance melts, and her whom want betrays;
Her who loves loneness best, and her who masks and plays;
Her whom the country formed, and whom the town;
Her who believes, and her who tries;
Her who still weeps with spongy eyes,
And her who is dry cork and never cries.
I can love her, and her, and you, and you;
I can love any, so she be not true.

In the first line the poet highlights his idea. He says that he can love a variety of women. In the lines that follow he extends the idea into details of this variety. He can love plump and lean, quiet and flirtatious, country bred and city bred, saintly and worldly, weepy-eyed and hard; and then to make the idea final, he finishes on an impersonal note—with the idea that he can love any woman, so long as she doesn't love only him—so long as she doesn't tie him down. The poem is really an identification of the case for those against constancy, against loving one person forever.

Now compare Donne's way of saying it with the prose treatment of the idea given in the above paragraph. Is there any question about which is more imaginative? emotional?

The poem by Donne and, in fact, poetry in general, derives its emotion and imagination from the use of *imagery*—or what are most often called *figures of speech*. There are many such devices, but three which are most important for you to learn to recognize are *simile, metaphor,* and *allegory*. A *simile* is a figure of speech which makes a comparison between two things, using the word "like" or other similar connecting words. For example, if a poet wrote "My love is like a red, red rose," he would have a simile.

A *metaphor* is also a comparison, but it omits the connecting word or words. So if the same poet wrote "My love is a red, red rose," he would have a metaphor. The implication in such a comparison is that the poet's lover has all the qualities of the red, red rose. The poem by Donne in this chapter is loaded with metaphors. The comparisons he implies are identified in the paragraph that follows the poem.

An *allegory* is an extended comparison. In short, a poem (or prose selection) which tells a story on more than one level of meaning is an allegory. Walt Whitman's poem "O Captain! My Captain!" is an example of allegory. The poem on the surface speaks of a sea captain and a sea voyage; yet, the captain is Lincoln, and the voyage, the Civil War. Read the poem with allegory in mind.

O CAPTAIN! MY CAPTAIN!

WALT WHITMAN

O Captain! my Captain! our fearful trip is done!
The Ship has weather'd every rack, the prize we sought
 is won,
The port is near, the bells I hear, the people all exulting,

While follow eyes the steady keel, the vessel grim
    and daring;
    But O heart! heart! heart!
    O the bleeding drops of red,
    Where on the deck my Captain lies,
    Fallen cold and dead.

O Captain! my Captain! rise up and hear the bells;
Rise up—for you the flag is flung—for you the bugle trills,
For you bouquets and ribbon'd wreaths—for you the shores
    a-crowding,
For you they call, the swaying mass, their eager faces
    turning;
    Here Captain; dear father!
    This arm beneath your head!
    It is some dream that on the deck,
    You've fallen cold and dead.

My Captain does not answer, his lips are pale and still,
My father does not feel my arms, he has no pulse nor will,
The ship is anchor'd safe and sound, its voyage closed
    and done,
From fearful trip the victor ship comes in with object
    won;
    Exult O shores, and ring O bells!
    But I with mournful tread,
    Walk the deck my Captain lies,
    Fallen cold and dead.

Allegory is not only found in poetry; fables, parables, many nursery rhymes, and other types of literature can be read on more than one level and thus, as extended metaphors, are allegorical.

Other figures of speech that you might wish to recognize and work with are these:

Personification is a device often used in which an object or an idea is given human qualities. Thus a poet might write of "opportunity knocking," "pines whispering," or of an animal "singing" to its mate. In his poem "The Express," Stephen Spender uses personification of the express train when he writes,

Without bowing and with restrained unconcern
She passes the houses . . .

Apostrophe is similar to personification in that the poet addresses an object or an idea as he would a person. Percy Bysshe Shelley speaks directly to the wind throughout his poem "Ode to the West Wind." At one point he pleads,
Make me thy lyre, even as the forest is . . .

Hyperbole is exaggeration used to make a point or heighten the effect of the poem. This figure of speech is used most often in humorous poetry, as in the case of Oliver Wendell Holmes' "The Deacon's Masterpiece," which is also known as "The Wonderful One-Hoss Shay." Only the first two stanzas are included here.

THE DEACON'S MASTERPIECE

or

THE WONDERFUL ONE-HOSS SHAY

OLIVER WENDELL HOLMES

Have you heard of the wonderful one-hoss shay,
That was built in such a logical way
It ran a hundred years to a day,
And then, of a sudden, it——ah, but stay,
I'll tell you what happened without delay,
Scaring the parson into fits,
Frightening people out of their wits,—
Have you ever heard of that, I say?

Seventeen hundred and fifty-five.
Georgius Secundus was then alive,—
Snuffy old drone from the German hive.
That was the year when Lisbon-town,
And Braddock's army was done so brown,
Left without a scalp to its crown.
It was on the terrible Earthquake-day
That the Deacon finished the one-hoss shay.

This poem, too, is an allegory. Look it up and see if you can detect the institution the poem satirizes.

UNDERSTANDING LITERATURE

Synecdoche is a figure of speech through which the poet attempts to identify the whole of something by naming one of its parts. Perhaps the easiest way to identify this figure of speech is to show how we commonly use the same device when we speak of seeing so many "heads" of cattle or we count "noses" or we leave town on "wheels."

Metonymy is akin to synecdoche in that the poet uses one word to suggest another. With metonymy, however, the poet may be working with a problem and its solution, a cause and its effect (or the reverse of these), or a symbol to stand for what it symbolizes. Thus a poet might use "the Crown" to refer to the royal family of England or to the ruling body of the country. He might use "The Eagle" as a reference to the United States, "The Lion" as a reference to England, and "The Bear" as a reference to Russia.

The implication in all of this for you as an interpreter of such literature is that you must be careful your investigation into meaning reveals the use of figures of speech in the works you choose to read. This does not mean that you should be able to name them as you confront them in literature, but you should understand why they were used and what they are intended to convey to your audience.

In addition to figures of speech, the content of poetry is marked by beauty and vividness of language. "The best words in the best order." The order of the words in poetry will be discussed later in the chapter, but more should be said about the best words.

Students often shun poetry because they feel it is phony, too artificial, too formal for their tastes. In reality, poetry is the most vivid, colorful, imaginative type of literature. Many times it would take a page of prose to say what is included in a few words of poetry. Read the following sonnet by Shakespeare and note all the implications it contains. After you have thought about it for a few minutes, ask yourself how many paragraphs of prose it would take to say the same thing with the same implications.

SONNET 18

WILLIAM SHAKESPEARE

Shall I compare thee to a summer's day?
Thou art more lovely and more temperate;
Rough winds do shake the darling buds of May,

And summer's lease hath all too short a date;
Sometime too hot the eye of heaven shines,
And often is his gold complexion dimmed;
And every fair from fair sometime declines,
By chance, or nature's changing course untrimmed.
But thy eternal summer shall not fade,
Nor lose possession of that fair thou owest,
Nor shall death brag thou wander'st in his shade
When in eternal lines to time thou growest:
So long as men can breathe, or eyes can see,
So long lives this, and this gives life to thee.

Another example should convince you that beauty, vividness, and concentration of idea into a few words are the chief distinguishing characteristics of the contents of poetry. This second sonnet of Shakespeare is an excellent illustration of those characteristics.

SONNET 73

WILLIAM SHAKESPEARE

That time of year thou mayst in me behold,
When yellow leaves, or none, or few, do hang
Upon those boughs which shake against the cold,
Bare ruin'd choirs, where late the sweet birds sang.
In me thou see'st the twilight of such day,
As after sunset fadeth in the west,
Which by and by black night dost take away,
Death's second self, that seals up all in rest.
In me thou see'st the glowing of such fire,
That on the ashes of his youth does lie,
As the death-bed whereon it must expire,
Consum'd with that which it was nourish'd by.
  This thou perceiv'st, which makes thy love more
   strong,
  To love that well, which thou must leave ere long.

The Shape of Poetry

That poetry exists in many shapes has already been stated. This section of the chapter will identify some of the characteristics of the shape of poetry that are important for the interpreter of literature. There are three general classes into which poetry may be put: narrative, dramatic, and lyric.

Long narrative poems (with a story line) are called epics. *The Iliad, The Odyssey, Beowulf, The Song of Roland,* and *The Aeneid* are all examples of poetry of this class. No doubt other examples come to your mind. Alfred Noyes' *The Drake* is an epic poem of our modern time. But a poem needn't be an epic in order to be classed as a narrative poem. Poetry abounds in the narrative form. Robert Frost's "Out, Out," John Keats' "Eve of St. Agnes," Alfred Noyes' "The Highwayman" are all examples; the list could go on and on.

Dramatic poetry is simply any poetry which utilizes techniques of drama in order to achieve its effects. Much of the drama that Shakespeare wrote is called poetic drama—dialogue written in poetic form. Robert Browning's *Pippa Passes* is an example of a more modern play written in this form. Dramatic poetry is usually marked by dialogue between speakers (perhaps just one speaker and another person who listens), a dramatic situation, and an unfolding of one or more qualities of the speaker or speakers. Robert Frost's *The Death of the Hired Man* is an excellent example of this class of poetry. Walt Whitman's *Come Up From the Fields, Father,* used in Chapter 4, is an example of a dramatic ballad.

The third class is called lyric poetry. Its mode is best identified by the fact that it reveals the personal feelings of the poet. It is usually short and always emotional. It, more than any other class of poetry, reveals the mood, the personality, the soul of its author. It is easier to cite authors of lyric poetry here than it is to identify particular poems because there are so many such "thoughts" revealed by poets like Emily Dickinson, Sara Teasdale, Conrad Aiken, A. E. Housman, Percy Bysshe Shelley, John Keats, and Walter de la Mare. Several lyric poems are included to illustrate the mode.

I'M NOBODY! WHO ARE YOU?

EMILY DICKINSON

I'm nobody! Who are you?
Are you nobody, too?
Then there's a pair of us—don't tell!
They'd banish us, you know.

How dreary to be somebody!
How public, like a frog
To tell your name the livelong June
To an admiring bog!

MY HEART LEAPS UP

WILLIAM WORDSWORTH

My heart leaps up when I behold
A rainbow in the sky:
So was it when my life began;
So it is now I am a man;
So be it when I shall grow old,
Or let me die!
The Child is father of the Man;
And I could wish my days to be
Bound each to each by natural piety.

TO HIS COY MISTRESS

ANDREW MARVELL

Had we but World enough, and time,
This coyness, Lady, were no crime.
We would sit down, and think which way

To walk, and pass our long Love's Day.
Thou by the Indian Ganges side
Should'st Rubies find: I by the Tide
Of Humber would complain. I would
Love you ten years before the Flood:
And you should if you please refuse
Till the Conversion of the Jews.
My vegetable Love should grow
Vaster than Empires, and more slow.
An hundred years should go to praise
Thine Eyes, and on thy Forehead Gaze.
Two hundred to adore each Breast:
But thirty thousand to the rest.
An Age at least to every part,
And the last Age should show your Heart.
For Lady, you deserve this State,
Nor would I love at lower rate.

     But at my back I always hear
Time's winged Chariot hurrying near:
And yonder all before us lie
Deserts of vast Eternity.
Thy Beauty shall no more be found,
Nor, in thy marble Vault, shall sound
My echoing Song. Then Worms shall try
That long preserv'd Virginity,
And your quaint Honour turn to dust,
And into ashes all my Lust.
The Grave's a fine and private place,
But none, I think, do there embrace.

     Now therefore, while the youthful hue
Sits on thy skin like morning dew,
And while thy willing Soul transpires
At every pore with instant Fires,
Now let us sport us while we may;
And now, like am'rous birds of prey,
Rather at once our Time devour,
Than languish in his slow-chapt pow'r.
Let us roll all our Strength, and all

Our sweetness, up into one Ball,
And tear our Pleasures with rough strife
Through the Iron gates of Life.
Thus, though we cannot make our Sun
Stand still, yet we will make him run.

So much for the classification of poetry. Now for a further look at its shape. Some poets write in verse. Verse is that highly structured form which sets arbitrary limits on line length (meter) and uses rhyme. Often the rhyming pattern and the metrical system used present problems for the beginning reader. The temptation is to read the poem the way the poet wrote it, without considering meaning. The sad result under these conditions is that the meaning is distorted or obscured, and the only element the listener hears is the rhythm. In a sense this situation presents a paradox for the reader of poetry. The only possible answer to the problem is to read poetry with concentration on the meaning; subordinate rhyme and meter to meaning in your reading and that amount of rhythm that should be apparent will be. If you read poetry in such a way that the rhyme and meter dominate, meaning is often lost.

A separate look at the two will help. A poem may be written in rhyme. Consider these lines from William Wordsworth's "Daffodils."

I wandered lonely as a cloud
That floats on high o'er vales and hills
When all at once I saw a crowd,
A host, of golden daffodils.

Did you notice that the final words in the first and third lines rhyme? And that the same is true of the second and fourth lines? The rhyme scheme for the poem is *a b a b*. Here is another example. Note that these lines from Andrew Marvell's *To His Coy Mistress* (the complete poem is included earlier in this chapter,) rhyme in an *aa bb* pattern.

Had we but World enough, and time,
This coyness, Lady, were no crime.
We would sit down, and think which way
To walk, and pass our long Love's Day.

UNDERSTANDING LITERATURE

Another kind of rhythm is achieved through three poetic devices called alliteration, assonance, and onomatopoeia. Alliteration is the repetition of the initial letter or sound of words or syllables in a line or in successive lines of poetry. Notice the repetitious use of the "s" sound in these lines by Wordsworth.

A SLUMBER DID MY SPIRIT SEAL

A slumber did my spirit seal;
I had no human fears;
She seemed a thing that could not feel
The touch of earthly years.
No motion has she now, no force;
She neither hears nor sees;
Rolled round in earth's diurnal course,
With rocks, and stones, and trees.

Assonance is a similar device except that it is a repetition of vowel sounds instead of consonants. Such repetition adds to the rhythm inside the lines of poetry. The following sets of words illustrate assonance. The fact that they also rhyme is incidental; rhyme is not a necessary characteristic of assonance.

first sweet sleep of night
vile and violence will suffice
the freedom of sleep
the tolling of the bell rang over the knoll.

The third device which heightens rhythm is *onomatopoeia*. Anytime a poet uses a word which suggests the sound it represents, he is working with onomatopoeia. Thus we read of the

buzz of bees
whirr of wind
drone of flies
hiss of snakes

and so on.

YOUR ROLE IN ORAL INTERPRETATION

All three of these devices add to the rhythm and beauty of
poetry and all three add to the problems of the beginning reader, as
he tries to concentrate on meaning.

Meter is another element of structure that tends to handicap
the beginning reader. Simply, meter is the system (and there are
several varieties) of choosing words in lines of poetry which follow
a prescribed pattern of stressed and unstressed syllables. A poem
will illustrate one such system and point up the inherent problem
that meter brings to oral interpretation. The poem recounts an
encounter with death—not a happy, light, carefree subject. But the
meter, if allowed to dominate the reading of the poem, will make it
seem light and carefree. A mark like this (u) indicates that the
syllable it appears above is not stressed, while this mark (/) indicates that the syllable is to be stressed.

THE CHARIOT

EMILY DICKINSON

Because I could not stop for Death—
He kindly stopped for me—
The carriage held but just Ourselves—
And Immortality.

We slowly drove—He knew no haste
And I had put away
My labor and my leisure too,
For His Civility—

We passed the School, where Children strove
At Recess—in the Ring—
We passed the Fields of Gazing Grain—
We passed the Setting Sun—

UNDERSTANDING LITERATURE

ᴗ / ᴗ / ᴗ /
Or rather—He passed Us—

ᴗ / ᴗ / ᴗ / ᴗ /
The Dews drew quivering and chill—

ᴗ / ᴗ / ᴗ / ᴗ /
For only Gossamer, my Gown—

ᴗ / ᴗ / ᴗ /
My Tippet—only Tulle—

ᴗ / ᴗ / ᴗ / ᴗ /
We paused before a House that seemed

ᴗ / ᴗ / ᴗ /
A Swelling of the Ground—

ᴗ / ᴗ / ᴗ / ᴗ /
The Roof was scarcely visible—

ᴗ / ᴗ / ᴗ /
The Cornice—in the Ground—

ᴗ / ᴗ / ᴗ / ᴗ /
Since then—'tis Centuries—and yet

ᴗ / ᴗ / ᴗ /
Feels shorter than the Day

ᴗ / ᴗ / ᴗ / ᴗ /
I first surmised the Horses' Heads

ᴗ / ᴗ / ᴗ /
Were toward Eternity—

In this particular poem each unaccented syllable is followed by one which received stress or accent. This pattern of meter (u /) is called *iambic*; the reverse (/ u), as in the word únder, is called *trochaic*. Two other metric patterns deserve mention. The word incorréct illustrates the pattern called *anapestic*. In this pattern two unstressed syllables are followed by one which is stressed (u u /). The reverse of anapestic meter is called *dactylic*, which requires that each stressed syllable be followed by two which are unstressed; the word yésterday illustrates dactylic meter (/ u u).

Metrical feet, whether they are iambic, trochaic, anapestic, or dactylic, are then combined into lines which are named according to the number of feet they contain. For example, the Dickinson poem is said to be written in *iambic quatrimeter*. This means that there are four iambic feet in each line or in most of the lines of the poem. Actually each line of iambic quatrimeter in the poem is followed by a line of iambic trimeter. But since the first line of the poem contains four iambic feet and the pattern is repeated in each of the six stanzas of the poem, the poem would be identified as having been written in iambic quatrimeter. It is enough, then, to recognize that one metrical foot per line is called *monometer,* two feet per line of poetry *bimeter,* three feet *trimeter,* four feet *quatrimeter,* five feet *pentameter,* six feet *hexameter,* and so on.

You couldn't help but notice the strong rhyme and meter even when you accented the words (not syllables) that carry meaning in the poem. Another way to concentrate on meaning in reading poetry with such a strong rhyme and meter is to write it out in sentences. Here is the Dickinson poem again written in that fashion.

THE CHARIOT

Because I could not stop for Death—He kindly stopped for me—The carriage held but just Ourselves—And Immortality.

We slowly drove—He knew no haste and I had put away my labor and my leisure too, For His Civility—

We passed the School, where Children strove At Recess—in the Ring—We passed the Fields of Gazing Grain—We passed the Setting Sun—Or rather—He passed Us—

The Dews drew quivering and chill—For only Gossamer, my Gown—My Tippet—only Tulle—

We paused before a House that seemed A Swelling of the Ground—The Roof was scarcely visible—The Cornice—in the Ground—

Since then—'tis Centuries—and yet Feels shorter than the Day I first surmised the Horses' Heads Were toward Eternity.—

Did it seem easier to concentrate on meaning in the second instance? Perhaps so, but remember that the reason for rewriting the poem is to make concentration on meaning easier. You must have noticed that rhythm was still present in your reading. The difference is that the rhyme and meter were not allowed to *dominate* your reading.

Look again at the poem "The Chariot" as Emily Dickinson wrote it. Notice that each group of four lines is set off from the other groups. These are the stanzas of the poem; a stanza might be likened to a paragraph of prose. A definite distinction must be made between the two terms, however. A paragraph (in prose) is generally regarded as a unit of thought. A stanza is a more arbitrary division of lines of poetry into whatever units the poet deems advisable or desirable, usually dictated by rhyme or rhythm.

The smallest stanza is, of course, the *couplet*—two lines of poetry which rhyme, separated from at least two other lines which also rhyme but on a different sound than the first two. The lines that follow were taken from Alexander Pope's "An Essay on Criticism." Note that each set of two lines rhyme. Had he chosen to do so Pope could have set each couplet apart from the others in separate stanzas. Rather, he chose to use stanzas of varying lengths according to the ideas they contain.

from AN ESSAY ON CRITICISM

ALEXANDER POPE

'Tis hard to say, if greater want of skill
Appear in writing or in judging ill;
But, of the two, less dangerous is the offense
To tire our patience, than mislead our sense.
Some few in that, but numbers err in this,
Ten censure wrong for one who writes amiss;
A fool might once himself alone expose,
Now one in verse makes many more in prose.

Stanzas three lines long are called *tercets;* those four lines long *quatrains.* And so on.

There is a great deal of material concerning the structure of poetry that has been left unsaid in this chapter. There are many books written on the subject and there are courses in college devoted to building the skill of understanding and appreciating poetry. It is the feeling of your authors, however, that the information presented here is essential to the effective oral reading of poetry. More information on the structure of poetry would add confusion rather than clarity.

YOUR ROLE IN ORAL INTERPRETATION

Reading Your Own Poetry and Verse

Students often ask whether or not they can read their own material. Our answer is *Yes, by all means!* But use care in selecting from the material you have written the poems you will read; be certain that they fit your audience. If you have your instructor's permission and you have chosen the poetry with your particular audience in mind, go ahead and try it on them. The final test of poetry and verse is whether or not it communicates with those who read and listen to it. Your audience will tell you quickly how successful you are both as poet and reader.

The chief problem in reading your own material is that you will, perhaps, get carried away with your writing skill and not concentrate on reading skill. Some of our greatest poets fail when they read their own materials for this very reason.

The poems that follow are excellent for oral interpretation. Their imagery is clear and vivid; their meaning is heightened through oral reading. They were written when Ester Lee was a college student. She has read them on many occasions before varied audiences, and they have always met with enthusiastic approval.

OH OF LITTLE WORTH TO DREAM

ESTER LEE

Oh of little worth to dream!
To muse in muted, vignetted projection;
Linger in obtrusive reality,
Remain only on the brink,
Hesitating to step for fear it is
But a cloud upon which you creep.

You merely play where fairies play,
Bend and sway with the breezes,
Sing and Laugh with the sunbeams,
Dance and cry with the raindrops,
And just stand by as life teases.
Oh of little worth to dream!

UNDERSTANDING LITERATURE

WAKE ME EACH MORNING

ESTER LEE

Wake me
    each morning
With your
    smiling face
All
    sadness
      and sorrow
    of yesterday eraced.
Let life and joy
Through my veins
Run with rapture
As I gaze upon you
And my journey renew.

Walk with me hand in hand
Through
    the
      day
And though we're parted
Let me feel your hand clasping mine
    Pulling
      when I slacken
    Tightening
      when I weaken
Caressing when I obey.
Carry me
    into the night;
Tuck me in
    in sweet surrender,
Knowing no fear
Of
  the
    night

YOUR ROLE IN ORAL INTERPRETATION

Because of your light,
Blanket me with your arms
And then
      gladly
           I bid the day
DEPART!

Summary

Poetry is characterized by content which is concentrated and imaginative; it is nearly always emotional.

There are three general classifications of poetry: narrative, dramatic, and lyric. Poetry is concentrated through the employment of figures of speech, which include metaphor and simile. An extended metaphor is an allegory, a poem which may be read on two or more levels of meaning. Other figures of speech of importance are *personification, metonymy,* and *synecdoche.*

The shape of poetry is determined at times by the poet's use of rhyme and meter. The four major metrical patterns are *iambic, trochaic, anapestic,* and *dactylic.* Metrical feet are combined into lines named according to the number of feet they contain. Assonance, alliteration, and onomatopoeia are devices of internal rhythm in poetry.

Rhyme and meter are characteristics of much poetry which present a special problem to the beginning reader, but it is a problem which can be overcome by concentrating on the meaning of the poem.

Don't be afraid to read your own poetry to your audiences so long as it meets the criteria of effective oral interpretation.

Additional Poetry for Practice and Study

JAZZ FANTASIA

CARL SANDBURG

Drum on your drums, batter on your banjoes, sob on the long cool winding saxophones. Go to it, O jazzmen.

Sling your knuckles on the bottoms of the happy tin pans, let your trombones ooze, and go husha-husha-hush with the slippery sand-paper.

Moan like an autumn wind high in the lonesome treetops, moan soft like you wanted somebody terrible, cry like a racing car slipping away from a motorcycle cop, bang-bang! you jazzmen, bang altogether drums, traps, banjoes, horns, tin cans—make two people fight on the top of a stairway and scratch each other's eyes in a clinch tumbling down the stairs.

Can the rough stuff . . . now a Mississippi steamboat pushes up the night river with a hoo-hoo-hoo-oo . . . and the green lanterns calling to the high soft stars . . . a red moon rides on the humps of the low river hills . . . go to it, O jazzmen.

MY SABBATH

EMILY DICKINSON

Some keep the Sabbath going to church—
I keep it staying at home—
With a bobolink for a chorister—
And an orchard, for a dome—

YOUR ROLE IN ORAL INTERPRETATION

Some keep the Sabbath in surplice—
I just wear my wings—
And instead of tolling the bell, for church,
Our little sexton—sings.

God preaches, a noted clergyman—
And the sermon is never long,
So instead of going to Heaven at last—
I'm going, all along.

THE PASSIONATE SHEPHERD TO HIS LOVE

CHRISTOPHER MARLOWE

Come live with me, and be my love,
And we will all the pleasures prove
That valleys, groves, hills and fields,
Woods, or steepy mountain yields.

And we will sit upon the rocks,
Seeing the shepherds feed their flocks,
By shallow rivers, to whose falls
Melodious birds sing madrigals.

And I will make thee beds of roses,
And a thousand fragrant posies,
A cap of flowers, and a kirtle,
Embroider'd all with leaves of myrtle;

A gown made of the finest wool,
Which from our pretty lambs we pull,
Fair-lined slippers for the cold,
With buckles of the purest gold;

A belt of straw, and ivy-buds,
With coral clasps and amber studs;
And if these pleasures may thee move,
Come live with me, and be my love.

The shepherd-swains shall dance and sing
For thy delight each May morning;
If these delights thy mind may move,
Then live with me and be my love.

UNDERSTANDING LITERATURE

THE NYMPH'S REPLY TO THE SHEPHERD

SIR WALTER RALEIGH

If all the world and love were young,
And truth in every shepherd's tongue,
These pretty pleasures might me move,
To live with thee, and be thy love.

Time drives the flocks from field to fold,
When rivers rage, and rocks grow cold,
And Philomel becometh dumb,
The rest complain of cares to come.

The flowers do fade, and wanton fields
To wayward winter reckoning yields,
A honey tongue, a heart of gall,
Is fancy's spring, but sorrow's fall.

Thy gowns, thy shoes, thy beds of roses,
Thy cap, thy kirtle, and thy posies,
Soon break, soon wither, soon forgotten:
In folly ripe, in reason rotten.

Thy belt of straw and ivy buds,
Thy coral clasps and amber studs,
All these in me no means can move,
To come to thee, and be thy love.

But could youth last, and love still breed,
Had joys no date, nor age no need,
Then these delights my mind might move,
To live with thee, and be thy love.

YOUR ROLE IN ORAL INTERPRETATION

SONNET 29

WILLIAM SHAKESPEARE

When in disgrace with fortune and men's eyes,
I all alone beweep my outcast state,
And trouble deaf heaven with my bootless cries,
And look upon myself and curse my fate,
Wishing me like to one more rich in hope,
Featur'd like him, like him with friends possess'd,
Desiring this man's art, and that man's scope,
With what I most enjoy contented least,
Yet in these thoughts myself almost despising,
Haply I think on thee, and then my state,
Like to the lark at break of day arising,
From sullen earth sings hymns at heaven's gate,
For thy sweet love rememb'red such wealth brings,
That then I scorn to change my state with kings.

A CONEY ISLAND OF THE MIND

LAWRENCE FERLINGHETTI

15

Constantly risking absurdity
              and death
    whenever he performs
             above the heads
                    of his audience

the poet like an acrobat
        climbs on rime
             to a high wire of his own making

UNDERSTANDING LITERATURE

and balancing on eyebeams
        above a sea of faces
    paces his way
        to the other side of day
   performing entrechats
       and sleight-of-foot tricks
and other high theatrics
       and all without mistaking
   anything
       for what it may not be
  For he's the super realist
       who must perforce perceive
   taut truth
       before the taking of each stance or step
in his supposed advance
       toward that still higher perch
where Beauty stands and waits
    with gravity
       to start her death-defying leap

And he
   a little charleychaplin man
       who may or may not catch
    her fair eternal form
       spreadeagled in the empty air
    of existence

SONG

JOHN DONNE

Go and catch a falling star,
Get with child a mandrake root,
Tell me where all past years are,
Or who cleft the Devil's foot,
Teach me to hear mermaids singing,
Or to keep off envy's stinging,

And find
    What wind
Serves to advance an honest mind.

If thou be'st born to strange sights,
Things invisible to see,
Ride ten thousand days and nights,
Till age snow white hairs on thee,
Thou, when thou return'st wilt tell me
All strange wonders that befell thee,
    And swear
    No where
Lives a woman true, and fair.

If thou find'st one, let me know,
Such a pilgrimage were sweet;
Ye do not, I would not go,
Though at next door we might meet;
Though she were true, when you met her,
And last till you write your letter,
    Yet she
    Will be
False, ere I come, to two, or three.

THE COLLAR

GEORGE HERBERT

I struck the board, and cried, "No more.
    I will abroad.
What? shall I ever sigh and pine?
My lines and life are free, free as the road,
Loose as the wind, as large as store.
Shall I be still in suit?
Have I no harvest but a thorn
To let me blood, and not restore
What I have lost with cordial fruit?
Sure there was wine
Before my sighs did dry it: there was corn

Before my tears did drown it.
Is the year only lost to me?
Have I no bays to crown it?
No flowers, no garlands gay? all blasted?
   All wasted?
Not so, my heart: but there is fruit,
And thou hast hands
Recover all thy sigh-blown age
On double pleasures; leavy thy cold dispute
Of what is fit and not. Forsake thy cage,
Thy rope of sands,
Which petty thoughts have made, and made to thee
Good cable, to enforce and draw,
And be thy law,
While thou didst wink and wouldst not see.
Away; take heed:
I will abroad.
Call in thy death's-head there, tie up thy fears.
He that forbears
To suit and serve his need,
   Deserves his load."
But as I rav'd and grew more fierce and wild
At every word,
Methought I heard one calling, Child!
And I replied, My Lord.

CHAPTER 13

How do I read children's literature?

THE LIMITLESS POSSIBILITIES for the interpreter in the area of children's literature are often overlooked—or relegated to a secondary position. In reality, the interpreter would do well to begin his study of oral interpretation by reading the fables, legends, fairy tales, nursery rhymes, adventure stories, animal stories, plays, or biographies that make up this vast literature.

Perhaps in no other branch of literature does the material involve such "getting out of oneself" as does children's literature. Many teachers have found that beginning a course in oral interpretation with the reading of a selection such as "Billy Goats Gruff" can do much to teach bodily and emotional involvement. In fact, the authors have used that story as an initial tension-reliever and as a first lesson in expressing emotion. Since the students realize that such a story, designed for children, calls for an exaggerated kind of characterization to make the goats and the troll vivid and real, it is comparatively easy to forget themselves and have fun with the characters. The results of such a practice session are an immediate recognition of the need for emotional involvement in interpretation and an easing of tensions as students realize that they can make literature live through oral reading.

Reading for children requires consideration of both the sensory appeals and the qualities in the literature designed to reach that appeal. Children like repetition of sounds; they like rhymes and it makes no difference whether or not the rhymes make sense; they like animals with human traits; they like suspense and humor and stories filled with dialogue; they like enthusiasm in the reader and bodily movement and facial expressions, plus noticeable varieties in volume and pacing.

You must be careful to observe all the above aspects of reading children's literature and to make each one impressive. Generally, you will read at a somewhat slower pace to make certain the children catch every new development, every new thought. And you will work to read any moments of suspense in the story with a good deal of dramatic involvement. In short, you will exaggerate the literary qualities to achieve the necessary response from a child. But at the same time, you must not produce an aura of superiority and talk down to your audience. Your focus is on them and the material.

If you were to read the same literature to an adult, however, you would not indulge in such exaggeration. The material would probably be read in a more sophisticated manner with only a suggestion of the characterization and suspense; it would be approached with the attitudes of the adult rather than with the heart and mind of the child. For an audience comprised of adults and children, on the other hand, you would do well to center your attention on the children's likes and interests. In doing so you might even succeed in transporting the adults back to their childhood days.

Nursery Rhymes

The nursery rhymes are a good example. Many of the nursery rhymes are favorites of the children. It doesn't matter at all that they do not make sense in a modern setting. Let us look at "Sing a song of sixpence." To a child, the fact that there is no relationship between pie and rye does not matter. And he does not question how blackbirds baked in a pie can be alive and singing when the pie is opened. All that counts is his fondness for the rhyme pattern and his own visualization of the theme. Read the selection to children with that in mind—with an emphasis on the rhyme. However, if you were to read it to an adult audience, you would have to consider the historical setting for the writing of this rhyme. "Sing A Song Of Sixpence" was a political satire of the time. The king referred to is King Henry VIII of England. The queen is his wife, Catherine of Spain. The maid is Anne Boleyn, handmaiden of Catherine and mistress of Henry. The blackbirds are the dark whispers about the indiscretions of the king. Specifically, the rhyme refers to the moves Henry made to divorce his wife so he could marry Anne Boleyn. The rhyme takes on an entirely different meaning in this context, but it is a context that would have no meaning to a child.

The same is true of "Georgie Porgie, pudding and pie—." This rhyme makes little or no sense if it is analyzed for what it says, but children do not care. They love to hear the rhyme pattern. To an adult, however, it takes on meaning when one considers that this too was a satire. Georgie Porgie was King George I of England. He was a lazy, indolent man who was lowly even in his sensual pleasures. The nursery rhyme is a biting satire on his inadequacies as a King and as a person.

Children also like a repetition in names given to animals or fowls or birds in stories. A good example of this is Henny-Penny. The repetition of the sounds in the first syllables of the name are important to the children in your audience. This device is carried out further in the story with Cocky-Locky, Goosey-Loosey, Turkey-Lurkey, Foxy-Loxy.

Repetition is also a feature in the rhyme "The Crooked Man" and "The Five Little Pigs."

> There was a crooked man,
> Who walked a crooked mile;
> He found a crooked sixpence
> Against a crooked stile;
> He bought a crooked cat,
> Which caught a crooked mouse,
> And they all lived together
> In a little crooked house.

> This little pig went to market
> This little pig stayed home,
> This little pig had roast beef,
> This little pig had none
> This little pig cried "Wee, wee, wee"
> All the way home.

UNDERSTANDING LITERATURE

The love of repetition of sound or idea is carried out further in "The Little Red Hen." The little hen asks, in each sequence, the dog, the cat, the pig, and the turkey to help her plant the wheat, cut it, thresh it, grind it, and bake the flour. In each case, the animals answer "I won't."

"I won't," said the dog.
"I won't," said the cat.
"I won't," said the pig.
"I won't," said the turkey.

And in each case, the hen answers, "I will, then," and adds, "Cluck, cluck." Then when it is time to eat the bread, the hen asks them who will eat the bread. Each says, "I will," but this time the hen says, "No, I will . . . Cluck, cluck."

The Fable

The repetition in dialogue in this story serves to emphasize the ambition of hen and the laziness of the others. The fable also teaches a lesson, illustrates a moral value.

Perhaps in no other form of children's literature is the moral element so heavily involved as in Aesop's *Fables*.

"Belling the Cat" is a good example.

One day the mice held a general council to consider what they might do to protect themselves against their common enemy, the Cat. Some said one thing and some said another, but at last a young mouse stood up and announced that he had a plan which he thought would solve the problem.

"You will all agree," said he, "that our chief danger lies in the unexpected and sly manner in which our enemy comes upon us. Now, if we could receive some warning of her approach, we could easily hide from her. I propose, therefore, that a small bell be obtained and attached by a ribbon to the neck of the Cat. In this way we could always know when she was coming and be able to make our escape."

This proposal was met with great applause, until an old mouse arose and said, "This is all very fine, but who among us is so brave? Who will bell the Cat?" The mice looked at one another in silence and nobody volunteered. Moral: It is easier to suggest a plan than to carry it out.

In the reading of such fables, the interpreter must make the problem very clear to the children; he must characterize the "young" and the "old" mouse in particular.

James Thurber satirizes many of the fables and stories in children's literature, thereby using these tales for the more sophisticated tastes of the adult. The incorporation of Thurber's versions would be good in a program for an audience composed of children and adults. His version of "Little Red Riding Hood," called "The Little Girl and the Wolf," is an example, as is "Unicorn in the Garden." He pokes great fun at the stories and then at the end makes his central point with a satirical version of the moral lesson. In "Little Girl and the Wolf," his moral is: "It's not as easy to fool little girls nowadays as it used to be," and in "Unicorn in the Garden," it is: "Don't count your boobies until they're hatched."

One of the more effective moral lessons—although it is not heavily labored but is rather subtly implied—is found in A. A. Milne's story from *Winnie the Pooh* of Pooh Bear's visit to Rabbit. Gluttony is the theme. Yet, while Milne has a moral, he is actually far more concerned with the characterization of Pooh and of Rabbit and with the story itself than with preaching a lesson. In fact, all of the stories from *Winnie the Pooh* emphasize the characters more— and the dialogue used. With Milne, of course, dialogue is a key element, as is humor. We can see this in a section from the story:

. . . Well, he was humming this hum to himself, and walking along gaily, wondering what everybody else was doing, and what it felt like, being somebody else, when suddenly he came to a sandy bank, and in the bank was a large hole.

UNDERSTANDING LITERATURE

"Aha!" said Pooh. (*Rum-tum-tiddle-um-tum.*) "If I
know anything about anything, that hole means Rabbit,"
he said, "and Rabbit means Company," he said, "and
Company means Food and Listening-to-Me-Humming
and such like. *Rum-tum-tum-tiddle-um.*"

So he bent down, put his head into the hole, and
called out:

"Is anybody at home?"

There was a sudden scuffling noise from inside the
hole, and then silence.

"What I said was, 'Is anybody at home?' " called out
Pooh very loudly.

"No!" said a voice; and then added, "You needn't
shout so loud. I heard you quite well the first time."

"Bother!" said Pooh. "Isn't there anybody here at
all?"

"Nobody."

Winnie-the-Pooh took his head out of the hole, and
thought for a little, and he thought to himself, "There
must be somebody there, because somebody must have
said 'Nobody!' "

Rabbit and Pooh become quite unique characters, and when an
interpreter reads this story, "Pooh Goes Visiting," he must make
certain that both Pooh and Rabbit are carefully characterized and
that, unlike many children's stories, the dialogue is not merely a
device but an integral part of the characterization.

The interpreter must also remember that these stories, like the
poems from *When We Were Very Young*, were written by Milne for
his son, Christopher Robin, who is the main character in all the
Pooh books. These were told over and over to Christopher when he
was a young boy. Few authors have been able so successfully to
enter into the child's world of fantasy as Milne in his poems "Corner
of the Street," "Lines and Squares," and "Halfway Down."

Milne used rhyme patterns in his poetry to heighten the child's
involvement and to make the poems memorable. So conscious was
he of rhyme in his poem "The Three Foxes" that he made up words
purely for the sake of rhyming, and we get "sockses" to rhyme with
foxes.

The interpreter must emphasize those words made up for

rhyme purposes, but he must also make the experiences of the three foxes seem to be very delightful.

One of the most effective of all of Milne's works for the interpreter is "Vespers," the lovely prayer of Christopher Robin. This poem could be read for an adult and a child in just about the same way because what it says has meaning for both.

Repetition as Learning

The Dr. Seuss books have been extremely popular in the realm of children's literature because, through the use of repetition and vivid illustrations, children are taught, among other things, how to distinguish colors and read the alphabet at the same time as they are being entertained. The unique role here for the interpreter is to make the characters very definitive.

In *The Cat in the Hat Comes Back*, Seuss helps a child to learn the alphabet with the characters of Little Cats, A, B, C, D, E, F, G, etc. Each cat has a purpose in the story. To further emphasize the alphabet, Seuss often uses it backwards as "Take your Little Cats G, F, E, D, C, B, A." Reading the story aloud would emphasize the use of the alphabet which is the real reason for the story.

Seuss' books have also been popular because of his unusual characters. The Cat in the Hat is by himself unique, as are the little cats. Equally distinctive are such machines as the car with all kind of arms to clean up the house. These symbols intrigue a child who loves to be a part of the world of fantasy. The unreal is very real to him and a reader must keep that in mind.

Evil and Good

Children's literature, particularly fairy tales, is also concerned with good vs. evil, with the very good and the very bad. Children love to be scared by such things as witches and bad animals like the fox and the wolf. The fox, for instance, appears in the fable of Henny-Penny and is the big badman of the Uncle Remus stories, which are excellent choices for the interpreter of children's literature because of the challenging characterizations they offer: Uncle Remus, the little boy, the rabbit, the fox, and the others. To read these stories effectively you must emphasize the suspenseful moments when

Br'er Rabbit seems to be in great danger at the hands of Br'er Fox and then at the last minute manages to escape. The climax occurs when Br'er Fox is foiled—again. Endow Br'er Rabbit with slyness, cleverness, and present Br'er Fox first as the villainous schemer and then as completely frustrated and angry when he is defeated once more. You must present Uncle Remus as the kindly, enthusiastic old man, and read the dialogue as the author intended and wrote—in dialect.

Witches and giants are also popular villains. The witch in "Hansel and Gretel" and in *Wizard of Oz* are graphic examples of the kind of evil that pervades most children's stories. The witches must be made very vivid and very real for children if they are to share in the suspense. In the same way, characters like Dorothy and Hansel and Gretel must be read with sensitivity. Both these stories contain a good deal of suspense, and the interpreter should read them so that the little heroes and heroines appear to be in very real danger.

In the Oz books by Frank Baum, the uniqueness of the characters offers wonderful challenges for the interpreter. The Cowardly Lion, for instance, is a very definite person. He is humorous and yet pathetic in his cowardice, and the interpreter must demonstrate both qualities. The Tin Woodman is certainly an unreal character, but not to children. They can believe he exists. He, too, must have sympathetic understanding on the part of the reader, as must the Scarecrow. The interpreter, then, in the reading of such stories must not allow himself to disbelieve in such unreal people— he must put himself into the world of the child and make fantasy seem to be reality if he is to move his audience to respond. He can never be totally objective in the reading of children's literature.

The Giant in "Jack and the Beanstalk" is a much different Giant from the one in "The Selfish Giant." The former is huge, menacing, gruff, belligerent, a form of danger. The interpreter would characterize him with a full voice, and a slower, more ponderous pace. The latter Giant, however, demands a different treatment. He begins as a gruff, selfish person, but then becomes kindly, a friend of the children, so there is far more contrast in his character. The interpreter would want to make him loved by his audience, to give him more sensitive qualities.

One could go on and on with a discussion of children's literature. There are adventure stories such as *King Arthur and His Knights of the Round Table;* the colorful Thornton W. Burgess animal stories, including *The Adventures of Buster Bear; Bambi,* a delightful challenge to the sensitivity of a reader; *Peter Pan; Tom Sawyer; Huckleberry Finn;* Walter Farley's *The Black Stallion; My Friend Flicka; Thunderhead;* many stories of history; and the wonderful tales of Hans Christian Andersen and the Brothers Grimm.

There is also "Snow White and the Seven Dwarfs," with the interpreter's need for precise characterization of the seven dwarfs to make each one different; there is "Cinderella" with the need to make the two daughters and their mother real (as witches) and to give reality to the other non-human characters who fill this age-old legend. And certainly one cannot forget *Mary Poppins* and her appeal to children of all ages.

An interesting new development in children's literature occurred recently when a sixth grade teacher was asked to have children in her class donate books to an impoverished neighborhood. Instead of doing this, she decided to have her pupils write their own stories. The results were interesting. The writings reflected the children's own tastes; although there was some repetition of theme, the stories differed in background, format, style, subject, and treatment. There was a general emphasis on humor and there was usually a moral lesson involved. The findings reported seem to pinpoint what children themselves consider most important.

You will discover when you wish to find children's material to read that there is an endless supply. You have very likely read many of the stories yourself as a child and can easily decide which to choose. If you want to find something different or unusual, such magazines as *The Saturday Review of Literature* often list new books for children, and several times a year there is a general survey of books worthy of note. In addition, browsing through a book store can provide many choices. At least in children's literature, the problem of selecting material is much simpler than it is for other forms of literature.

It is significant that as interpreters you are called upon to show emotion and feeling, to make characters believable. The world of fantasy, the world of the child, offers the best place for a basic study of both these essential characteristics.

Summary

Children's literature makes a good beginning point for the interpreter, for in characterizing the people involved you can learn the essential qualities of characterization, bodily movement, and contrast in tone and pace. In reading the role of a goat or a fox, for instance, you need not worry about appearing ridiculous because you think more of appealing to a child than to an adult. You forget yourself; and consequently, the pressure is less.

Reading for children requires a specialized style. Pay careful attention to rhyme in such literature as nursery rhymes because children love repetition of sound. Emphasize dialogue since it is easy for them to follow and read at a slower pace than you would for other forms of literature to make certain each incident and sequence is clear. Over-exaggerate in most cases and over-dramatize action and suspense sequences. But do not "talk down" to an audience by emphasizing yourself more than the material. Concern yourself with the material and its demands. The child does not see you as a reader—he sees you as a storyteller bringing to life real beings.

Reading children's literature for an adult audience requires more subtlety, less exaggeration, and a consideration of the reasons for the writing of such literature as nursery rhymes. More concern is given to the political satire that is implicit in such rhymes.

Characterization is essential in the reading of children's literature because children regard animals as humans and they feel a real identity with both the non-human and human characters. A. A. Milne's Pooh stories as well as the Dr. Seuss books offer excellent opportunities for the interpreter to devise unique characterizations to delight the children in his audience.

Moral lessons are taught in children's literature, especially in fables; and good and evil are personified in many works, including fairy tales, Uncle Remus stories, the Oz books, "Hansel and Gretel," and "Snow White and the Seven Dwarfs."

Among the types of children's literature available to the interpreter are legends, fairy tales, fables, nursery rhymes, biographies, and histories.

Exercises

1. Read the story of the Three Little Pigs. Imagine yourself as each of the three pigs. Devise your own characterization and then read this story aloud. Also decide whether the wolf is to be a sophisticated wolf, a not-so-bright wolf, an educated wolf, or what.

2. Try "Billy Goats Gruff." Change your voice level for each

little goat. Decide how each is different from the others. Then feel a surge of energy and of expansion within the body as you read the troll. How do you pace him—slowly, ponderously? Then instill slyness and authority in the last Billy Goat. Read the "Trip, trop, trip, trop" with contrasts in pace and tone to convey the heaviness or lightness of each goat.

3. Read "Snow White and the Seven Dwarfs." Carefully decide how you want to read each dwarf, what kind of voice you want to use, what kind of pacing. Is one to be nervous and excitable? Is one to be shy and reserved? Then read the parts. Call in your little brother or sister or any of the children in the neighborhood and read the story to them. See how they react—and what they say to you about it. Ask them if they liked the reading. They'll tell you.

4. Read the *Wizard of Oz*. First, read the scene of the tornado. See if you can successfully create, by use of faster pace and excitement, the fury of the tornado. Have you ever been in a big windstorm? If so, try to remember it. Now—read the witch as she threatens to take Dorothy's dog. What level are you going to use? Usually, she is read with a high, screechy voice and with a slight nasal quality, but how do you see her? Characterize the Tin Woodman, the Scarecrow, and the Cowardly Lion.

PART FOUR

THE FUTURE

❧ CHAPTER 14

Where do I go from here?

So NOW we come to the end of our discourse on the art of oral interpretation. But—we have also reached the beginning.

It would be unfortunate to assume that oral interpretation is something only to be involved in when you are taking the course. It can be a lasting experience. Think for a moment of what has happened to you during this course. Are you not better able to express yourself emotionally? Have you not gained a wider appreciation of literature? Do you not know more of the emotional values in literature—and the freedom that infuses you as you express those values?

You can add to this experience and make yourself grow even more if you look at the opportunities offered you to continue your participation in oral interpretation. For one thing, you should take advantage of every chance to hear artists in the interpretative field. Check your newspapers to see what colleges, professional organizations, and civic groups are offering experiments in Readers' Theatre, concert readings of new plays, readings of poetry or prose or drama. And note, too, what TV is offering. There are many examples of the art of interpretation that have been presented on TV, as for instance, Hal Holbrook's *Mark Twain Tonight*. In addition, each month brings new recordings of readings and performances by the greatest artists of the day. Caedmon Records, for instance, has a wide repertoire of interpretative readings by artists such as Julie Harris, Lotte Lenya, Cyril Ritchard. And Sir John Gielgud has graced the recording field with his *Ages of Man* albums. The Shakespeare Recording Society and the Theatre Recording Society have done remarkable work with their presentations of Shakespearean and representative contemporary plays. Some feel that the albums of these societies are more theatre than interpretation. But remember that the artists, in the recording session, assemble in a room and read the roles without any use of physical action, lights, costumes, or props. Their voices and their voices alone must do the job for them, must bring to life their characters and the play. So, in reality, the recordings are an even greater challenge to the artists than would be the case if they gave concert performances of the plays; by appearing in person the actors would have the extra benefit of facial and bodily expressions to help convey the richness of the works.

Often students approach interpretative recordings with a "Do I have to listen to that?" attitude. Yet, just as often, once they have heard the recordings, they find them exciting and worthwhile. So make certain you at least give yourself the chance to hear these renowned artists in performance.

Now, what can *you* do to continue your work? At the local or civic level, you could arrange programs of interpretative reading. Let it be known that you are willing to be part of an entertainment program in your community. Encourage others, who have ability, to do the same. And to extend this kind of participation even further, you could initiate a Readers' Theatre program in which you could do a concert reading of a play written by one of the people in your area. You could also hold an evening of reading from noted plays— or from works of recognized poets and authors. The recordings of *Brecht on Brecht,* of Edgar Lee Masters' *Spoon River Anthology* are two examples of the types of program that can be arranged on the writings of one author.

The important thing is that you start to do something. And it is equally necessary to be inventive in the types of programs you plan. Perhaps you'd like to add music as background for readings. It has been done—and is becoming accepted even more. An example of the intermingling of music and reading would be Rod McKuen's *The Sea,* with orchestral background. Music can do much to help set a mood, although of course it is the reader who basically must create the moods. There was a time when it was thought that the interpreter must do nothing but read and interpret and that any other effects took him out of the realm of true interpretation. There are sufficient indications now to prove that such theories are becoming outdated.

Interpretation can also be a good medium for the entertainment of children. A program, geared to the children in your community, could be made up of excerpts from nursery rhymes, fairy tales, and other forms of children's literature.

In a like manner, a concert reading could be done in your church with various people reading excerpts from the Bible. You could build a reading around the Beatitudes, or deal with the challenging statements of the prophets in the Old Testament. Or you could create a program from the seven last words of Christ. For an even more ambitious project, a concert reading of some of the exciting religious plays might be presented. One such play is *Christ in the Concrete City* by P. W. Turner, available through Baker's Plays in Boston, Massachusetts. This lends itself particularly well to a Readers' Theatre presentation.

The field is limitless—and so are the possibilities. The important thing is to do something, to start a program. Don't let what you have learned go to waste.

The Professional Viewpoint

Much has been written in this text about the art of interpretation, but too often textbooks ignore the views and ideas and techniques of the prominent artists engaged in this field. We have asked for— and received—the opinions of six of the best known interpreters. They are also, we must add, among the finest actors in the world today.

Sir John Gielgud:

Sir John Gielgud has done much to give impetus to interpretation with his world-wide tours of *Ages of Man,* a program of Shakespearean readings. The show has also been recorded. No finer example of the art of the interpreter exists than this particular recording. When he first conceived *Ages of Man,* he was not certain how to handle it, but then, after much experiment and selective effort, he said: "I devised *Ages of Man* to combine a certain amount of improvised relation directly with the audiences in a very slight and unacademic manner, making links between the excerpts.

"I chose speeches mostly with some veins of consecutive narrative interests as well as with poetic contrast in mood, rhythm, and content, and only acted 'full out' in two or three of the most obviously dramatic and powerful excerpts. The intense concentration, keeping of gesture and physical movement to a minimum, the difficulty of attacking each excerpt with full confidence of the character to be implied and the fact of remaining on stage alone for so long a time were the main problems to be solved. The conclusion, necessary to each speech, was also difficult to determine. One needs great experience in the playing of the whole scene and in interpreting the different styles of writing in the various plays chosen.

"In my own case, I took as great care in presenting the young characters, to indicate vocally the age and vigour of the personages, as I would in directing a young actor. Thus I feel the attempt to *imply* rather than *impersonate* is far more likely to be successful, besides being an effective contrast to the older, more dramatic characters. I was also careful to place the sonnet and poems in places where rests were needed both for actor and audience and not to have too many love or death scenes together. The idea of doing Romeo's death and following with that of Lear seems extremely successful, for instance, though at first it seemed hard to reconcile that Romeo speech with the section depicting age."

Sir John Gielgud's comments are of particular value to a young person who is attempting to arrange a program. In addition, his views on characterization of age are significant, with special emphasis on his views of implication and impersonation. It is also well to listen to the wide tonal range of his voice for a lesson in the beauty of the voice and its importance in interpretation.

It would pay a student to spend several hours listening to Sir John Gielgud's *Ages of Man*.

Cyril Ritchard:

Cyril Ritchard has made several recordings in the interpretative field, and one of his most successful has been *Alice in Wonderland*, which he did for Caedmon.

Mr. Ritchard believes firmly in the close relationship between actor and interpreter. As he says, "I think an actor *is* an interpreter. But for recording purposes, a good interpreter, or reader, need not be a good actor except vocally.

"In the reading of poetry, prose, or drama, the main thing is to study the inner meaning of the literature and then to rehearse it aloud until it eventually becomes your own. However, it is important not to be carried away by the music of your own voice. It is necessary that an interpreter be caught up emotionally with the emotions of the text, to be involved."

YOUR ROLE IN ORAL INTERPRETATION

As to his views on the primary obligation of the interpreter, Mr. Ritchard says firmly, "The greatest challenge the reader faces is to interpret—in the complete sense and with the complete dedication to the poetry, drama, or prose."

One notices immediately Mr. Ritchard's dedication to his material in the many recordings he has made. In addition to his views of interpretation, his superb diction is a model to follow.

Julie Harris:

Julie Harris, one of the finest actresses on the stage today, has made an impressive recording of *The Poems and Letters of Emily Dickinson* for Caedmon Records. When undertaking this assignment she may have found the material and her role different, but she merely remarked, "They seem the same to me."

When she prepares a reading, she uses much the same technique that she does when she is preparing for a role in a play or a film.

"Whether I'm reading poetry or prose or drama, I try to digest the material thoroughly by reading it over and over to myself every day. Naturally, such rehearsal is always oral. I feel my involvement in my material must be total, at least for the time of study or of performance."

It is also her view that it is rather forbidding for a person who has not been used to displaying emotion to be confronted with the need for such outpouring of feeling as is required in interpretation.

For those students who find the reading of poetry awesome, a conscientious listening to Miss Harris' Emily Dickinson album would be advisable.

Lotte Lenya:

Lotte Lenya, the prominent German actress, is an authority on the interpretation of the works of Bertolt Brecht in particular, although her talents are extensive enough to enable her to handle any dramatic demands. It is simply that her association with Brecht has been given considerable emphasis.

One of her records has been *Brecht on Brecht* which was a form of Readers' Theatre presenting the works of Brecht. She has also done other recordings, such as *The Stories of Kafka*.

"In order to play a role, I must become the character," Miss Lenya states. "I feel the same about interpretation. My interpretation comes through my conceptions of the character as a human

THE FUTURE

being under any circumstances, whether presented in the play or not. In other forms of literature, such as poetry and prose, to understand completely, the meaning and intent of the author is necessary. The reading follows without further preparation or technique.

"Whatever I am doing, whether it is as an actress in a play or an interpreter of poetry or prose, I must become totally involved to interpret to others my conception of material."

Her background in German theatre has made her feel even more intensely the importance of involvement since European artists are inclined to work on the theory of *becoming* rather than *implying*.

"What can I say to the beginning interpreter? I can only say how I feel about the work. Well, to me the challenge is to give to listeners the meanings which I have derived from intensive study. They may differ, but if they have been stimulated, I have met my greatest challenge."

Agnes Moorehead:

Agnes Moorehead, who has appeared on the stage, in motion pictures, and on television, is also a renowned interpreter. Her one-woman show has played to capacity audiences all over the country, and she has appeared on several albums in the Readers' Theatre form.

Miss Moorehead's views differ to a degree from those expressed above since she is very much inclined to make a specific distinction between interpretation and acting.

"The interpreter," she remarks, "acts with his mind—the actor uses movement. This does not mean that the actor does not interpret also, but he can use movement. The interpreter must use primarily his voice—and creative imagination—as the main instruments.

"My strongest advice to the beginning student, then, is to work with the voice and use imaginative creativity in the voice. Study it and characterization as much as would the actor. Know what effects you can use, such as music or sound effects. *Know your material cold.* But, above all, the voice must be used with depth."

As to the question of involvement, Miss Moorehead says, "The interpreter should not involve himself—he cannot get involved since he must go from dialogue to the narrative form. He must *represent*, therefore, the character rather than *be* it."

Miss Moorehead has had ample opportunity to test her theories

YOUR ROLE IN ORAL INTERPRETATION

in her one-woman show. She has learned from it that the interpreter cannot merely stand and read.

"He must have movement. When an interpreter presents a show, such as Sir John Gielgud's *Ages of Man,* or my own show, he is not really doing oral interpretation. He is presenting theatre. I do not feel an audience will sit still for two hours of readings of Elizabeth Barrett Browning's poetry. But an audience will be attentive for an hour of this if it is interpreted with good voice and movement. The big advantage for a person like Sir John Gielgud is that the public sees him in an acting form. And he is wise in that he picks material that is dramatically compelling and that those who see it can identify with.

"To me, there is no one form of material that is more difficult to do than another. All that counts is: Is it an exciting piece? Does it move an audience? Can it sustain you for two hours? So—it's all very well and good to believe you must remain true to the material, but you cannot forget that the audience is out front and it is they you must please. So choosing your type of material is a vital necessity."

Miss Moorehead's comment is similar to Miss Lenya's:

"If they have been stimulated, I have met my greatest challenge." That should be the emphasis for every student in oral interpretation—to be stimulated first of all yourself and then to stimulate others by making the literature speak through you. Make the words you read leap out of the pages and become alive!

And so we come to the beginning—there is no end unless you close the book yourself.

THE FUTURE

Index

DATE DUE
